I0729548

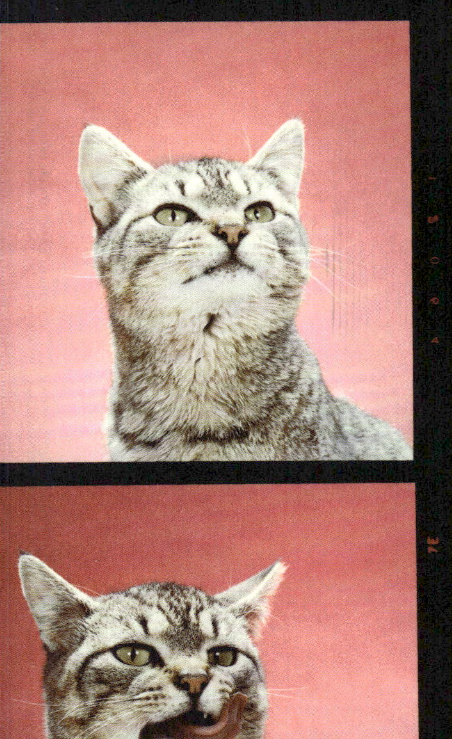
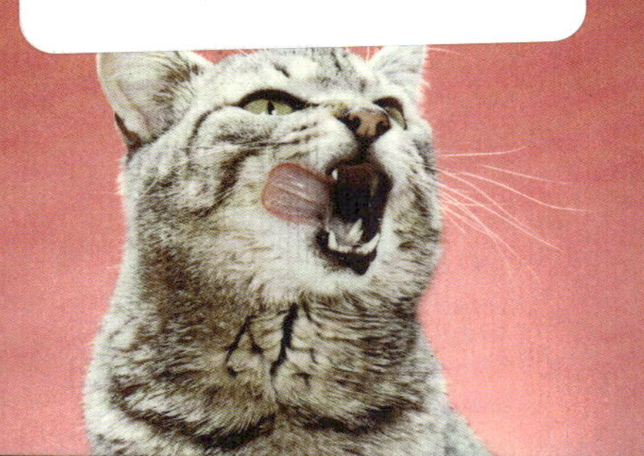
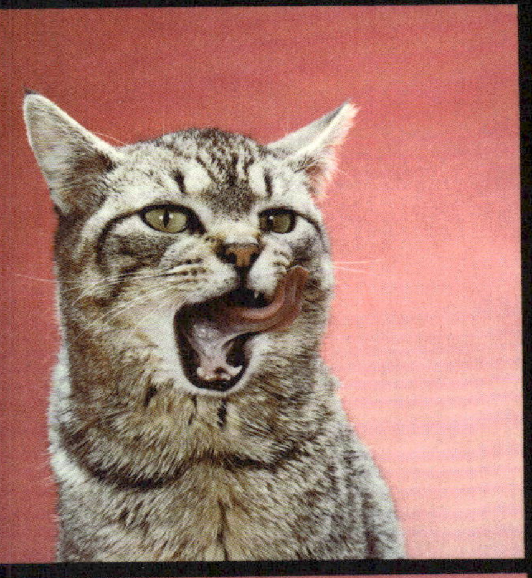
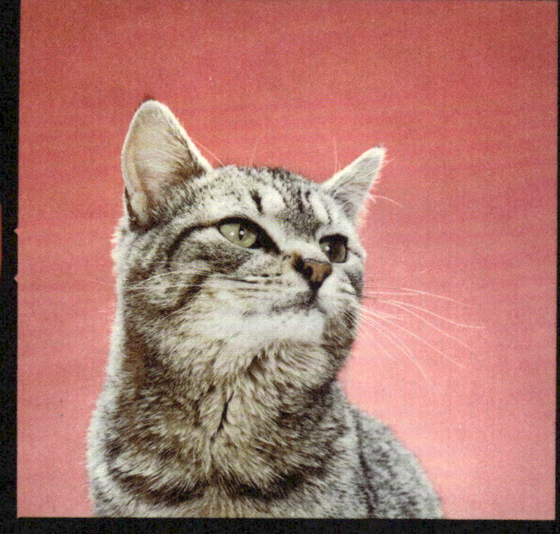
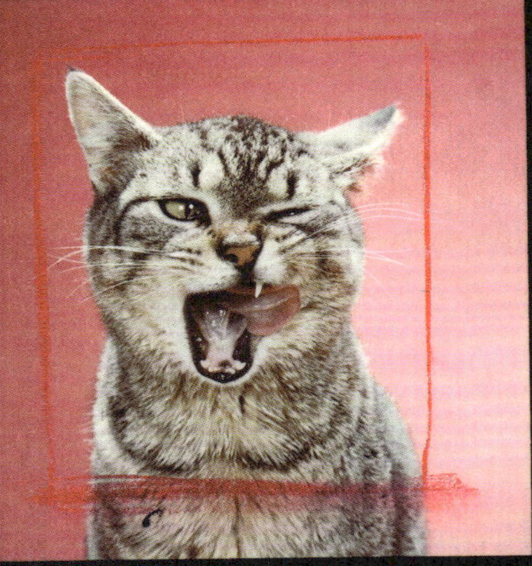
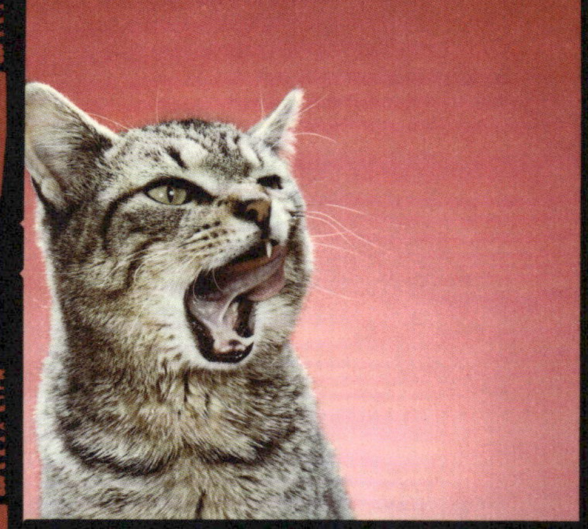

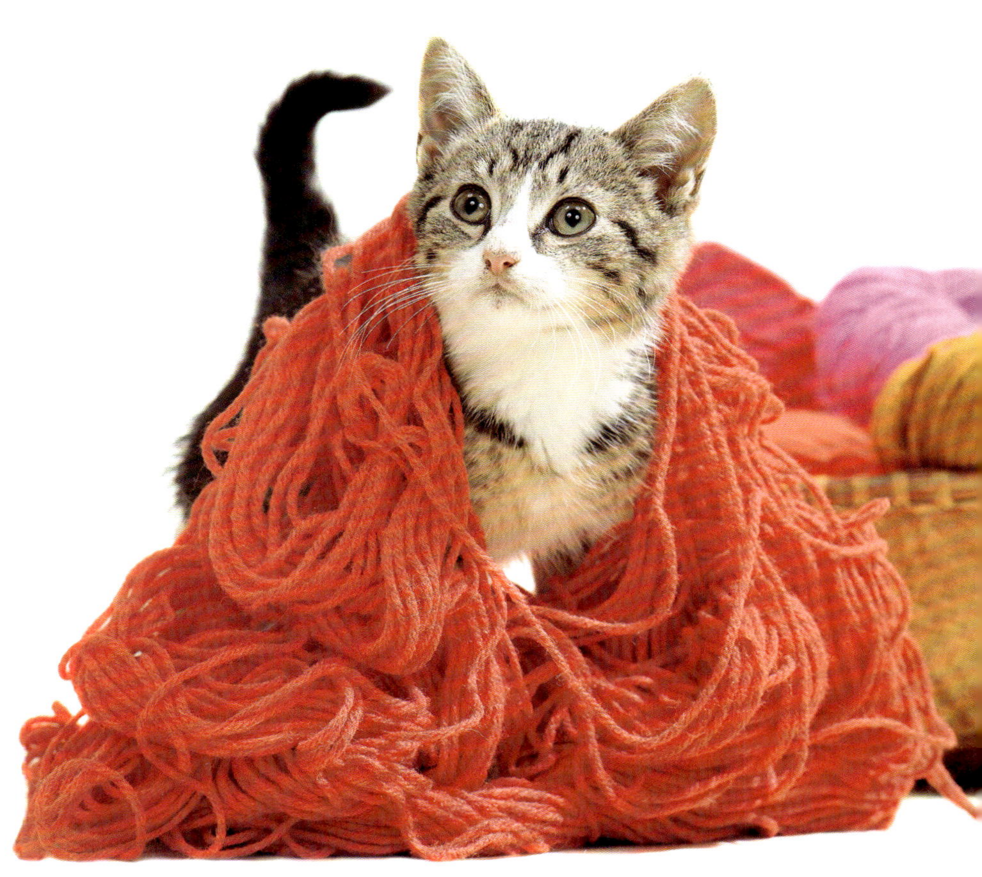

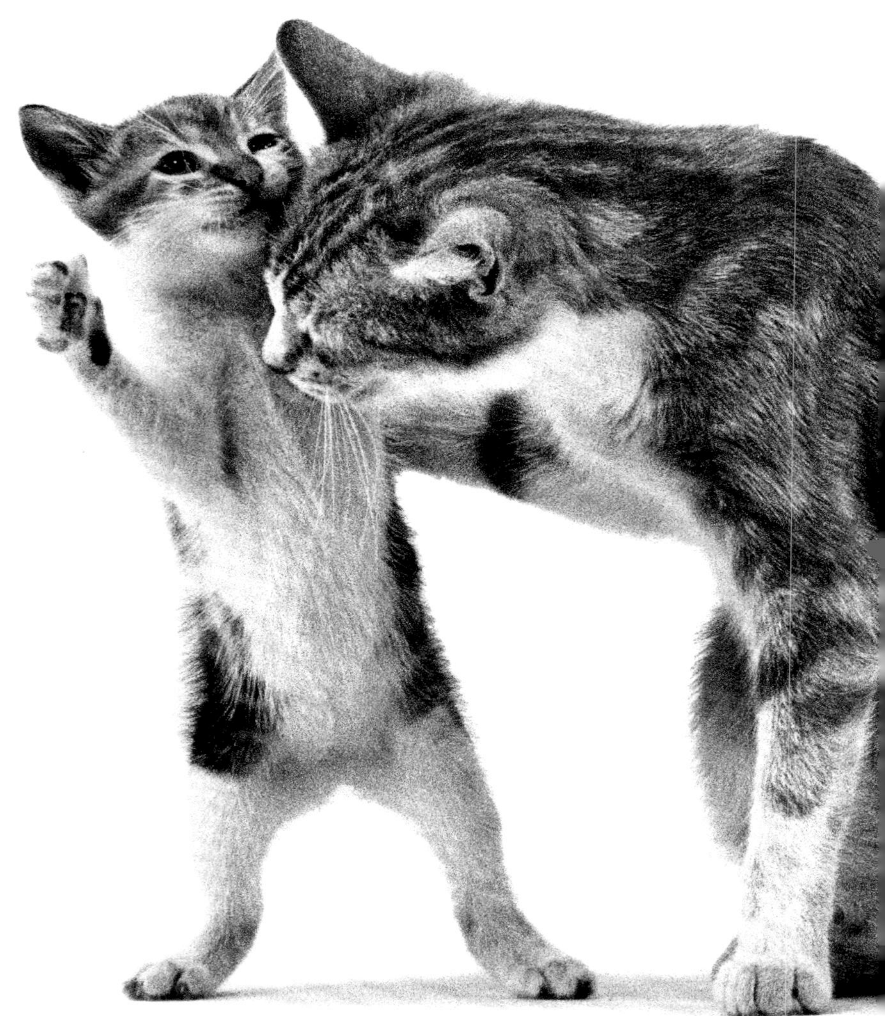

WALTER CHANDOHA

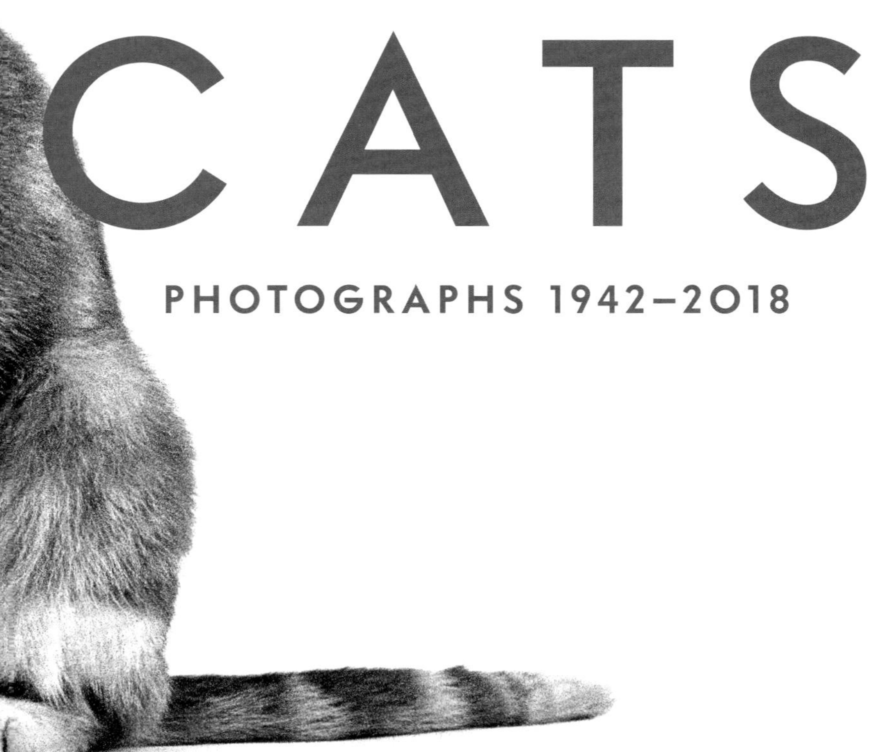

CATS

PHOTOGRAPHS 1942–2018

TASCHEN

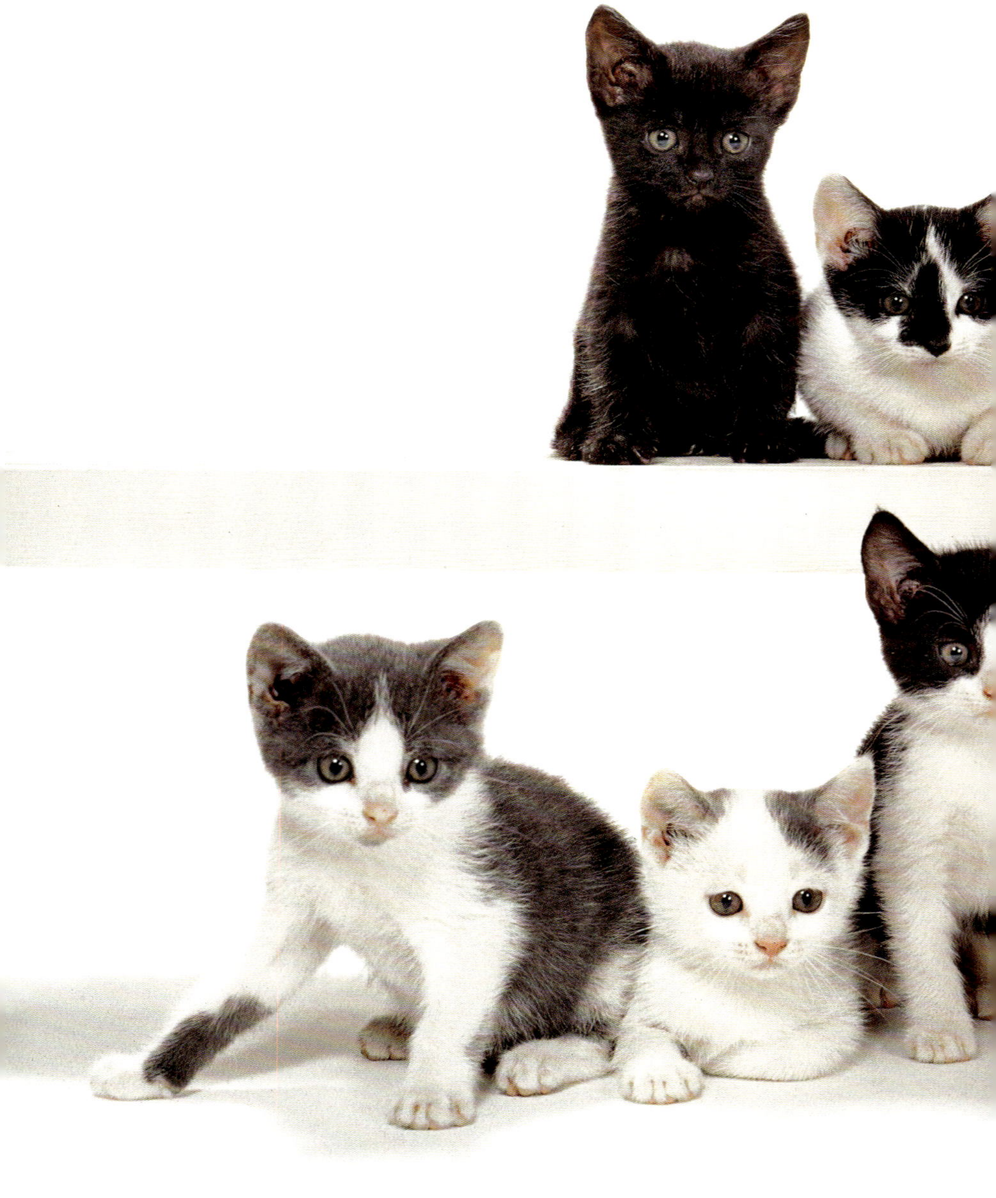

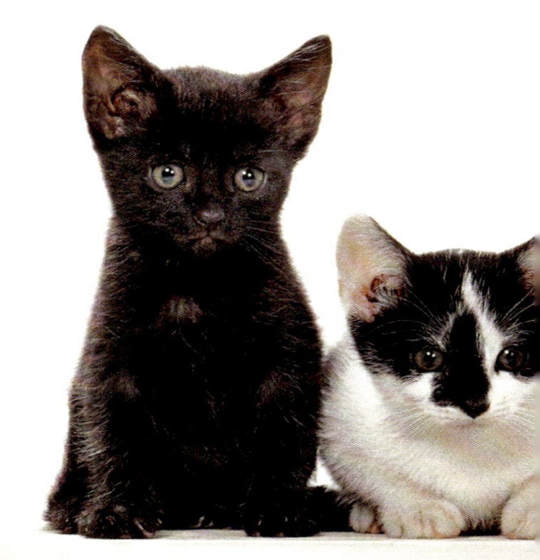

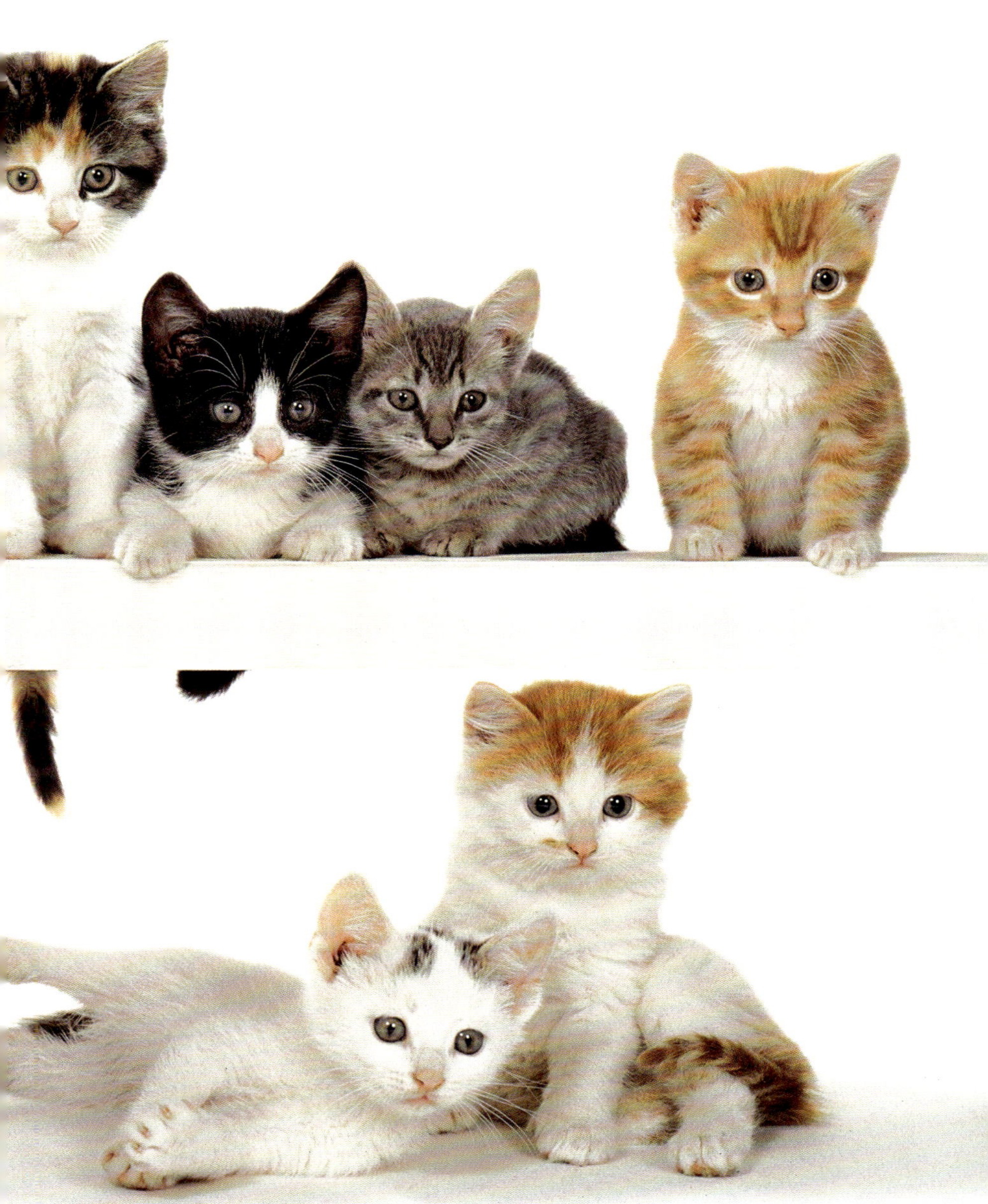

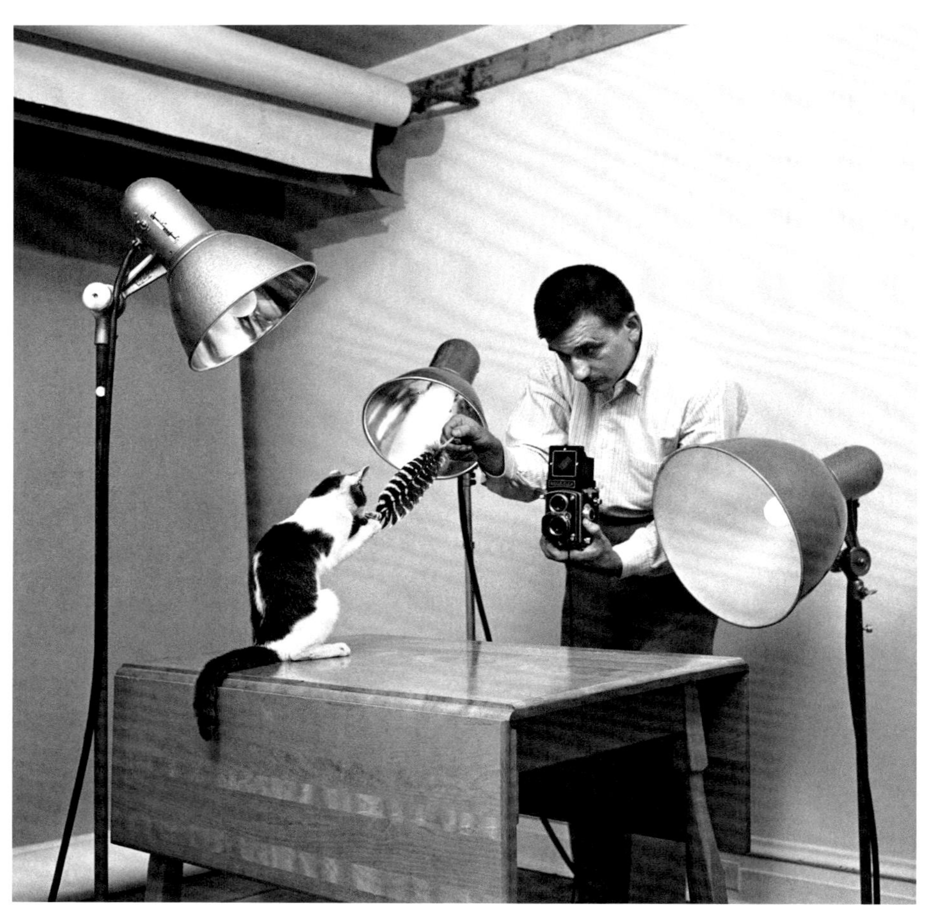

Previous: A seemingly impossible feat
with 11 entranced kittens. New Jersey, 1964.

Photographer and subject, taken in
Chandoha's Long Island studio, 1955.

MY LIFE WITH CATS

FOREWORD BY WALTER CHANDOHA

My fascination with photography began in the late 1930s as a student at Bayonne High School in New Jersey. I read every photography book I could get my hands on at the local library and tinkered with my family's folding Kodak camera, practicing what I had learned. But I needed to know more, so I joined the local Lens Club, whose experienced members and guest speakers began to unravel the many mysteries of the medium. Expert printers could be found in the club's darkrooms, and with a lot of trial and error in my home makeshift darkroom — consisting of a closet and some of my mother's soup bowls — I soon became a fairly good darkroom technician. A year after graduating from high school, I got a job in New York City as an apprentice with Leon de Vos, a top advertising photographer at the time, for $12 a week. Even then the pay was low, but I was discovering the science and magic behind lighting portraits, still lives, and location shots, and understanding how a strong backlight can make a good picture even better and more impactful. This later became one of my photographic signatures.

After a brief stint as a portrait photographer in studios in New Orleans and Newark, I was drafted into the U.S. Army following Pearl Harbor. The army was impressed with my photographic skills, and I became a staff press photographer for a G.I. newspaper at Fort Dix, New Jersey, and later transferred to the Signal Corps as a combat photographer in the Pacific. In war I quickly learned the value of thinking on your feet and resourcefulness, improvising with available equipment and makeshift tools to get the shot.

In 1946 I returned home and enrolled in New York University under the G.I. Bill, majoring in marketing, but I used every free moment I had to photograph daily life in New York City — from Penn Station before it was demolished in 1963 to laundry day in Harlem. On the way home from classes one winter night, I found a kitten shivering in the snow and decided to bring him home as a gift for my wife, Maria. She gave him food, made a bed for him, and he responded in kind, quickly acclimating himself to our home. Late that night, he started running around the periphery of each room of our Queens apartment. After about a minute, he stopped as quickly as he started. He would repeat this brief performance just before midnight every night. Like a man possessed, my wife said, and so we named him Loco. Captivated by his antics, I grabbed my camera and started shooting — and shooting.

We were truly thrilled with the success of those first pictures of Loco and began to seek out other cats to photograph. We found them at local shelters and cat shows, from other cat owners, and on the streets of New York. I relished the challenge of making photographs of cats and quickly saw the potential of attempting to capture their naturally expressive personalities. The photographic possibilities and challenges seemed endless.

In all these years I've spent making thousands of images of every kind of cat, I'm still surprised to find yet another who is completely different from their peers. From Loco to Maddie, my current cat and an adoptee from a local animal shelter, we have had dozens of assorted cats living in our house. Sometimes they were the sole spoiled potentate, but more commonly there were as many as four in the house and a number in the barn. Every one of these cats had their own distinct manner and set of characteristics —whether it be engaging or enigmatic, active or lethargic — but they were always part of the family. And it was Loco and his unusual personality that set me on this journey of befriending and photographing these charming critters for over 75 years.

—Walter Chandoha, 2019

This foreword was written just before Walter Chandoha's passing at age 98 in January 2019.

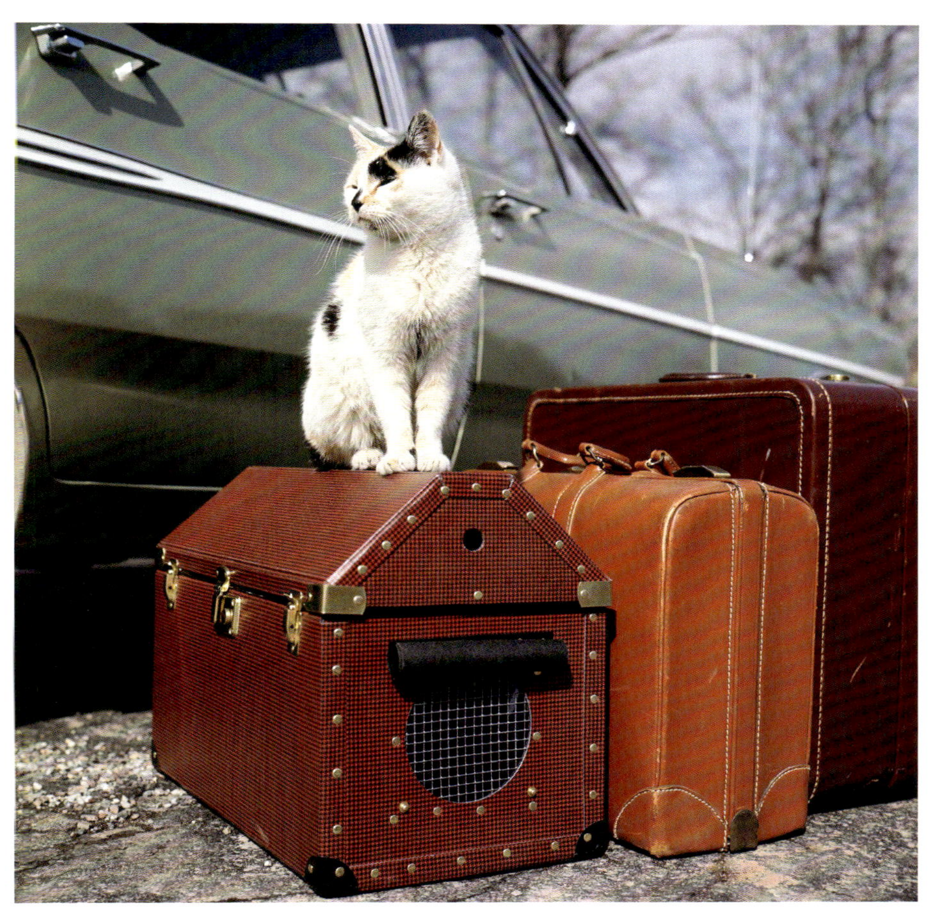

New Jersey, 1968.

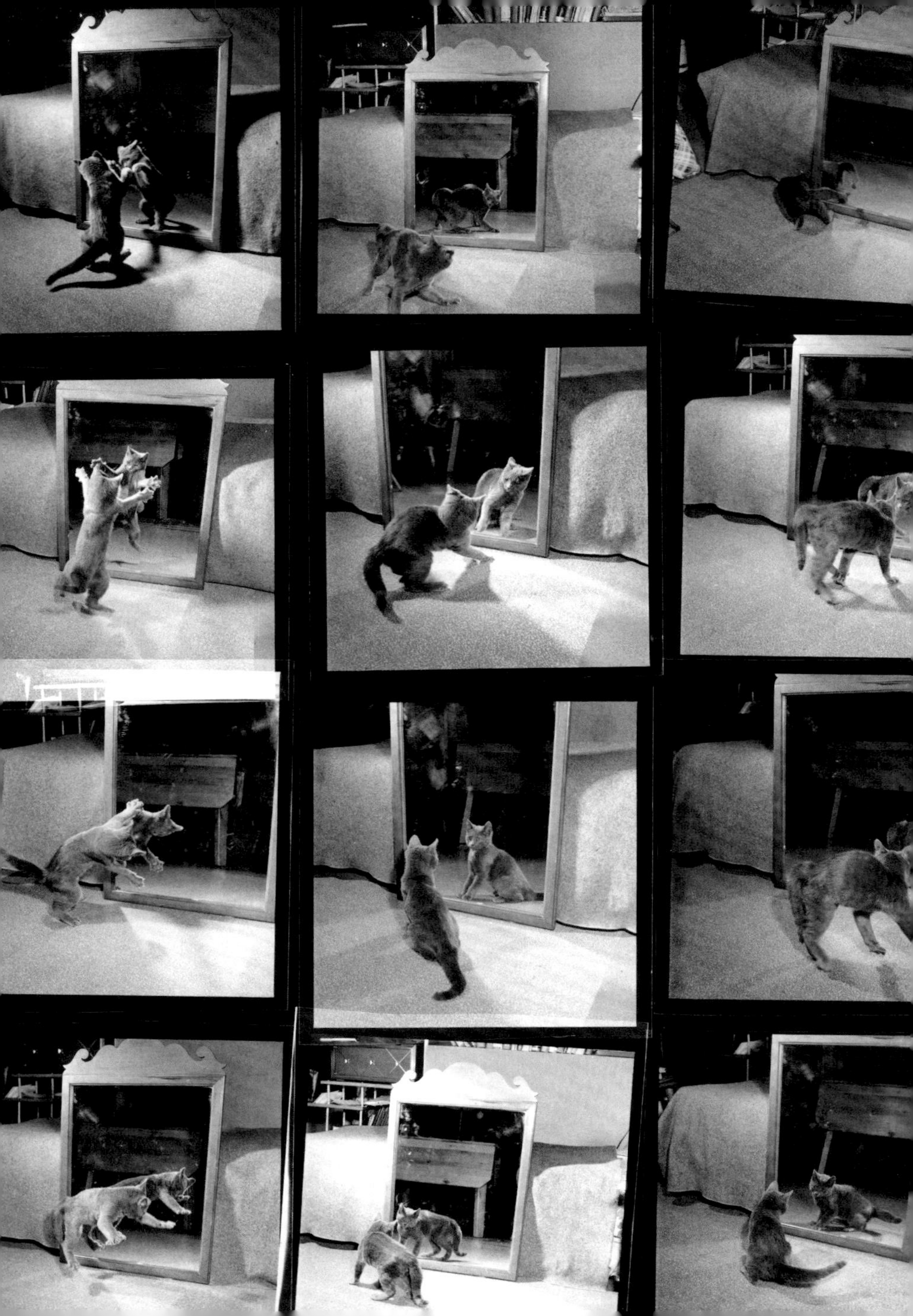

THE ANIMAL INSTINCT OF WALTER CHANDOHA

STORY BY SUSAN MICHALS

Actor W. C. Fields once said, "Never work with children or animals," but photographer Walter Chandoha debunked that statement many times over. Witness the artist's most famous melding of the two subjects in his 1955 photograph *Paula and Kitten*, a close-up shot of daughter Paula and a tiny feline friend and a perfect example of the Chandoha instinctive technique. The kitten was sans mother, and the photographer directed his daughter to coddle the youngster and eventually put her on her shoulder. Paula had lost her front teeth, and the kitten also appeared to be missing a few. In an instant, the child and the cat seemed to smile in unison like two best friends (though the cat is actually meowing). There is an innate whimsy to the work; they are both slightly off-kilter, almost about to regard each other, making one wonder: Was this a secretly hatched plan by the two moppets or merely jovial happenstance?

Paula and Kitten is recognized as one of Chandoha's most iconic images, yet the love affair between man and feline began much earlier. In 1949 Chandoha was on his way home one evening when he heard it — that tiny but mighty cry. A gray kitten in a New York City alleyway caught his eye; the animal was abandoned and alone. Chandoha scooped up the furry infant, tucked him in the pocket of his army mackinaw, and brought him home to his wife, Maria. The couple named him Loco, and aptly so; like clockwork every night, at 11 P.M., the cat would scurry about their three-room Astoria apartment in Queens, bouncing off the walls and scaring himself when catching a glimpse of his image in a mirror. This would last for about a minute, then, just as fast as he went berserk, he would become the pinnacle of calm. Chandoha began taking photos of Loco's nightly antics and submitted them to newspapers, magazines, and photo contests.

Photography had always been part of Chandoha's life. After immersing himself in the medium during high school and serving as a combat photographer during the Second World War, he had the initial goal of becoming a Madison Avenue genius, and received a marketing degree from NYU through the G.I. Bill. Newly married with a baby on the way, marketing and advertising seemed more lucrative than photography in the scheme of things. But Loco changed everything. Soon magazines like *Look* and *Women's Home Companion* came calling, launching a lifelong career and a love affair — one that would be at once familial, familiar, and four-legged in nature.

Cats are having a moment, and in the annals of pop culture, the feline reigns supreme. Yes, the *Felis catus* (domestic cat) has amused, bewildered, and coaxed us since the days of ancient Egypt, where they were considered sacred and worshipped as gods (and, most assuredly, in a cat's mind they are). Yet their idolatry has now surpassed even this. The Internet is their virtual pantheon where they are worshipped daily. Cats online — in the forms of photographs, GIFs, memes, and videos — provide us with much-needed mental respite from the nonstop barrage of opinions or news (fake or otherwise) that has divided us politically and culturally. They have transcended the role of mere companions. Cats with names like Lil BUB, Hamilton the Hipster Cat, and White Coffee Cat have pounced onto the scene as influencers, promoting products and amassing followers in the millions on social media. Hashtags like #purrfect and #catsofinstagram dominate, and the word "caturday" is part of our colloquial language. And

Previous: One of numerous photo shoots with Loco that launched Chandoha's feline photographic journey. Published worldwide beginning in the early 1950s, including in the April 1964 issue of *National Geographic*, titled "The Cats in Our Lives." Astoria, Queens, 1949.

Daughter Chiara and Tiger, a Domestic shorthair tabby, New Jersey, 1960.

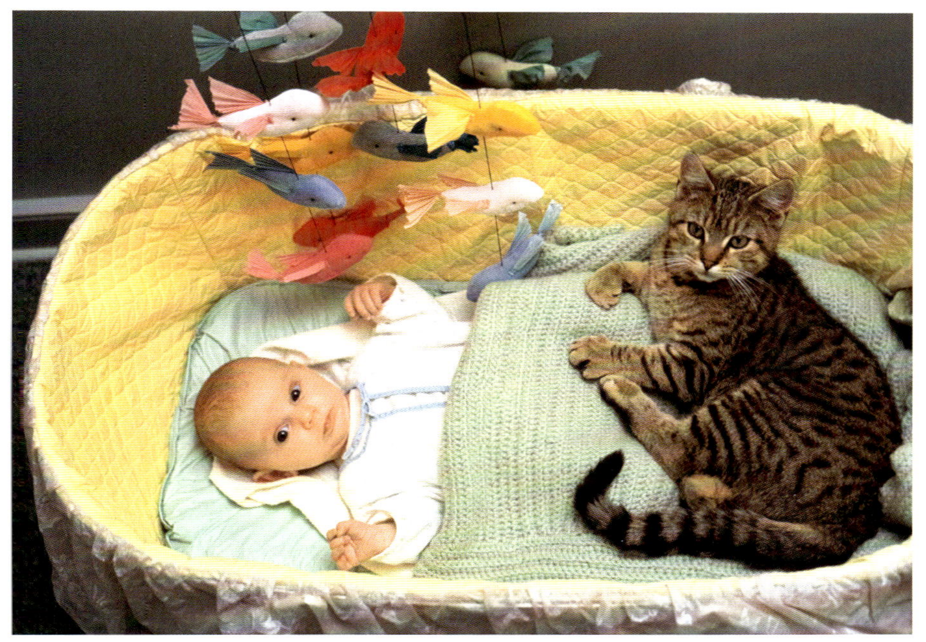

conventions melding all things feline and pop culture dot the land-
scape, from Los Angeles to London.

Chandoha spent over 75 years creating photos that meld our love of cats
with the American way of life. For one assignment he might create a
perfectly staged, high-definition, and color-saturated composition with,
at its epicenter, a beautiful ball of fluff; then he'd switch gears and bring
forth intimate, Rockwellian scenes of family life, resplendent in black and
white. His work graced over 300 magazine covers, hundreds of pet food
packages, and thousands of advertisements, and he published 33 books
(14 books on cats and other animals alone). Countless greeting cards, cal-
endars, and jigsaw puzzles also bear the Chandoha signature aesthetic,
one that would define the visual vocabulary of animal portraiture for gen-
erations. With over 200,000 photographs in his archives, he solidly captured one of the most unpredictable yet beloved creatures on Earth with
what may be one of the largest portfolios on the subject ever amassed.

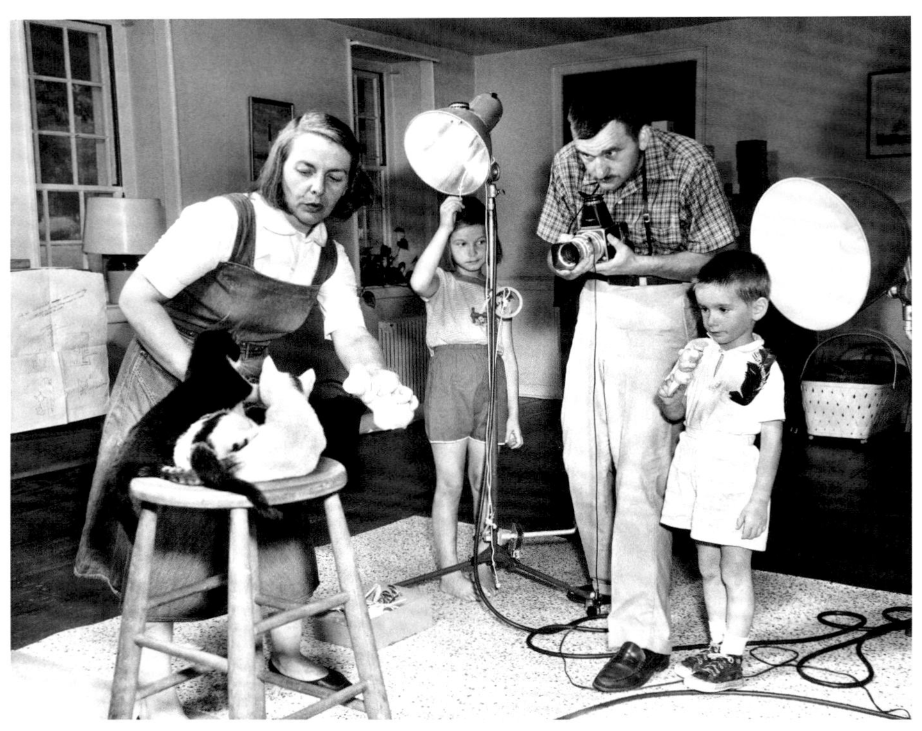

"The expressions dogs make are pretty limited," said Chandoha. "They don't get into real exciting postures, as a cat will." Cats have an unusual level of flexibility; they also lack a collarbone and have the ability to decrease their terminal velocity. The feline's physiology has been depicted both artistically and scientifically for hundreds of years; one of the most famous studies, *Falling Cat*, was created by scientist and chronophotographer Étienne-Jules Marey in Paris in 1894. Marey built a camera that had the capacity to capture animals in motion at 12 frames per second. He filmed the cat being dropped from an upside-down position in an effort to show what is now known as the cat-righting reflex, the animal's uncanny ability to reorient its body while falling — no matter its position — and land on its feet. He was a trailblazer for what would become the moving picture and, in essence, created the first cat video.

Like Marey, Chandoha was a pioneer when it came to capturing feline nuance through his photographic lens. In the 1950s, the advertising industry was hitting its stride in a postwar era of consumerism, fulfilling the need of a rising baby boomer population. Family was paramount, a powerful commodity, and animals were part and parcel of living the American dream. Ad men recognized the potential of integrating animals into their campaigns, and Madison Avenue came calling. Quickly, he became their go-to for *gato*, as well as an adviser to creative directors and ad executives trying to innovatively determine the way into the hearts of American consumers. He created diverse imagery of everything from undergarments to shoes, as well as virtually every pet food package around. Chandoha commented on the omnipresence of his work in the 1950s and '60s: "If you went into a supermarket when I was doing all these packages, there would be dog food on one side and cat on the other. Almost all of the photographs were mine!"

Perhaps his secret weapon was that he was a die-hard cat man and loved the animals through and through. His prowess with the purr set was enviable, and his instinct

Walter's wife, Maria, was also his partner in work and essential in readying the cats for a shoot. "She had magic in her hands." With children Maria and Sam, she assists Chandoha in one of the many photo shoots that took place in their home. New Jersey, 1961.

Domestic shorthair, Long Island, 1957.

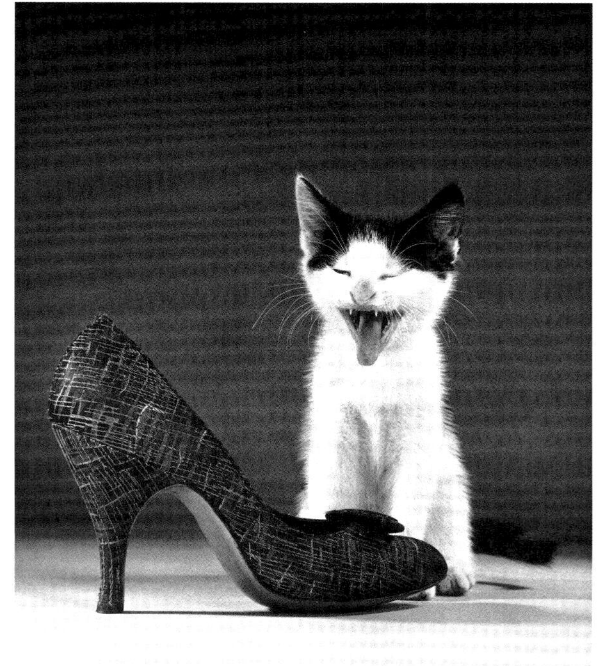

undeniable. He frequently got down to their eye level to generate a level of comfort and perfectly capture their bewhiskered intimacies. While working as an adviser for the advertising agency Leo Burnett, the art director asked what they could do to make a commercial with a mother and her kittens a real standout. "In every litter of kittens…there's a crybaby," recalled Chandoha. "You'd have to take that crybaby out of the basket and away from the group. The mother would have her kittens with her, but they get nervous because a sibling is crying and uncomfortable. The mother is torn between calming the ones in the basket with her or

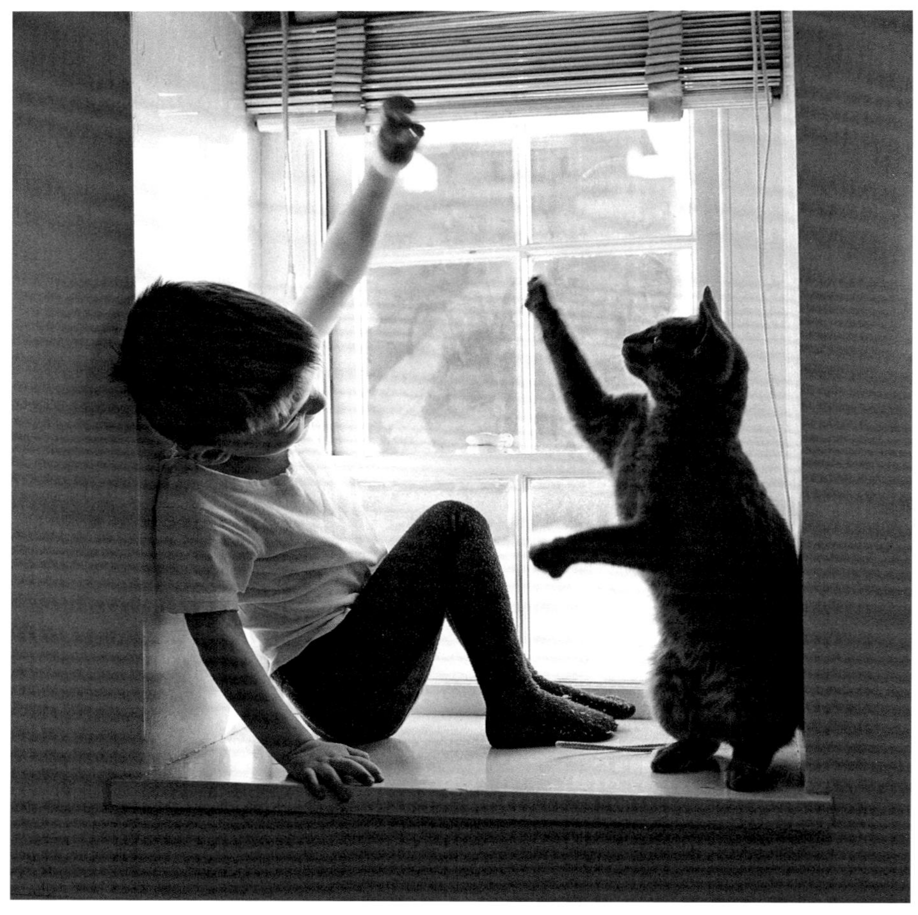

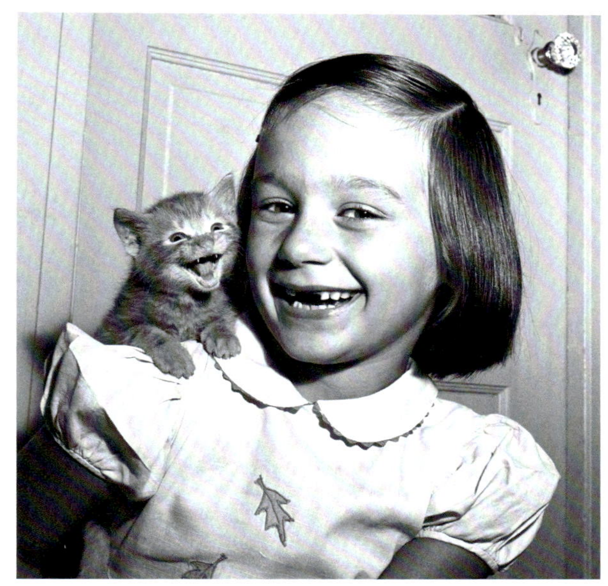

"Cats would often become hypnotized when they were with the kids," Chandoha said. "They had a rapport that was phenomenal. There was no reticence on the part of the cat to get out of the way as they would do with an adult forcing their attention on them." New Jersey, 1962.

"I said to my daughter Paula, 'I think she's looking for her mother. Why don't you hold her?' Paula was losing her front teeth at the time, and the kitten's teeth were growing in." *Paula and Kitten* is one of Chandoha's most iconic photographs. Long Island, 1955.

jumping out and getting the crybaby. Eventually she walked across the room, perfectly in focus, picked up the baby, and they got their shot." Getting that perfect shot was not so easy. "You can't use a view camera, where you have to keep the shutter open, focus, and then put a film holder into the back of the camera, pull the slide out, and set the aper-ture…" said Chandoha. "[By] that time the action you saw is gone. This is why you had to use a camera like a Hasselblad, an RB67, or a Nikon, where you can see the image constantly. This is how I got the shots."

Take the unlikely pairing of a rabbit and a kitten. Cats are already capricious, but throw a bunny into the mix and a whole new set of challenges emerges. As the pictorial story unfolds, any hint of relationship seems tenuous at best. Patience, as always, was Chandoha's comrade in arms, as evidenced by two miraculous shots — one of the Siamese kitten jumping high into the air over the rabbit, followed by the rabbit challenging the situation and putting the kitten on notice. A later frame from the same shoot shows Chandoha's sense of humor as it is now the hunted — not the hunter — who becomes the most foreboding.

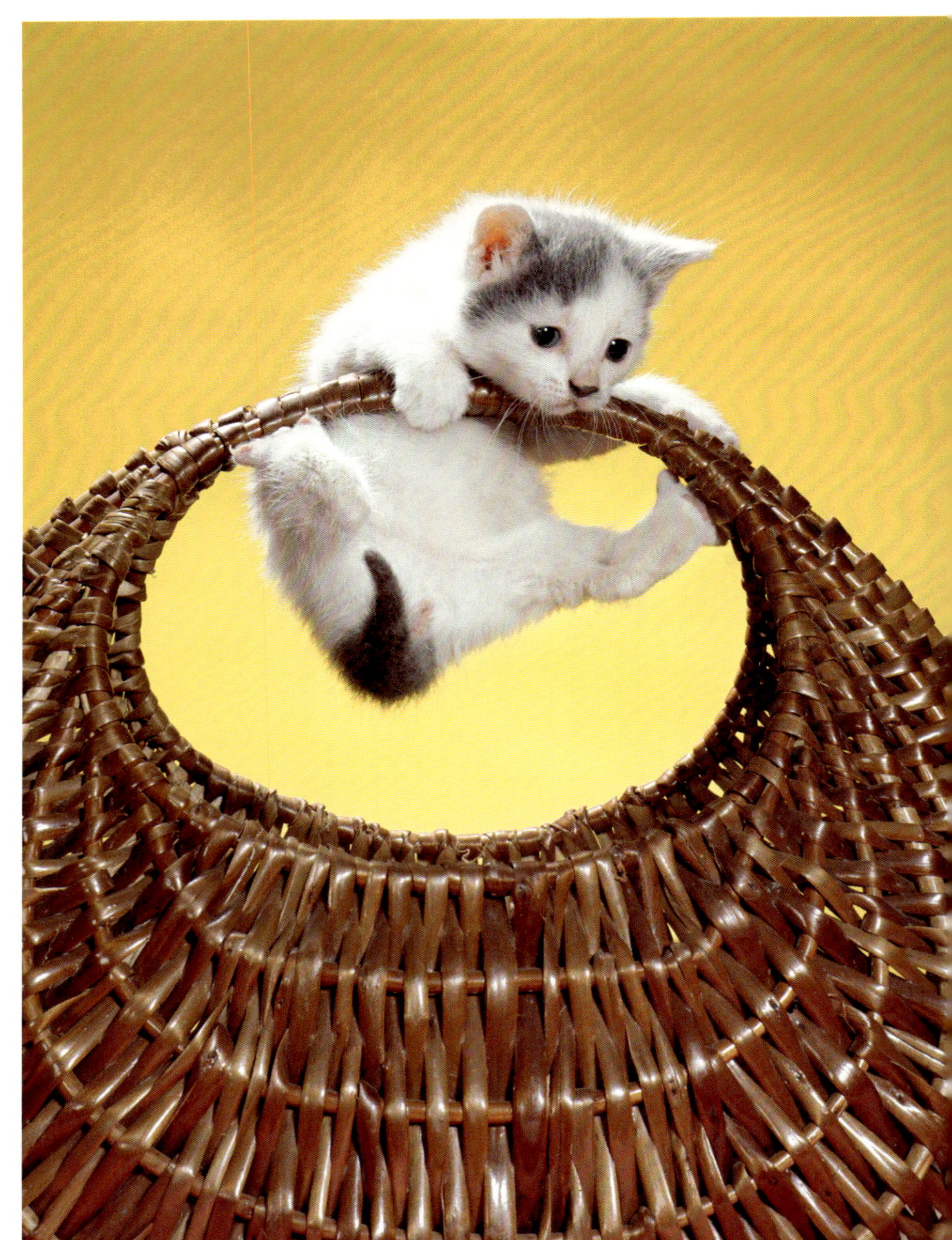

Chandoha had many influences, including artist Théophile Alexandre Steinlen (1859–1923), whose work focused heavily on animals. "We were in the same business — advertising," said Chandoha, referring to the fact that they both worked in commercial art. When looking at some of Steinlen's most famous works such as *Compagnie Française des Chocolats et des Thés* or *Lait Pur Stérilisé de la Vingeanne*, one can spot the similarities; both men had an affinity for like-minded subject matter, depicting everyday life and interactions between cats and children. Tsuguharu Foujita (1886–1968) also resonated greatly with Chandoha. Unlike Steinlen, who created work on myriad different subject matter, Foujita took his intense love for cats and put them in just about everything he created, alongside beautiful women, often in repose. Like Chandoha, he made a living at it with his paintings, printmaking, and various books.

But the artist who had the most impact on Chandoha was Dutch painter Johannes Vermeer (1632–1675). "The way he presented his subjects with light and shadows is something I use in all my pictures," explained Chandoha. Lighting was one of the key elements of the photographer's

Chandoha had an uncanny ability for capturing cats in their most winsome postures. Domestic shorthair, New Jersey, 1977.

Chandoha's first magazine cover: a beribboned kitten for the December 1954 Christmas issue of *Woman's Home Companion* magazine.

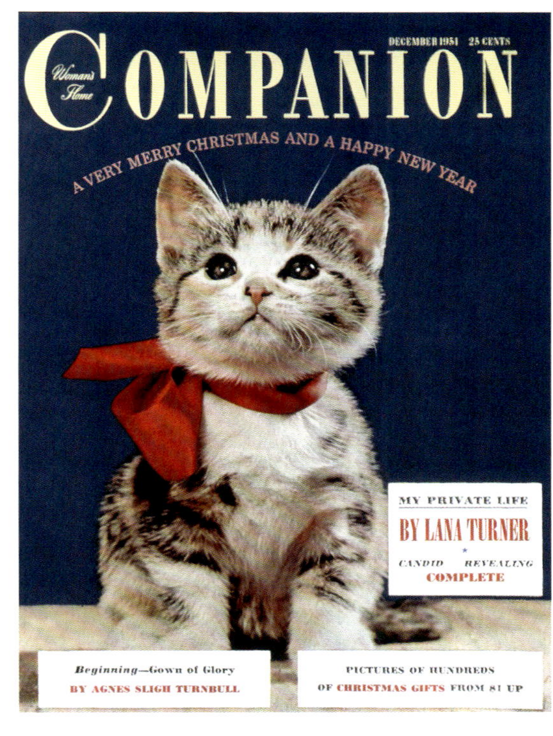

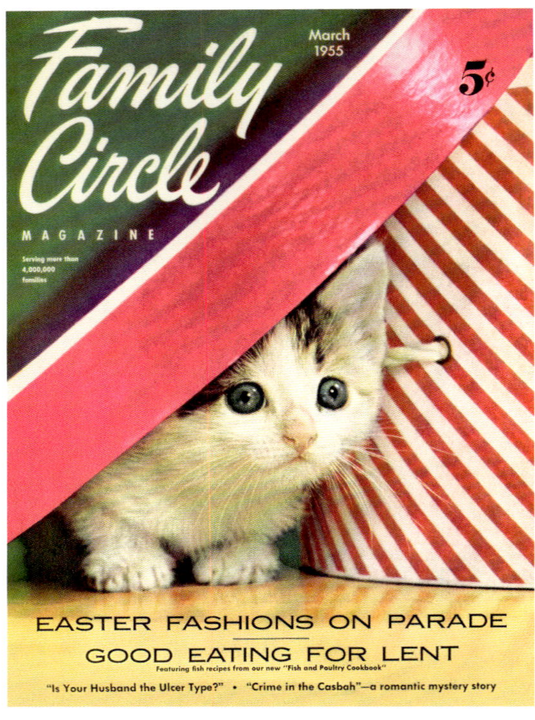

success and became his signature. Typically, in the studio he would use six lights: a main light and a fill, two backlights behind the cat to get a highlight, and two more on the background. Using this technique, he made the forms of his subjects stand out, highlighting their fur, their whiskers, the wisps of hair inside their ears.

With these multiple lights, he created consistency and balance and, ultimately, intense color. He preferred black-and-white photography as his modus operandi; however, he knew the importance of mastering the art of color when it came to advertising: striking color catches the eye and sells the product.

One can see why Chandoha felt so strongly about his black-and-white works. One photograph lets the viewer determine Loco's stance in the moment. He could be looking onward with authority, or he could be pensively assessing the life he has lived. His bewhiskered face shows maturity, his fur perfect as it transitions from light to dark. Another work, one of his most famous, also would not have had the same impact should it have come about in color. Chandoha shot many of his images on his 46-acre farm. "At any given time, we'd have up to half a dozen cats, as well as barn cats to keep the mice out." The animals would frequently follow him around because

By the mid 1950s his work graced magazine covers around the globe. *Family Circle* magazine, March 1955.

Puss'n Boots cat food advertisement, 1955.

Chandoha would feed them. One day, while walking down the road with his camera, a gang of cats began tailing him. He dropped down to his stomach and took an image that would become *The Mob*, five determined cats ambling toward the camera. "Most people consider cats to be loners, but they're very gregarious and are very much like a family," mused Chandoha. The gang walks in perfect harmony. They are mysterious and foreboding, with the black cat — the ringleader — obviously the Michael Corleone of the group, while the tabby lingering on his heels is reminiscent of the godfather's ultimately unlucky brother, Fredo.

Chandoha was himself an artistic influence. It is said that Andy Warhol was an early fan and used *All Kinds of Cats* (1952), Chandoha's second book, as reference material for his cat illustrations released in 1954.

Unlike the dog, their occasional domestic companion, cats can rarely be obedience-trained, but Chandoha managed to pull it off. After being on assignment for Ringling Bros. and Barnum & Bailey, the photographer was fascinated by the trainer's ability to get the tigers to sit up and beg. The animal trainer filled him in on what was needed: "You're going to need patience, sound, and food. Patience, we know you've already got. Food is a given. As you feed the cat, make a sound that can be repeated time and time again." Chandoha invested in a clicker and his muse, Loco, was his student. The outcome is a series of incredible images that look like a sequence, yet each picture was made with one exposure only. *Loco Leap* is the standout. The determination of his stare, compounded by Chandoha's backlighting on his fur and legs, gives him a majestic quality, one of authority, not unlike his cousins in the wild. Leaping with perfect precision and intensity, he is the overseer of his domestic kingdom and chief magistrate of this living room.

The Financial Times described the ubiquity of Chandoha's work during the height of the advertising boom: "Walking the supermarket pet-food aisle in the 1960s was like attending a Chandoha gallery opening." Close-up from a Puss'n Boots shoot, Persian, New Jersey, 1960.

Not only was Chandoha seminal as the most popular feline photographer on Madison Avenue, he was

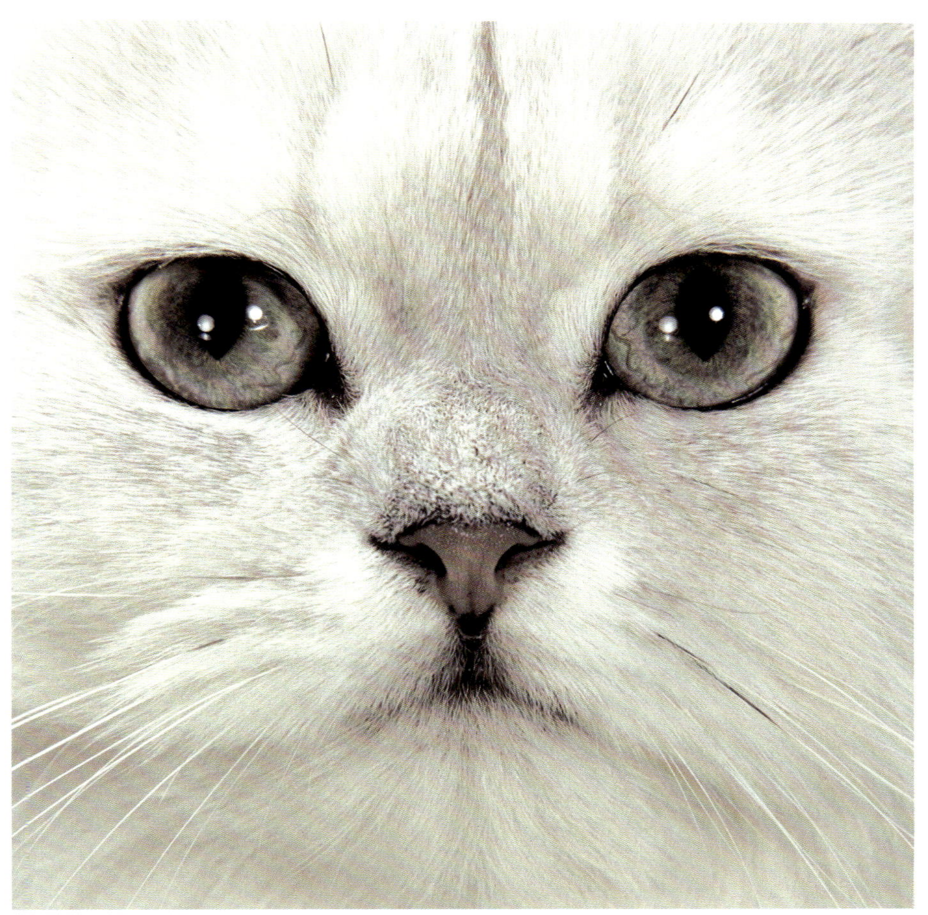

clso a pivotal contributor to the history of LOLcats, better known as cat memes. "In 1950, I got a request from Ethicon, a division of Johnson & Johnson," said Chandoha. "They wanted to do a little booklet for the personnel in operating rooms [and] wanted the pictures to coincide with the funny captions." The term LOLcat debuted in 2006 and married cat photos with sayings, frequently misspelled or idiosyncratic in nature. However, earlier iterations can be found as far back as the 1870s from photographer Harry Pointer (1822–1889), who used his personal clowder to create postcards with amusing sayings. In every issue of Ethicon's

Cat-a-log, the first page of the booklet states: "The current epidemic of picture books prompted us to get in the act with one of our own, relating to fields of mutual interest — nurses, doctors, and their patients.

"As to cats, we owe the name, at least, a salute. The larger percent of our business is in supplying catgut — an age-old misnomer for surgical gut made of sheep intestines. Further, we are happy that cats are not the source of this essential suture material for many of us are fond of the beautiful little creatures. We hope that both ailurophiles and ailurophobes will enjoy this CAT-A-LOG."

In one picture, you see a kitten gazing off into the distance, lingering under the hint of a blanket. The photo is captioned: "Nurse…I had to ring that bell four times!" In another, two felines are in the midst of a catfight; one is poised to attack, standing on its hind legs, while his opponent takes a step back, leering in mid-hiss. The caption: "Now, Doctor, let's be professional!" The Cat-a-logs were a huge hit. According to Chandoha, "The original press run for that first *Cat-a-log* was 10,000, and it quickly went into eight more printings totaling over a million copies."

His wife, Maria, was always by his side and his secret weapon, right from the beginning with Loco. (Sadly, she passed away in 1992.) "[She] was my assistant…" said Chandoha.

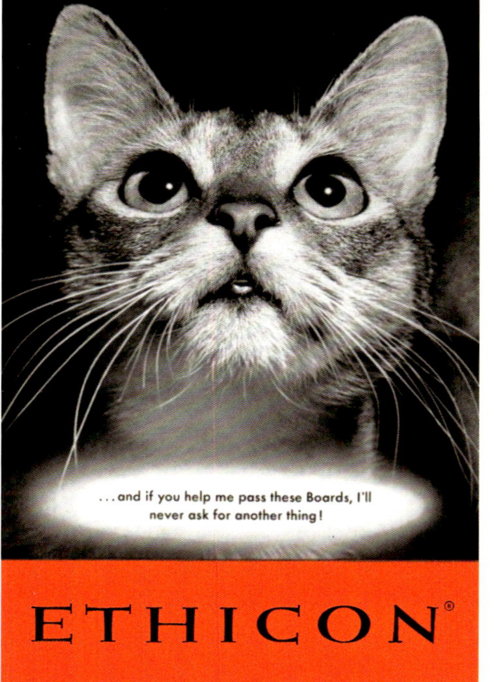

The Ethicon booklets were created to bolster the morale of hospital operating room staff. They proved so popular that numerous editions were produced, with print runs totaling millions of copies, 1953.

Loco, Queens, 1951.

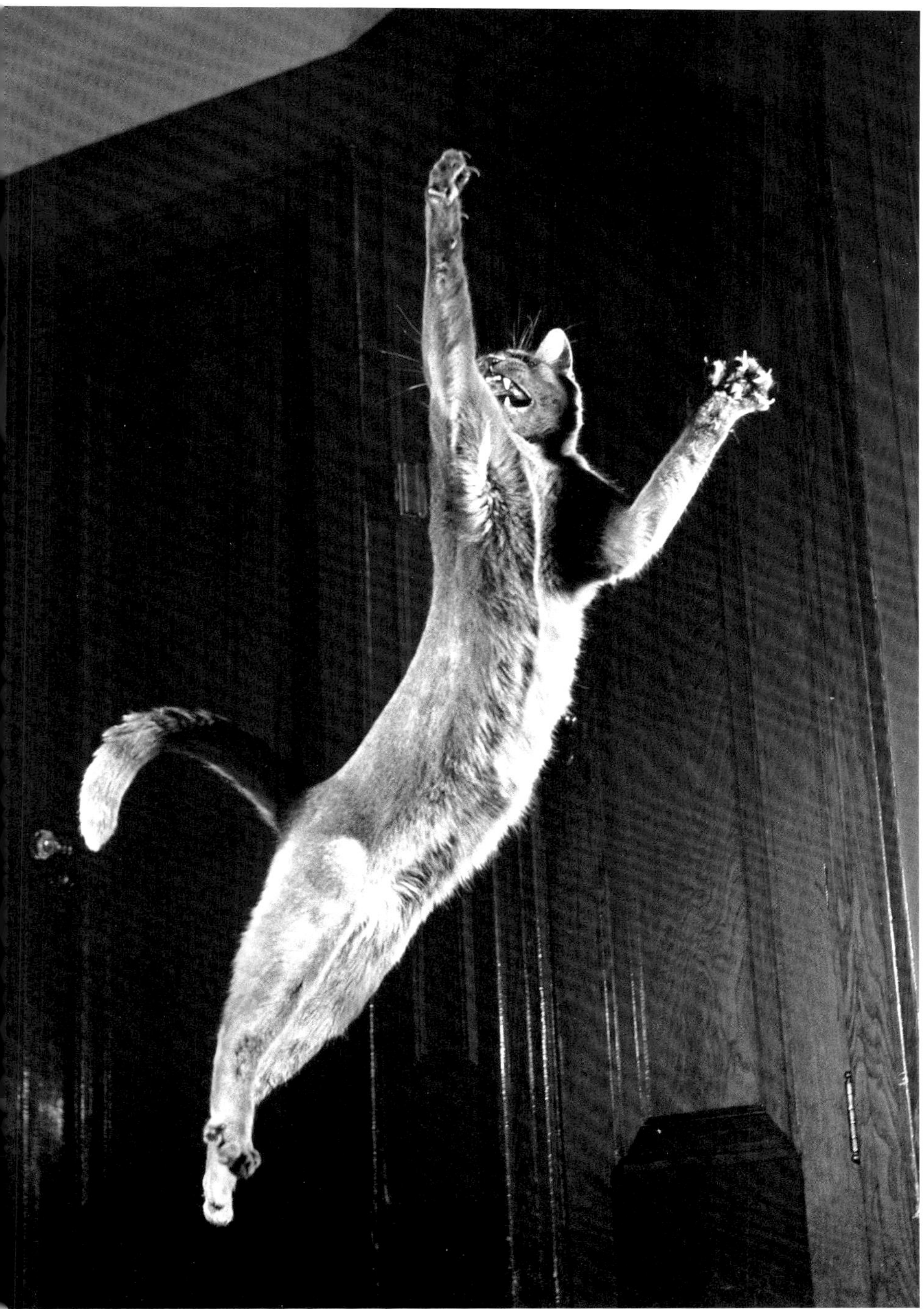

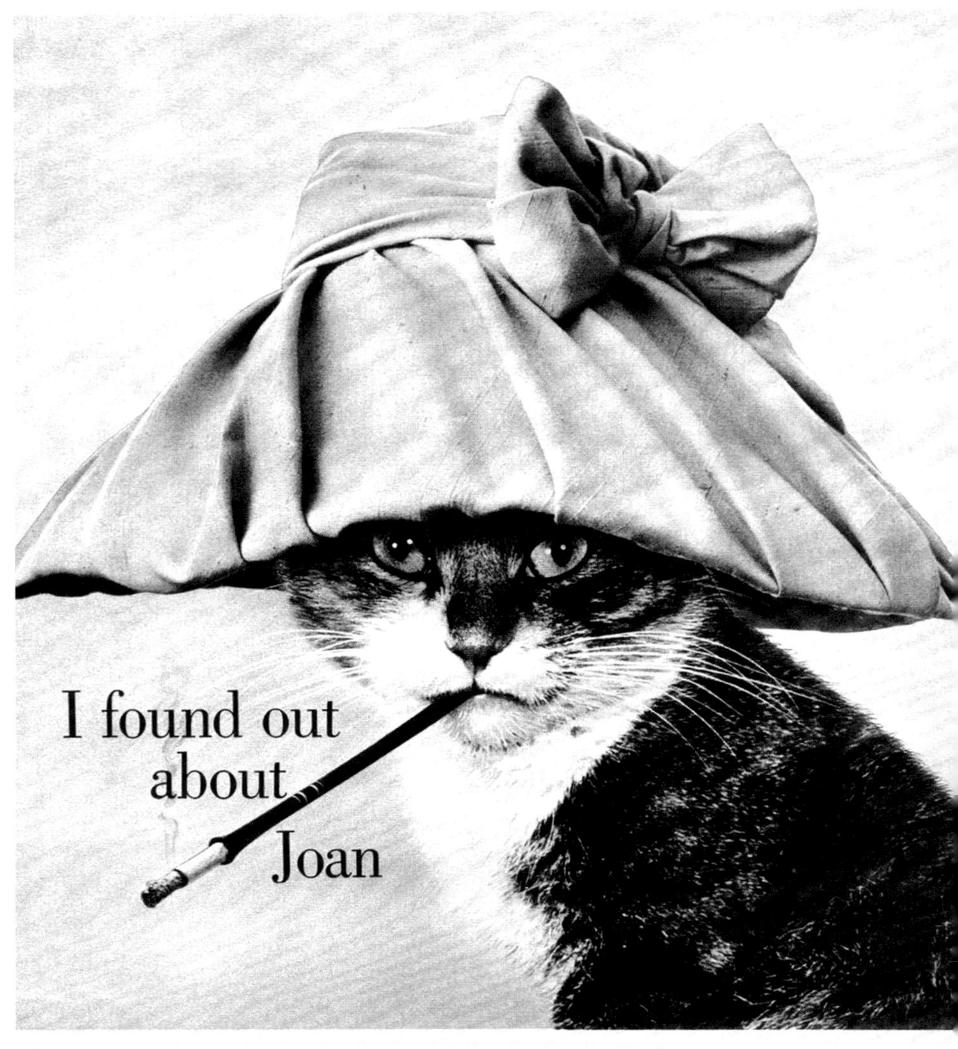

The way she talks, you'd think she was in Who's Who. Well! I found out what's what with *her*. Her husband own a bank? Sweetie, not even a bank *account*. Why that palace of theirs has wall-to-wall *mortgages!* And that car? Darling, that's horsepower, *not* earning power. They won it in a fifty-cent raffle! Can you imagine? And those clothes! Of course she *does* dress divinely. But really...a mink stole, and Paris suits, and all those dresses...on *his* income? Well darling, I found out about that too. I just happened to be going her way and *I saw Joan come out of Ohrbach's!*

Ohrbach's

© 1958 by Ohrbach's Inc.

34TH ST. OPP. EMPIRE STATE BLDG. · **NEWARK** MARKET & HALSEY · "A BUSINESS IN MILLIONS, A PROFIT IN PENNIES"*

26

"Without her, we wouldn't be here talking today." And what a pair they were. Like Walter, Maria was intrinsically in tune with their feline subjects, a veritable Houdini in her own right. "She had magic in her hands," mused Chandoha. Maria would let her husband know when he could take the shot; she prepped the animal for the shoot, petting them, talking to them. "She could feel by the muscular tension whether the cat was relaxed or tense. Then she'd say, 'Walter, he's ready,' and sure enough, the cat would get into a great pose. She'd pull her hands away, and I'd get my picture."

Maria was the stalwart yin to his creative yang; this harmonious partnership allowed them to work together in a situation most people at that time could only dream of — from home and with their children. "Our parents worked from home — we didn't know what it was like to have your parents go somewhere for work," states daughter Chiara.

As their household grew, work and life became even more intertwined with their children stepping into the picture. Over the years, the cat

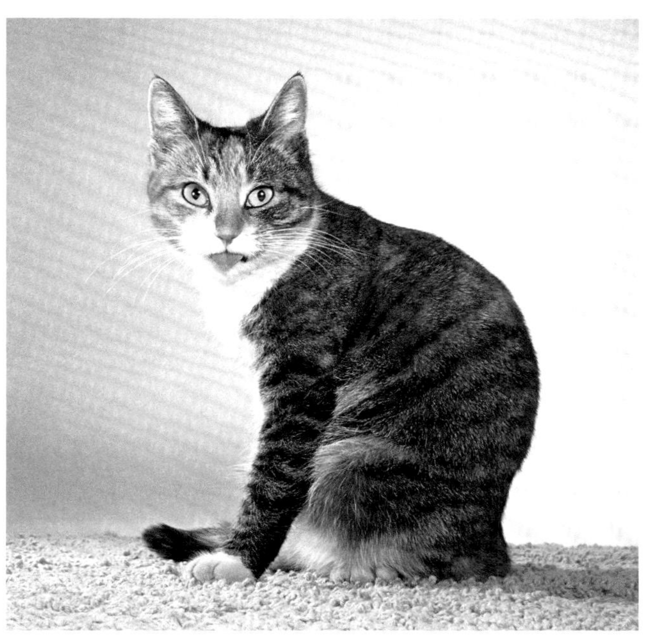

Mad Men—era legend Bill Bernbach of the Doyle Dane Bernbach agency created this seminal 1958 advertising campaign for Ohrbach's department store. It employed a maverick approach — with a catty headline.

The original photograph for the Ohrbach's advertisement. Domestic shorthair, Long Island, 1955.

family and the Chandoha clan melded into one — a perfect collaboration. Chiara, a photographer, said her dad was always on. "He had his camera with him always…no matter what we were doing." They were tasked with traditional chores such as feeding a group of caterwauling mousers, and sometimes even those turned into picture-perfect fodder, like when a very young Chiara became one with her kitty compatriot, joining her in a saucer of milk on the floor.

In another series, a Chandoha family feline just can't seem to get enough of one of the six siblings — and rightly so. The cat is in the crib sidling up to the infant; he obviously enjoys the smell of the child and the coziness of the crib. "The baby liked it, the cat liked it, so how could I miss?" reminisced Chandoha. It is a touching sight to see — the juxtaposition of the child's innocence and the curiosity of the cat. As the series evolves, the child is the more inquisitive creature, and the cat is the innocent.

Perhaps Chandoha's ethos could be best summed up by fellow cat lover and artist Leonardo da Vinci: "Simplicity is the ultimate sophistication." Through his lens, Chandoha gave us 75 years of scenes from American life and culture; some suffused in delectable color, others in his favorite, silken black and white. His observational narrative uniquely depicts the human–animal bond. He knew he could not command these cats, these feline nonconformists, but his work undoubtedly showed them gloriously being themselves — grooming, napping, caring for their babies, and caring for each other. Although we cannot hear the purr, the angry hiss, or the meow of sheer longing, Chandoha captured it all — seemingly effortlessly, viscerally. To spend time with his photos is much like a cat's afternoon in the summer sun: carefree, tranquil, and a meditation in beauty, purrs and all.

Chandoha's last feline companion,
Maddie, a rescue Domestic shorthair,
New Jersey, 2018.

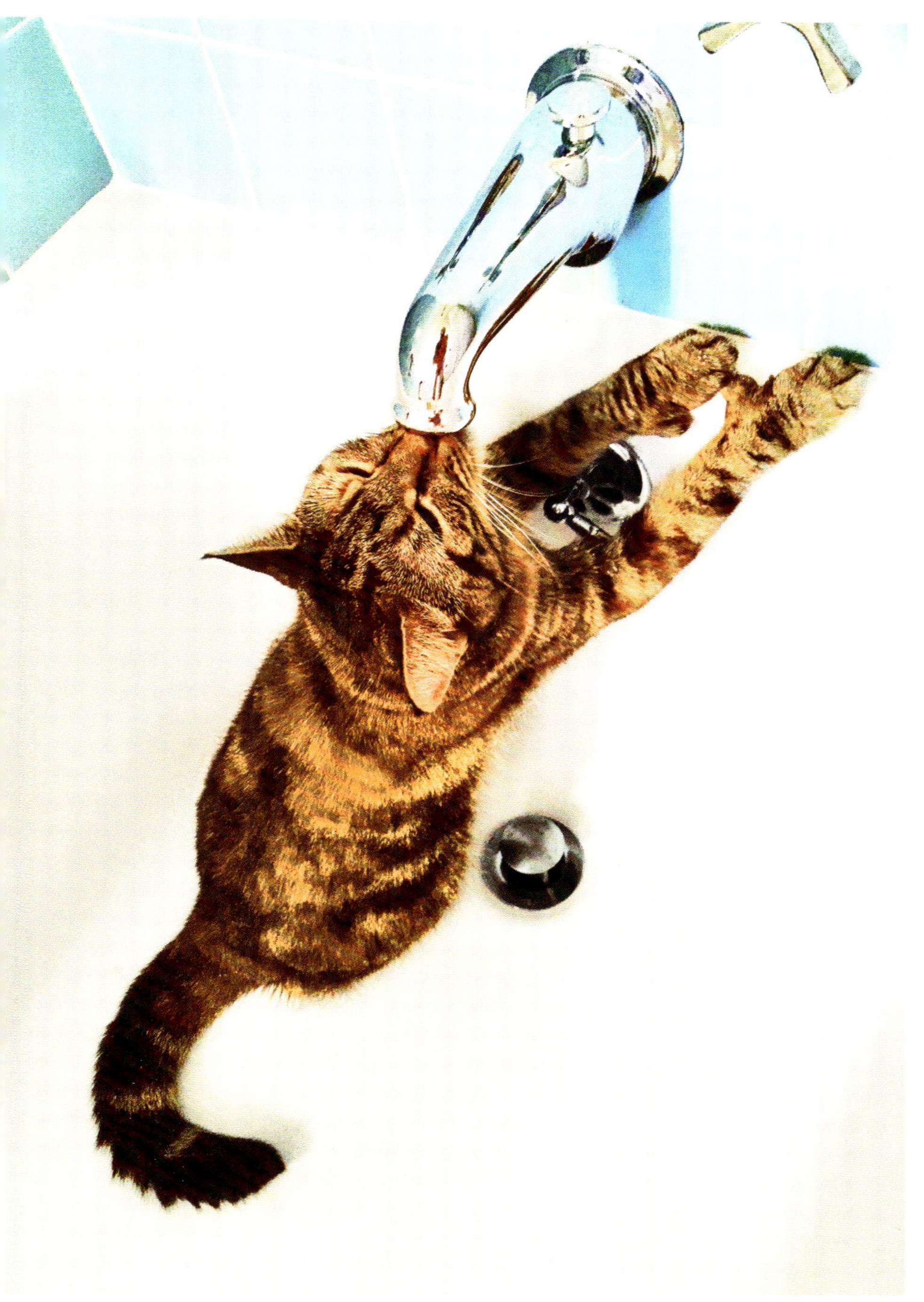

Domestic shorthair, New Jersey, 1988.

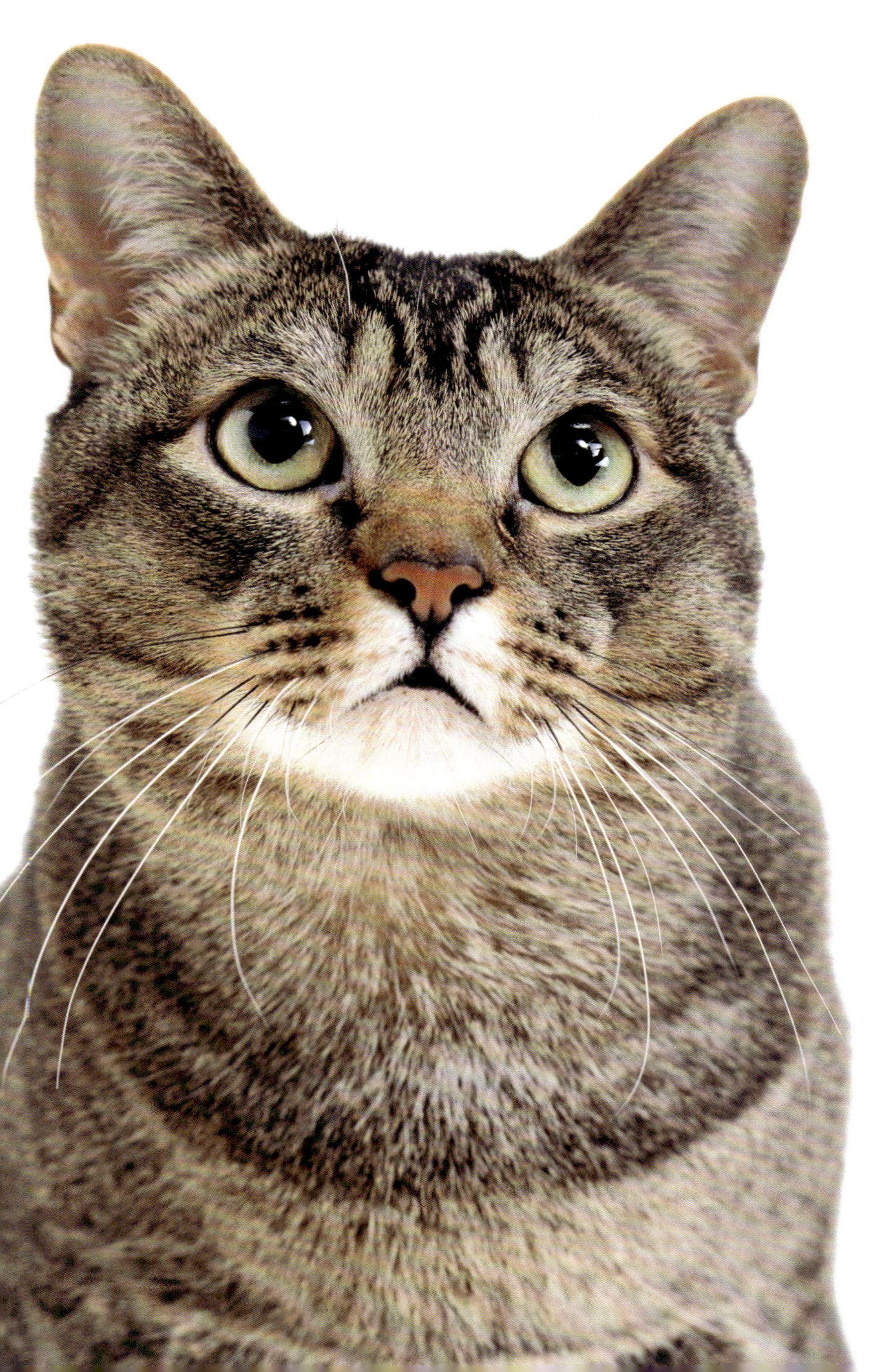

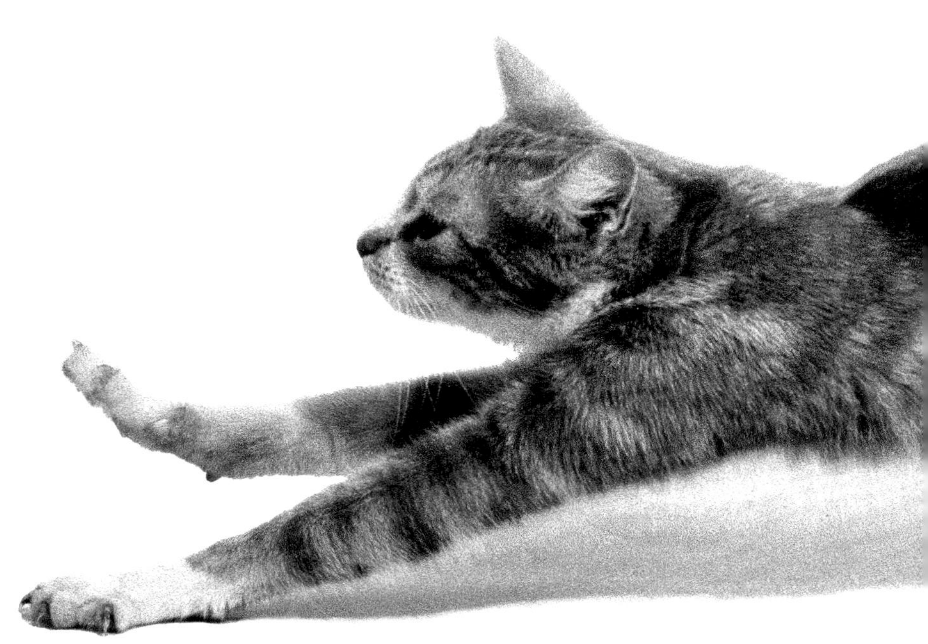

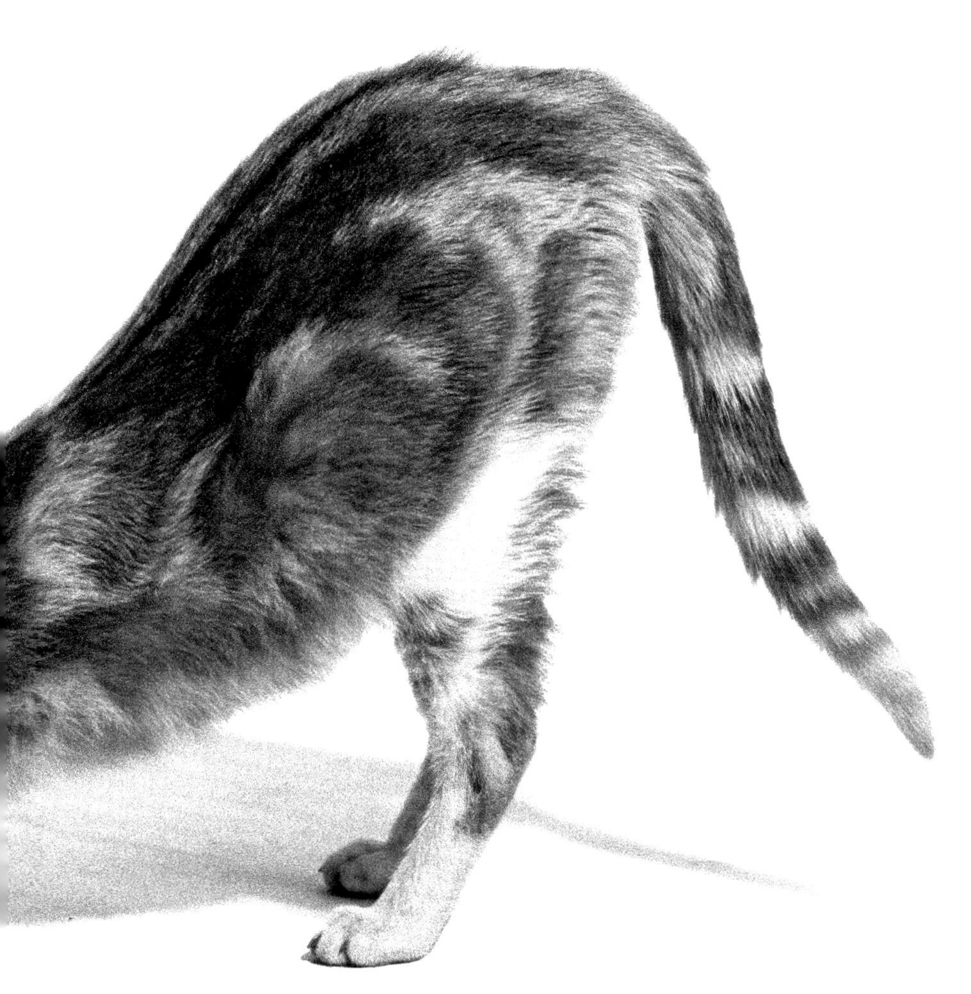

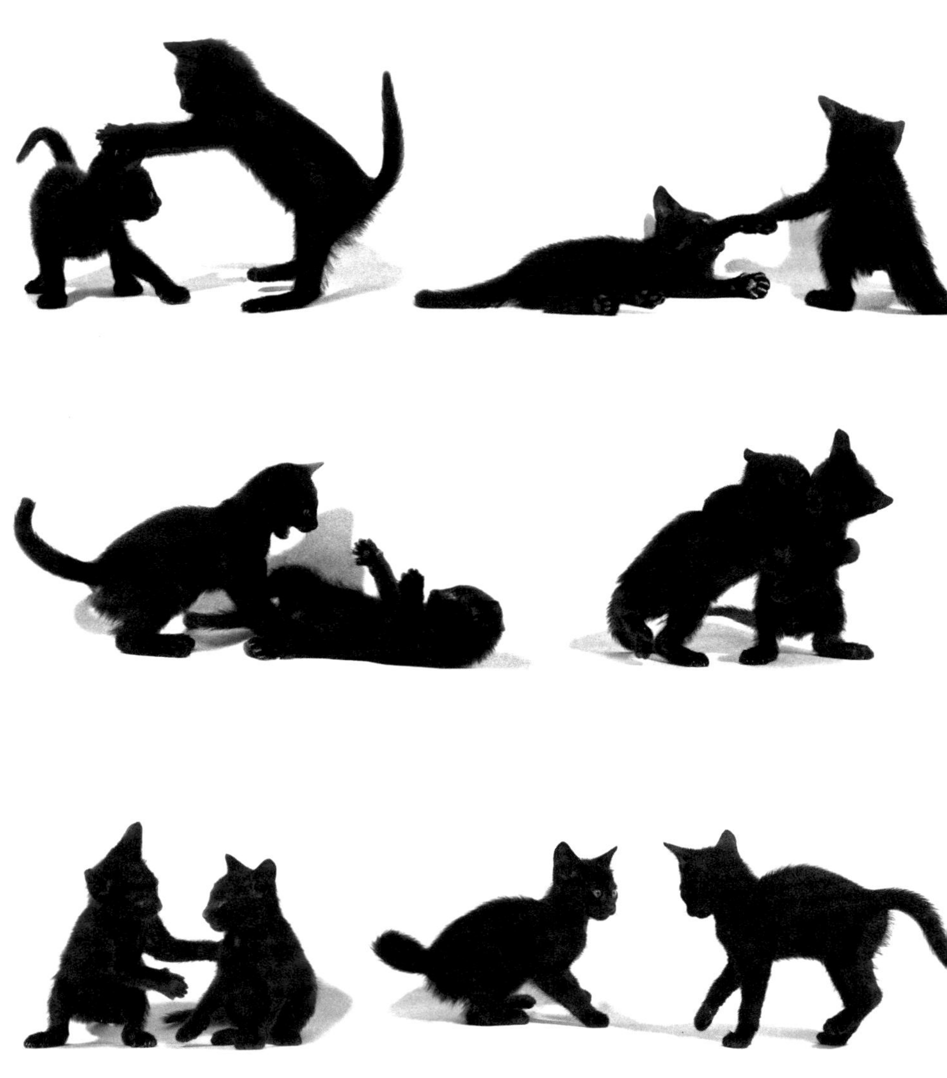

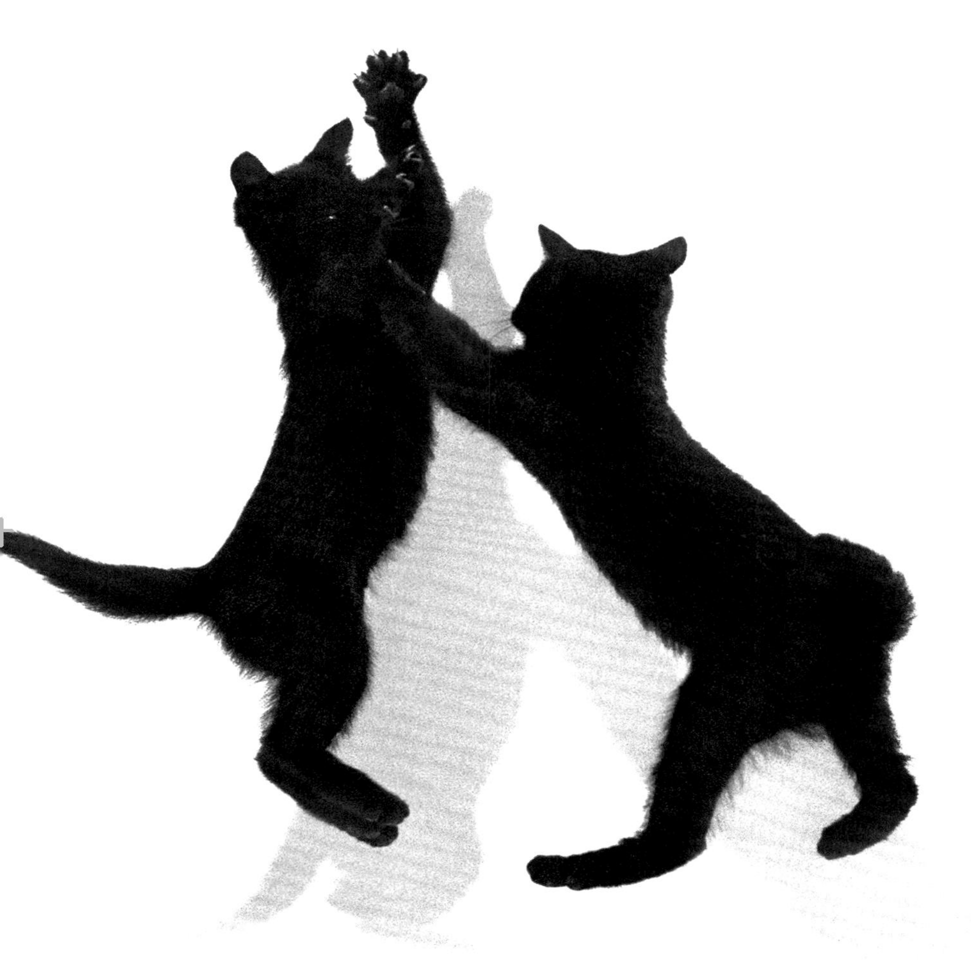

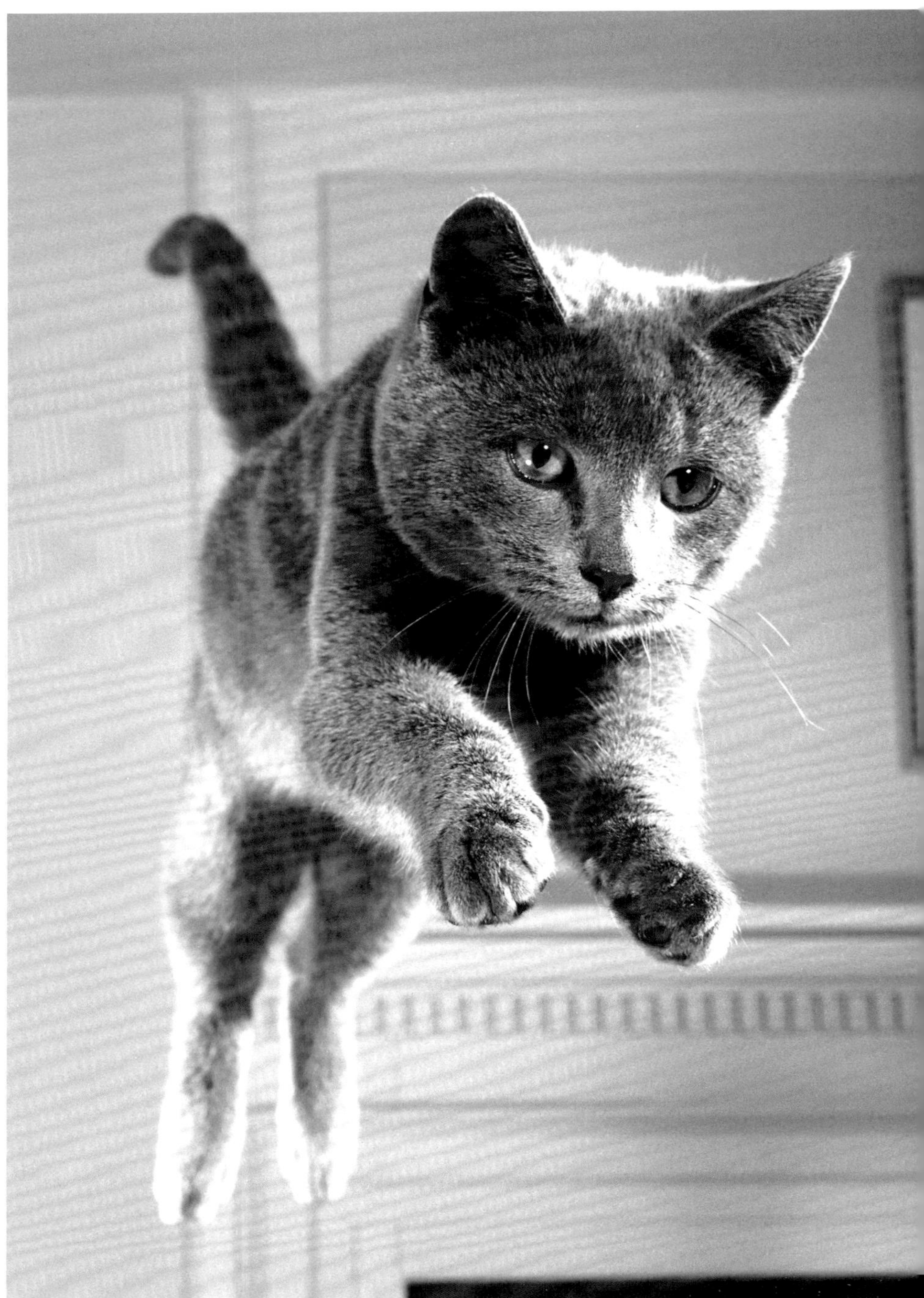

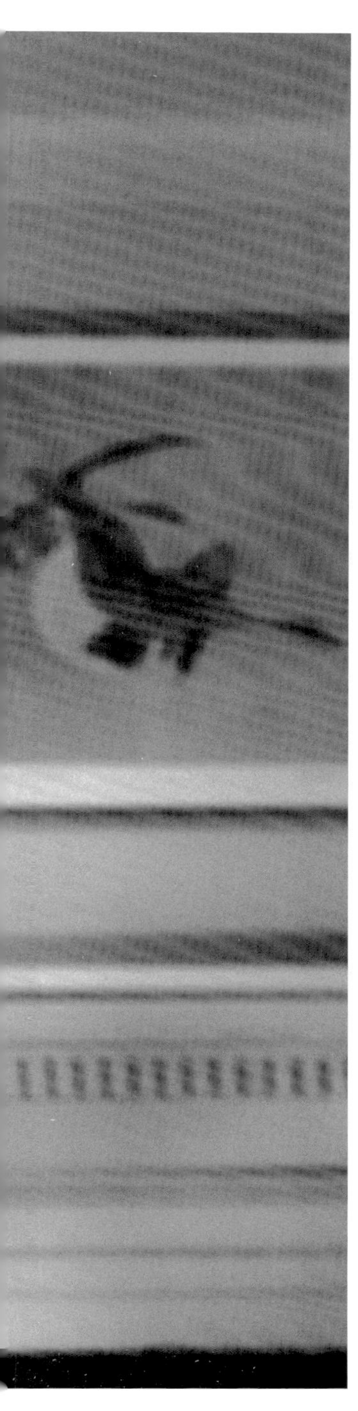

Loco, New Jersey, 1960.

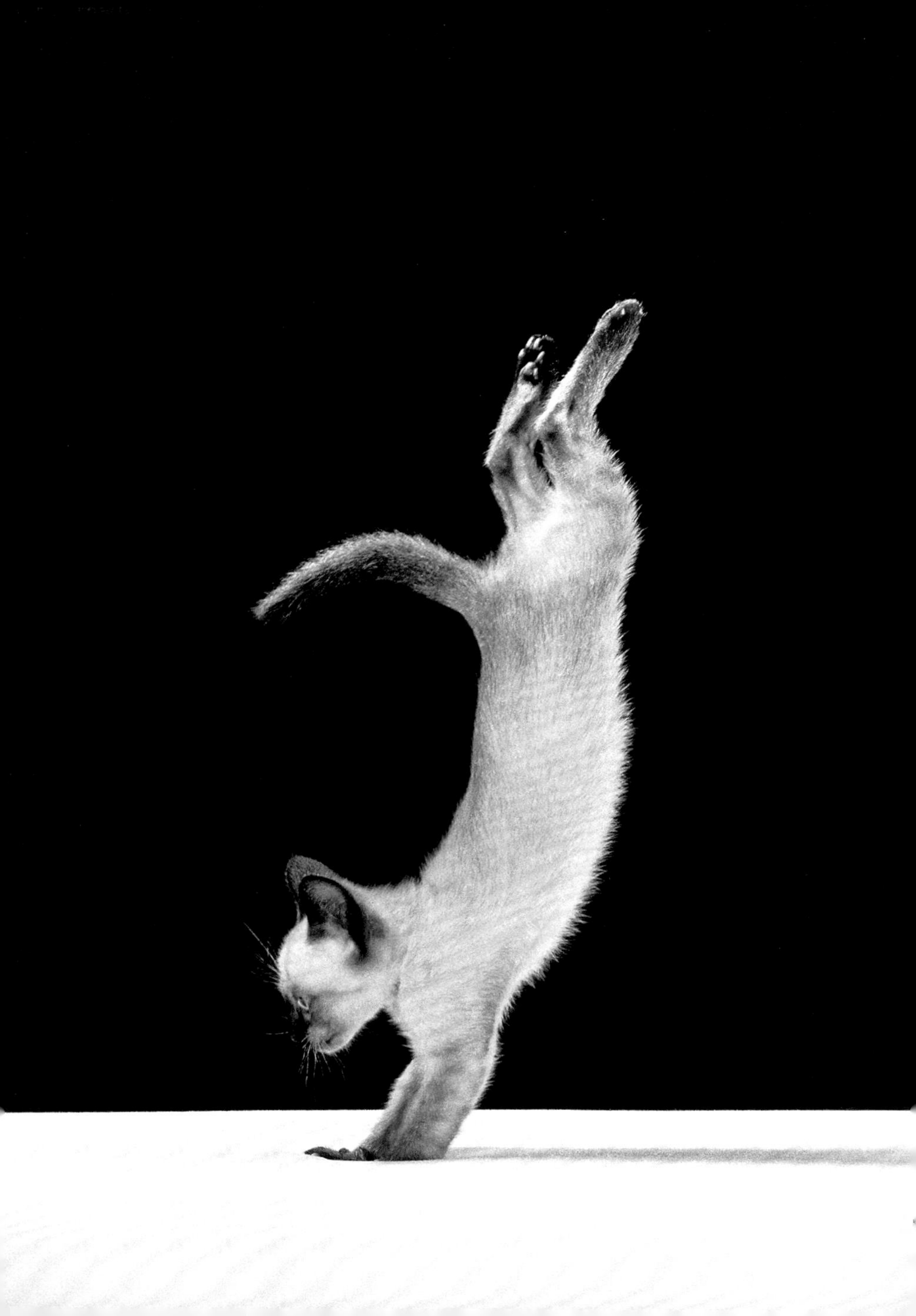

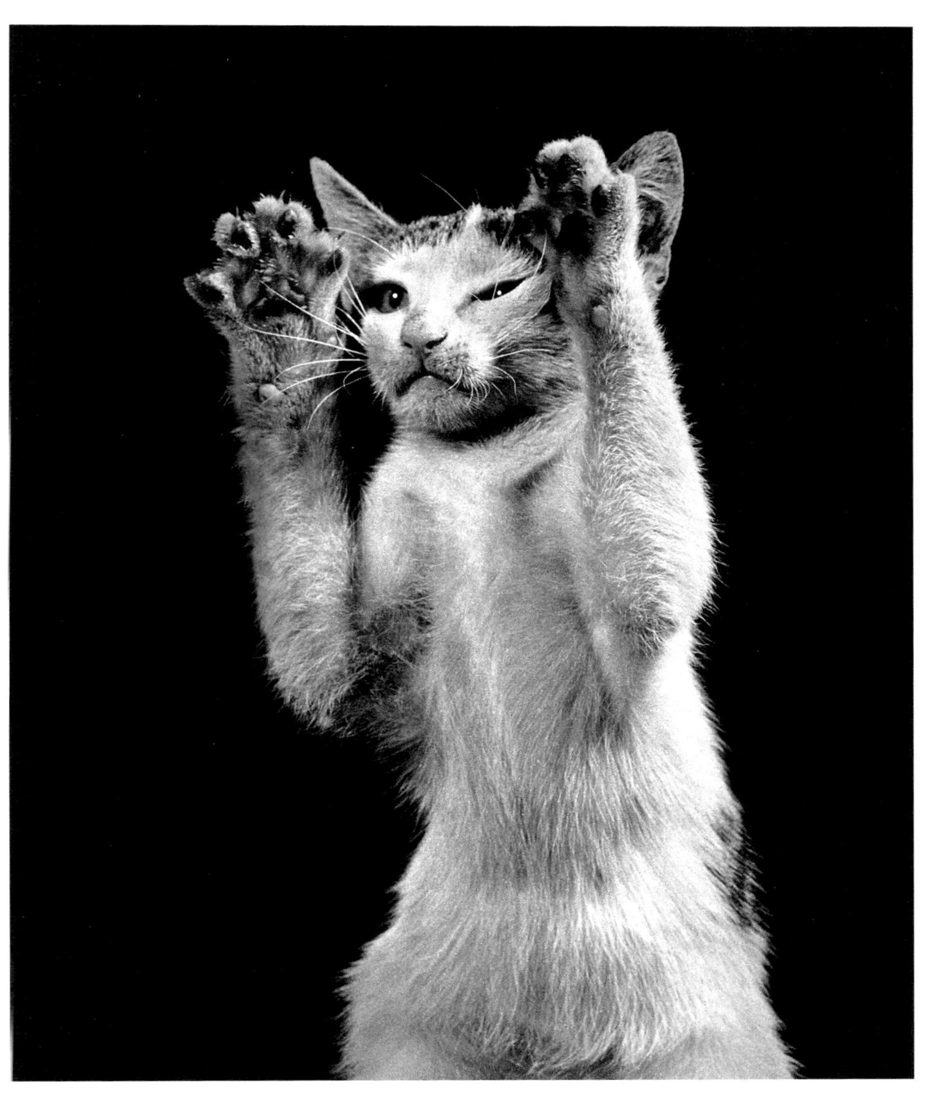

Siamese, New York City, 1949.

Domestic shorthair, New York City, 1949.

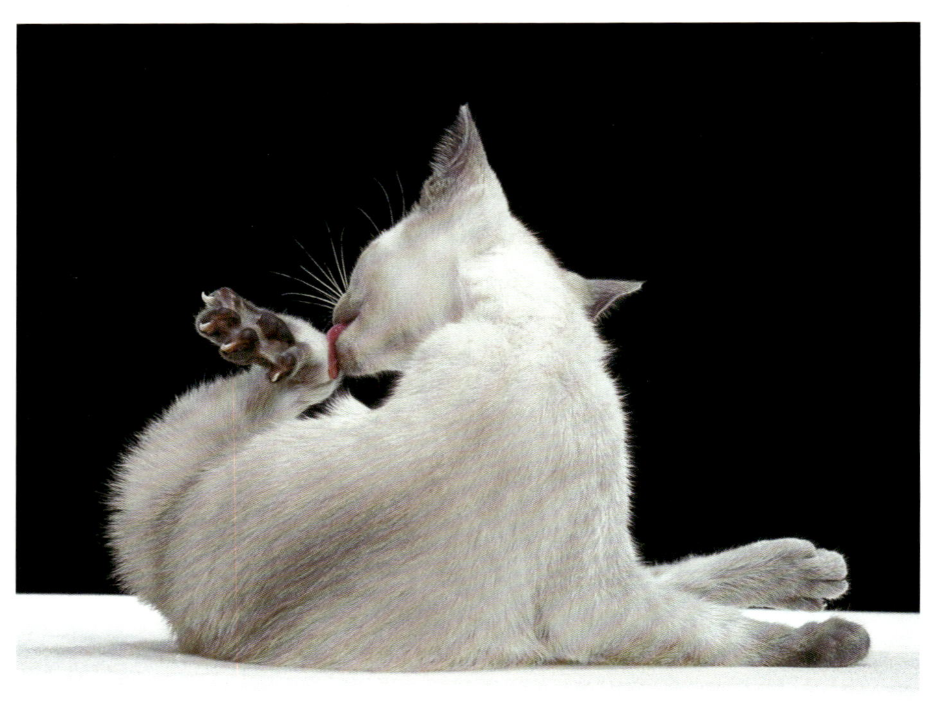

Siamese, New Jersey, 1982.

Loco, Astoria, 1950.

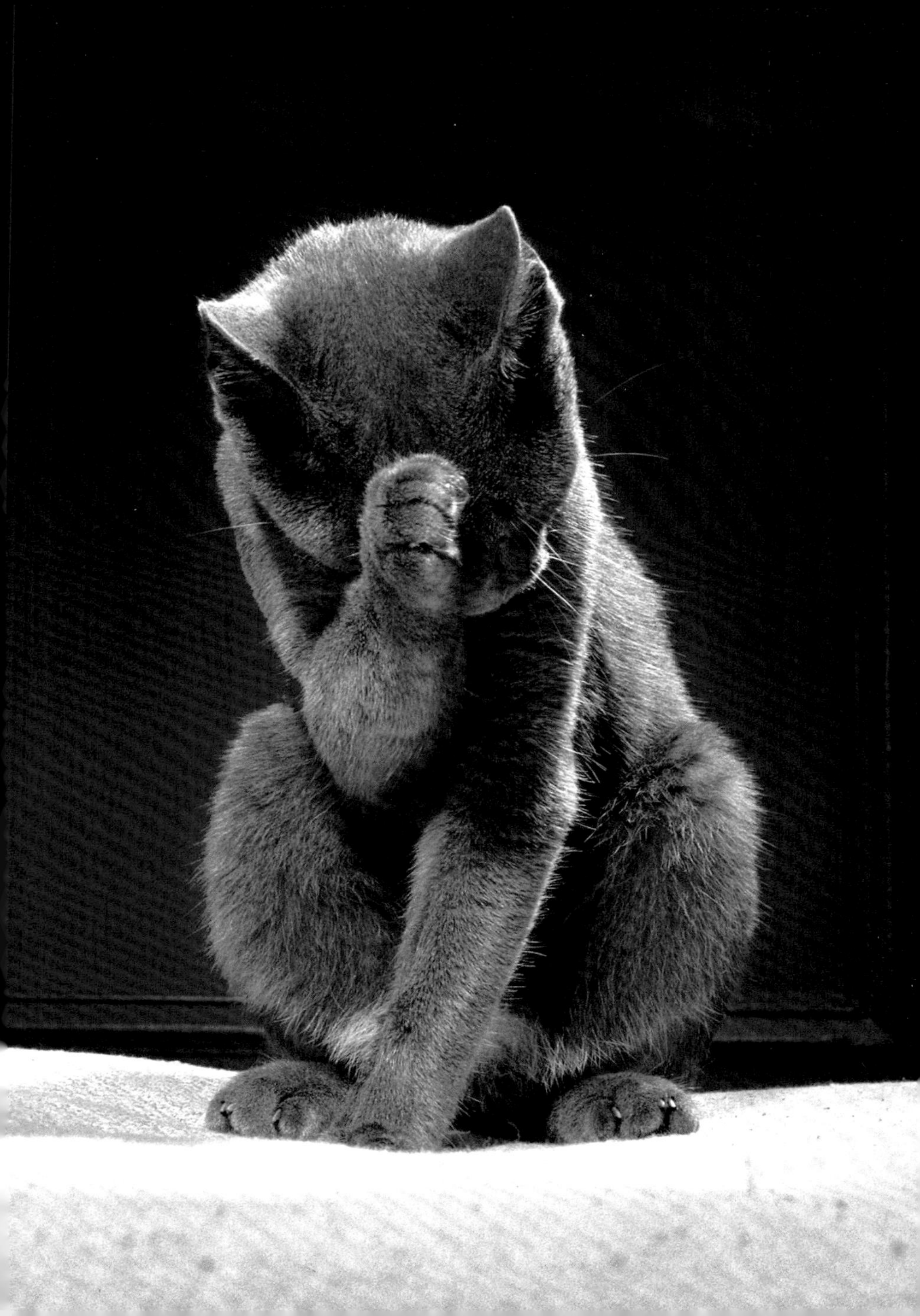

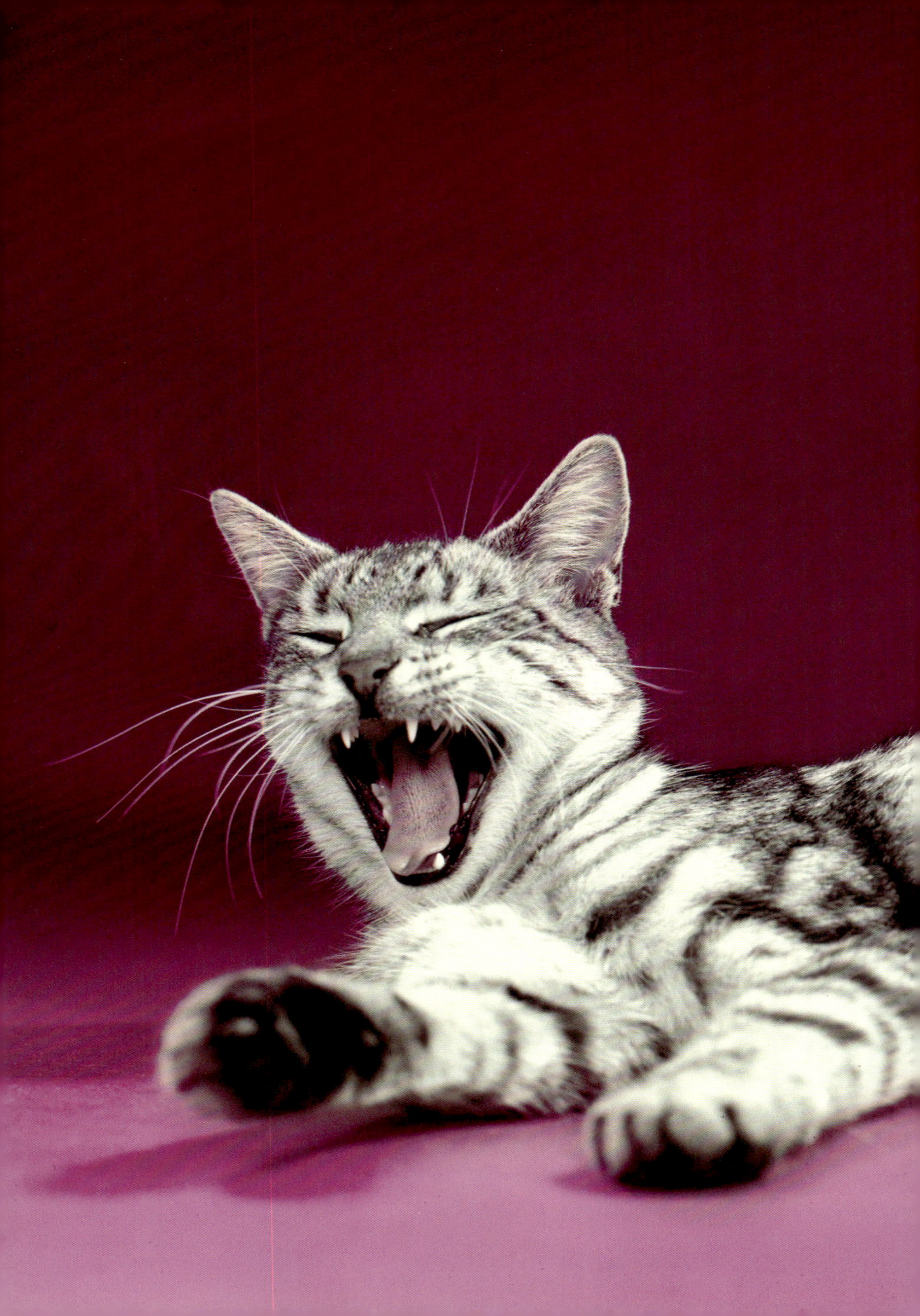

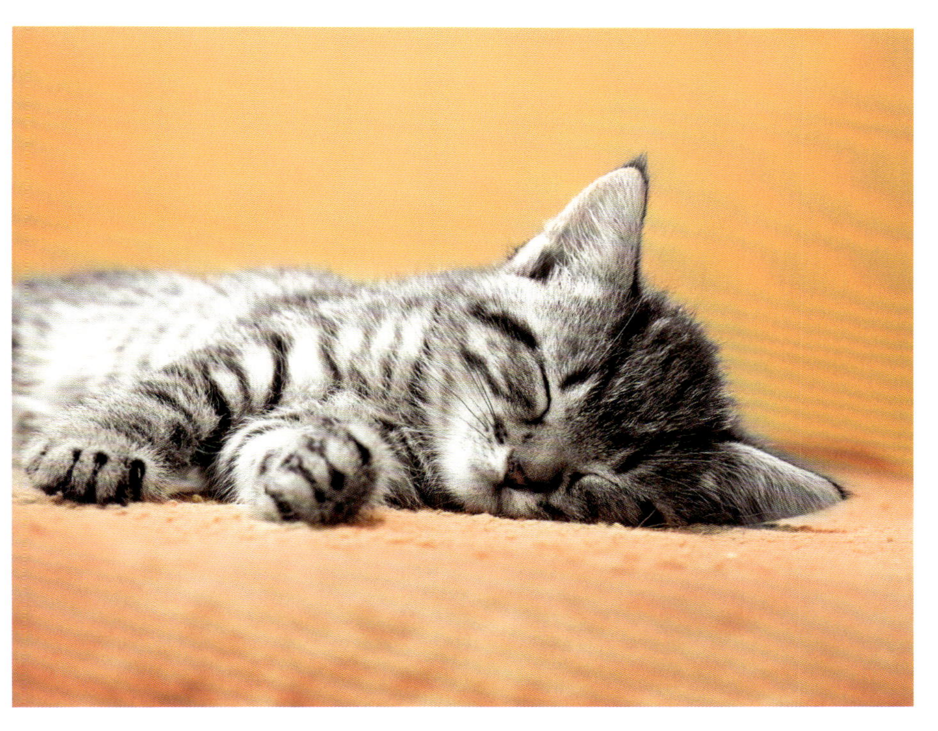

Domestic shorthair tabby, Long Island, 1953.

Domestic shorthair, New Jersey, 1973.

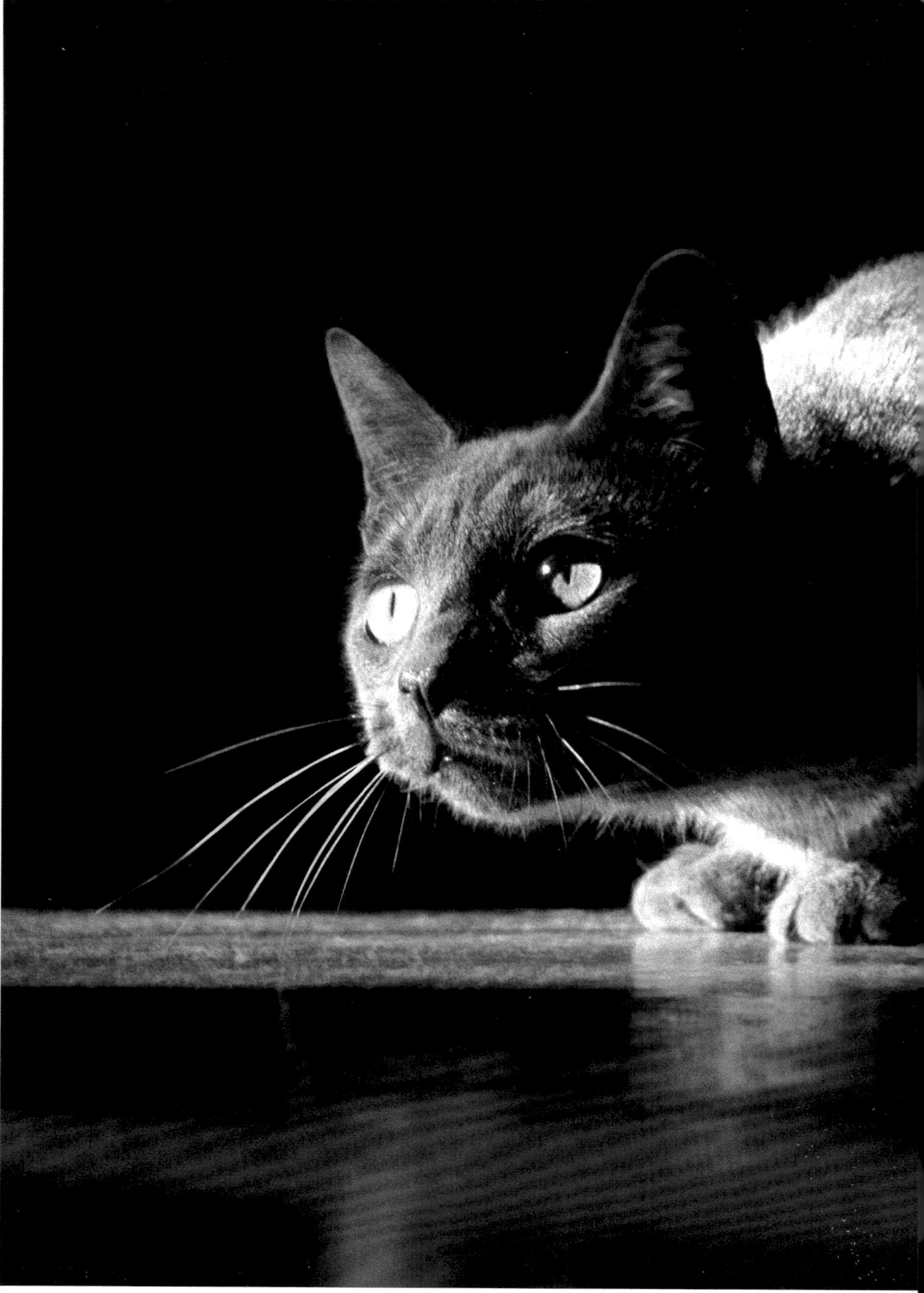

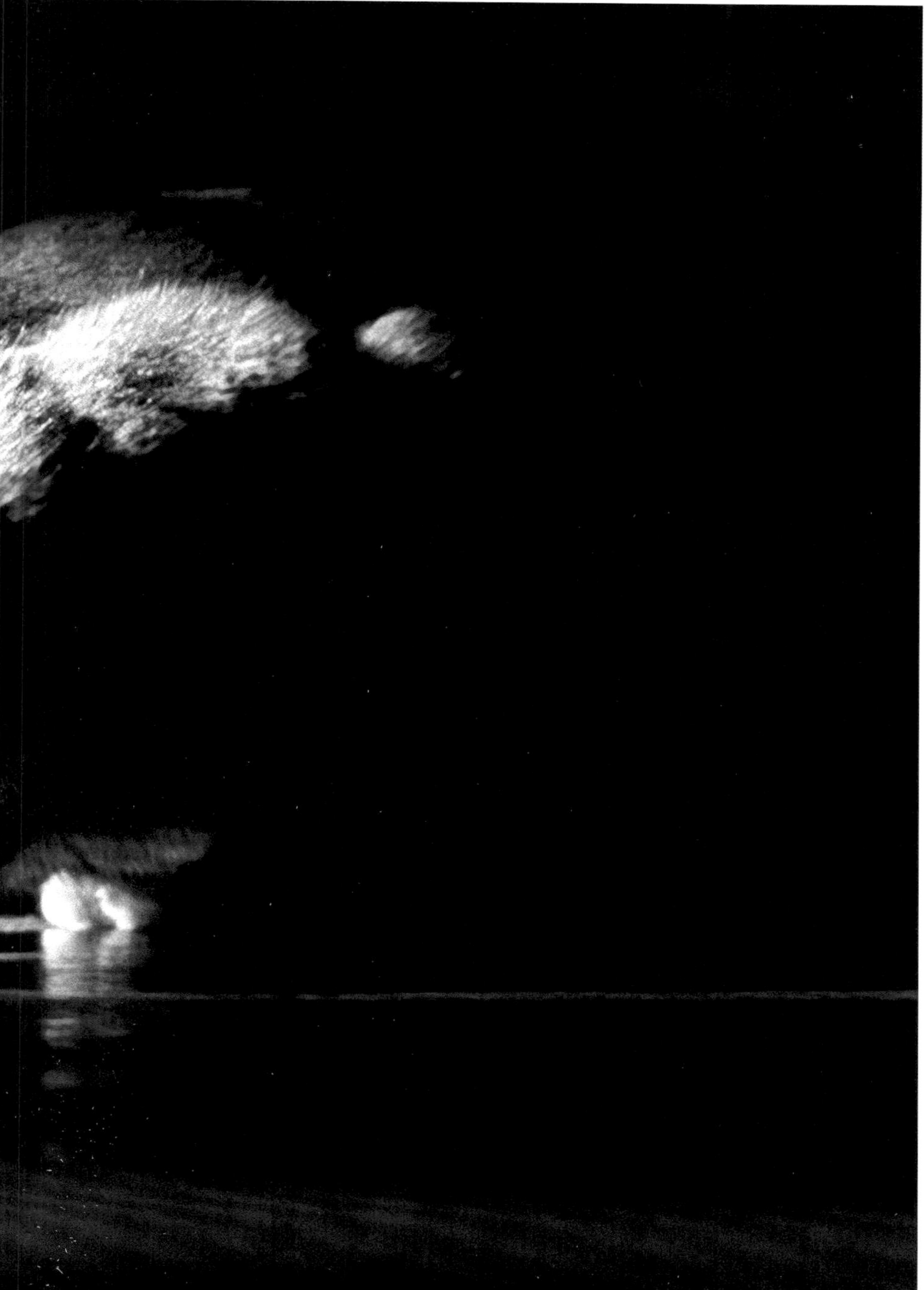

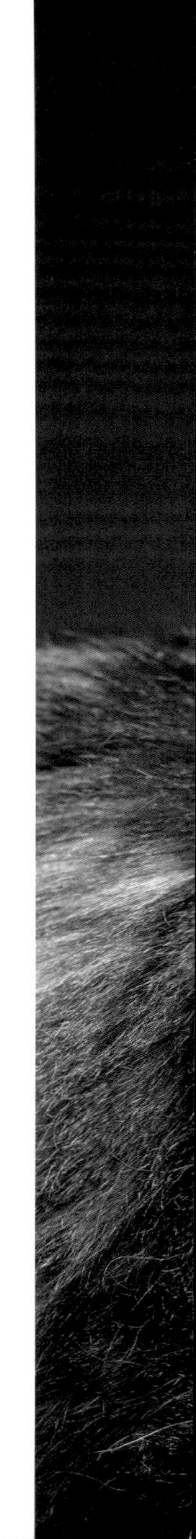

Previous: Loco, Astoria, 1950.

Maine coon, New Jersey, 1989.

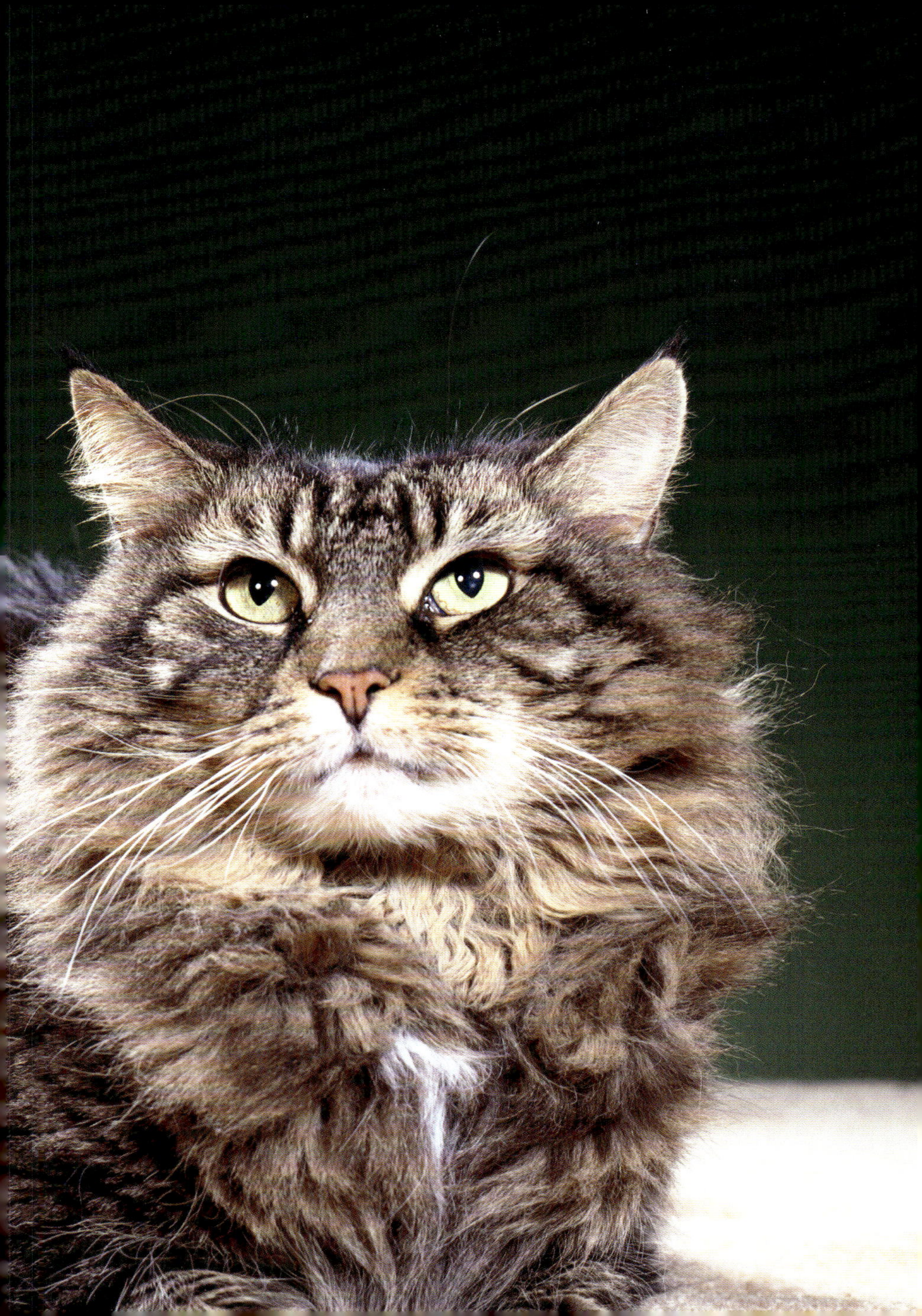

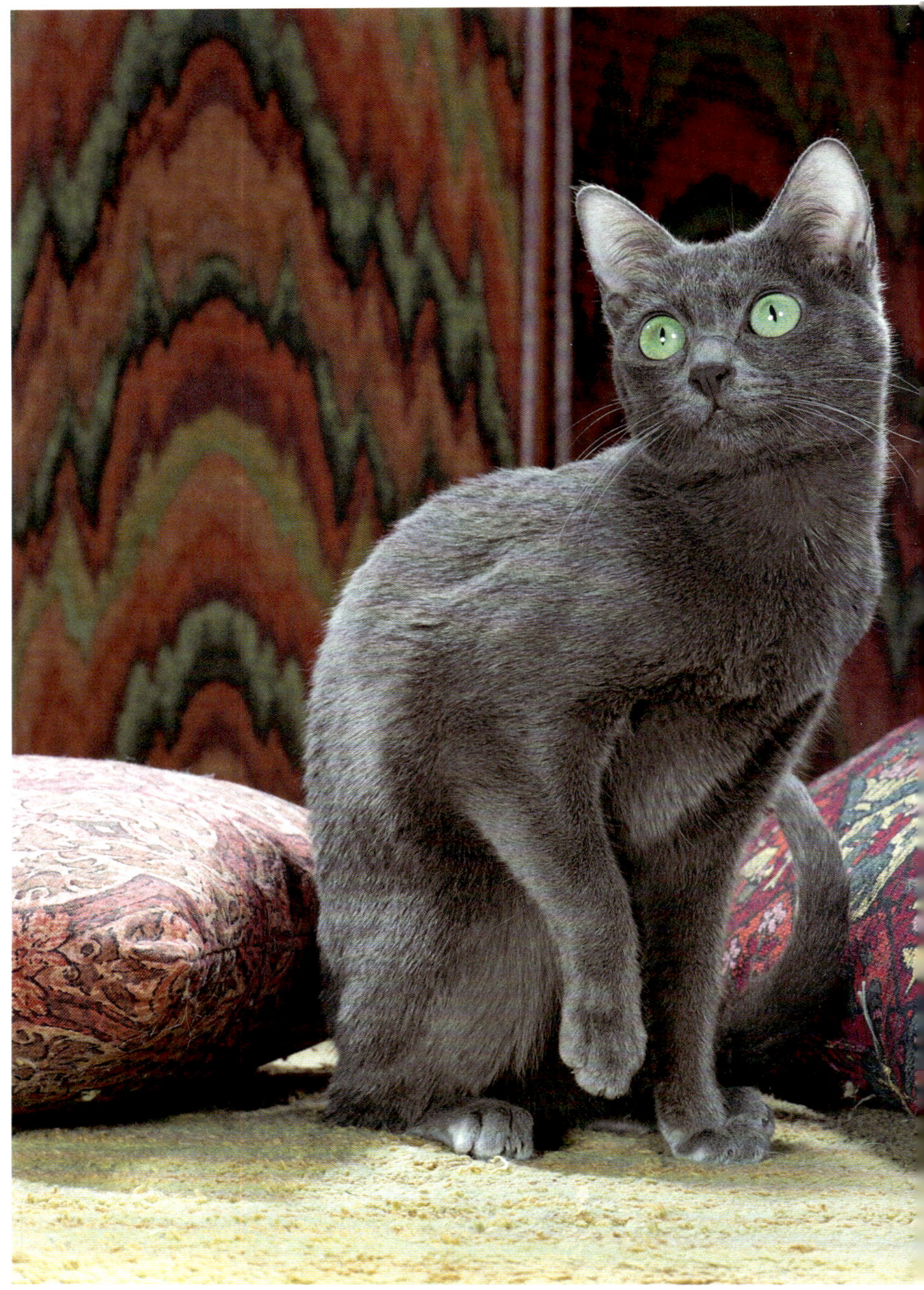

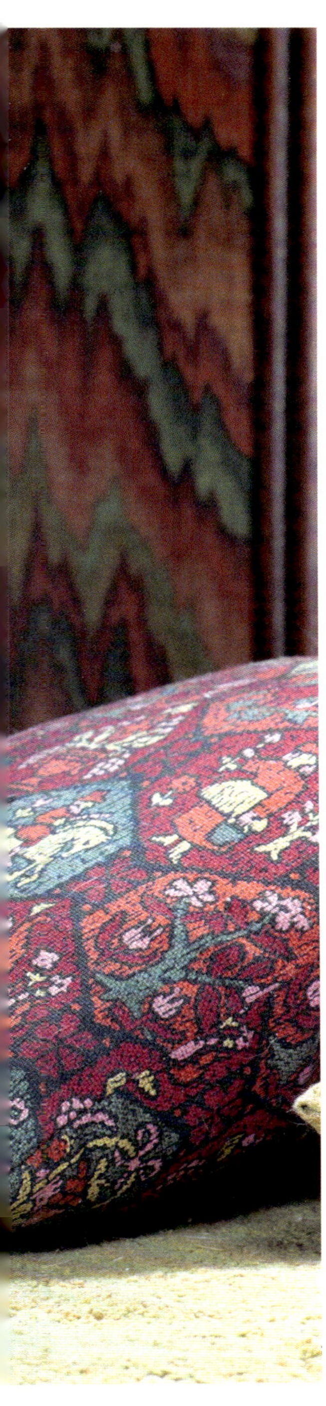

Korat, New Jersey, 1968.

Persian, New Jersey, 1961.

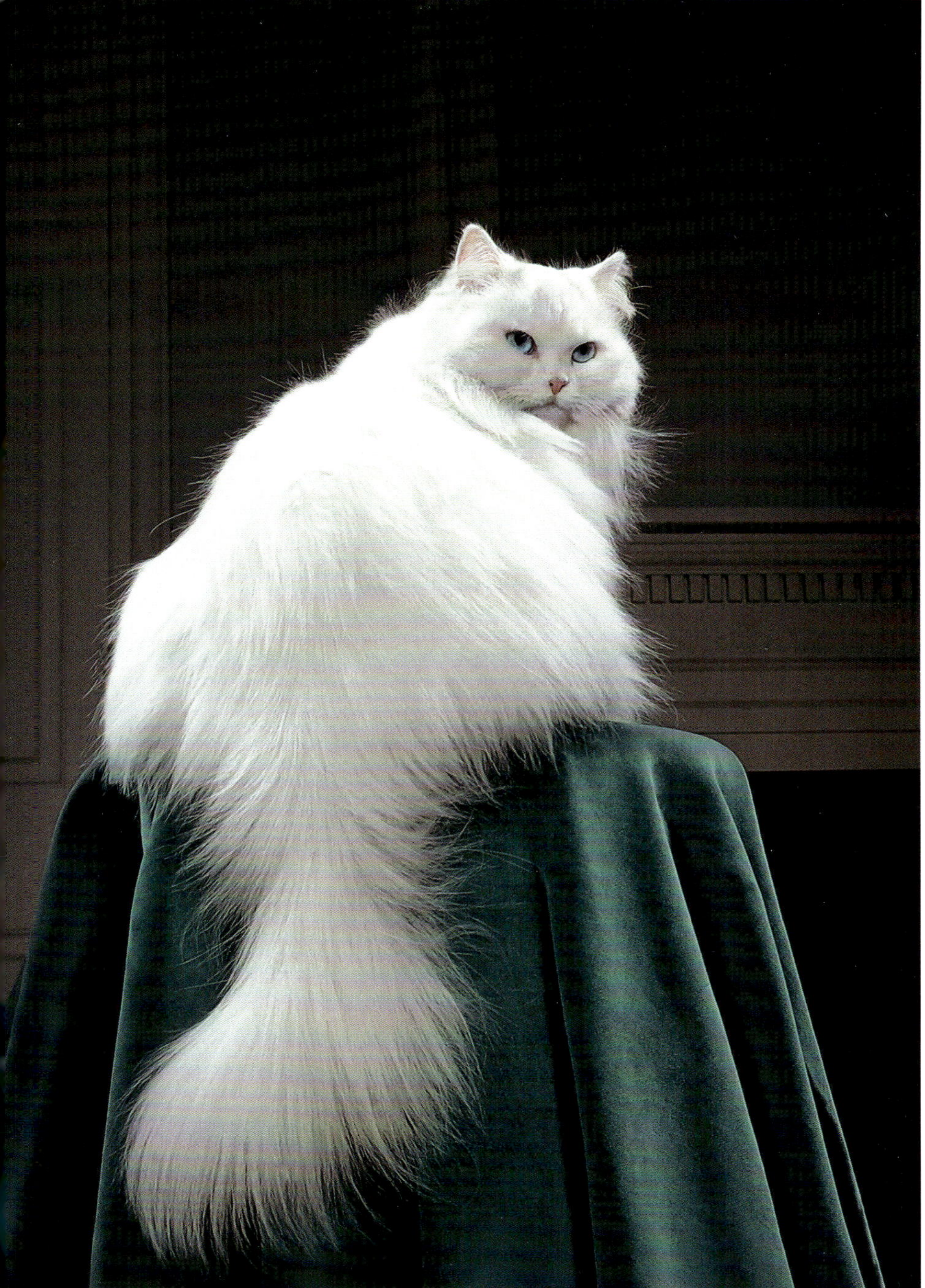

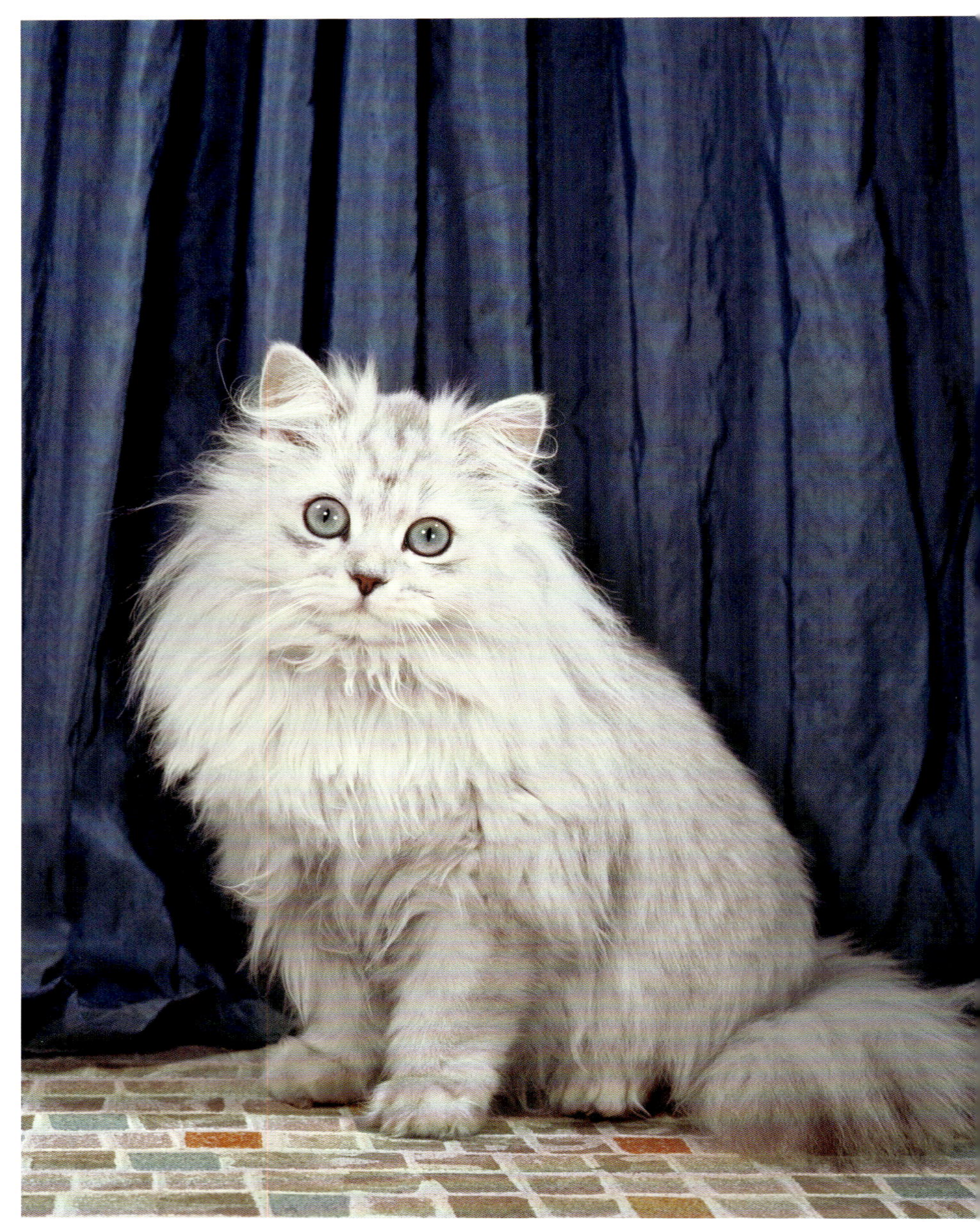

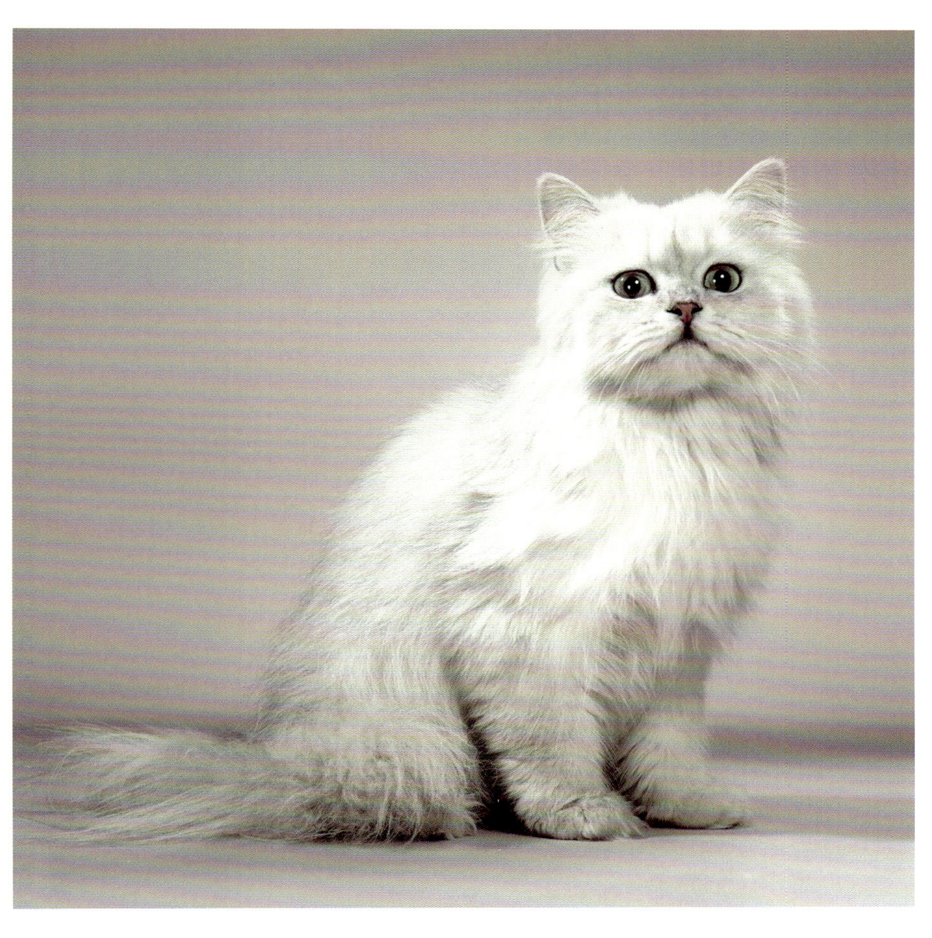

Silver Persian, Long Island, 1956.

Persian, New Jersey, 1974.

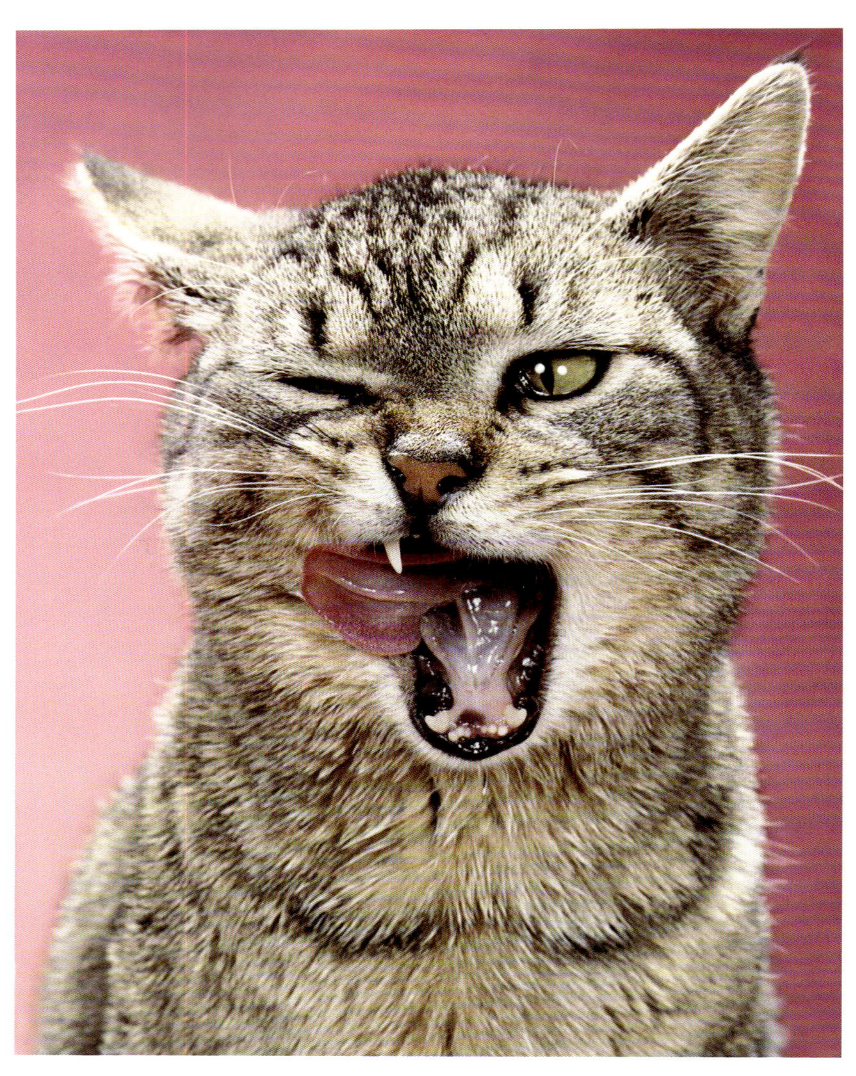

Domestic shorthair, New Jersey, 1966.

Siamese, New Jersey, 1984.

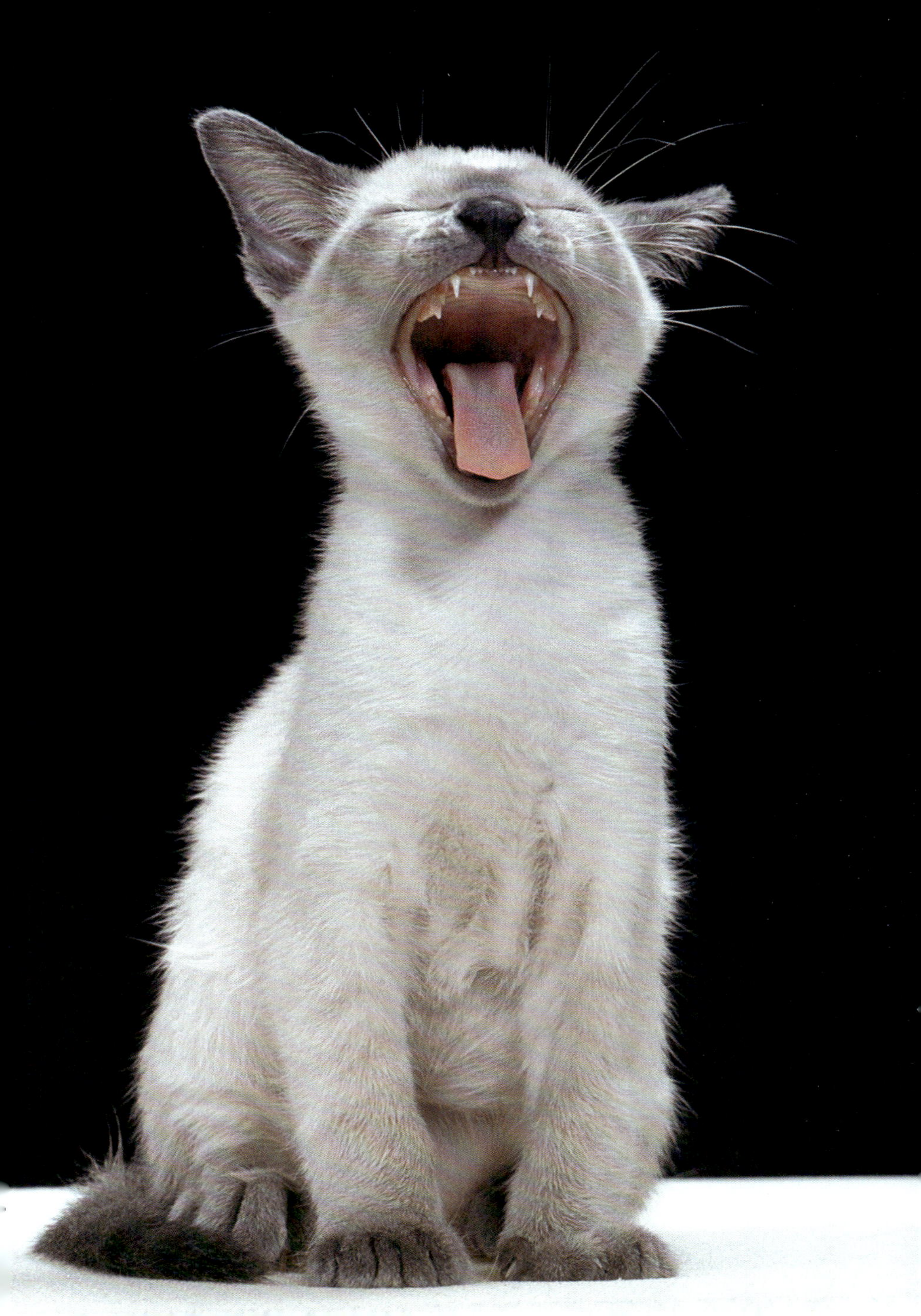

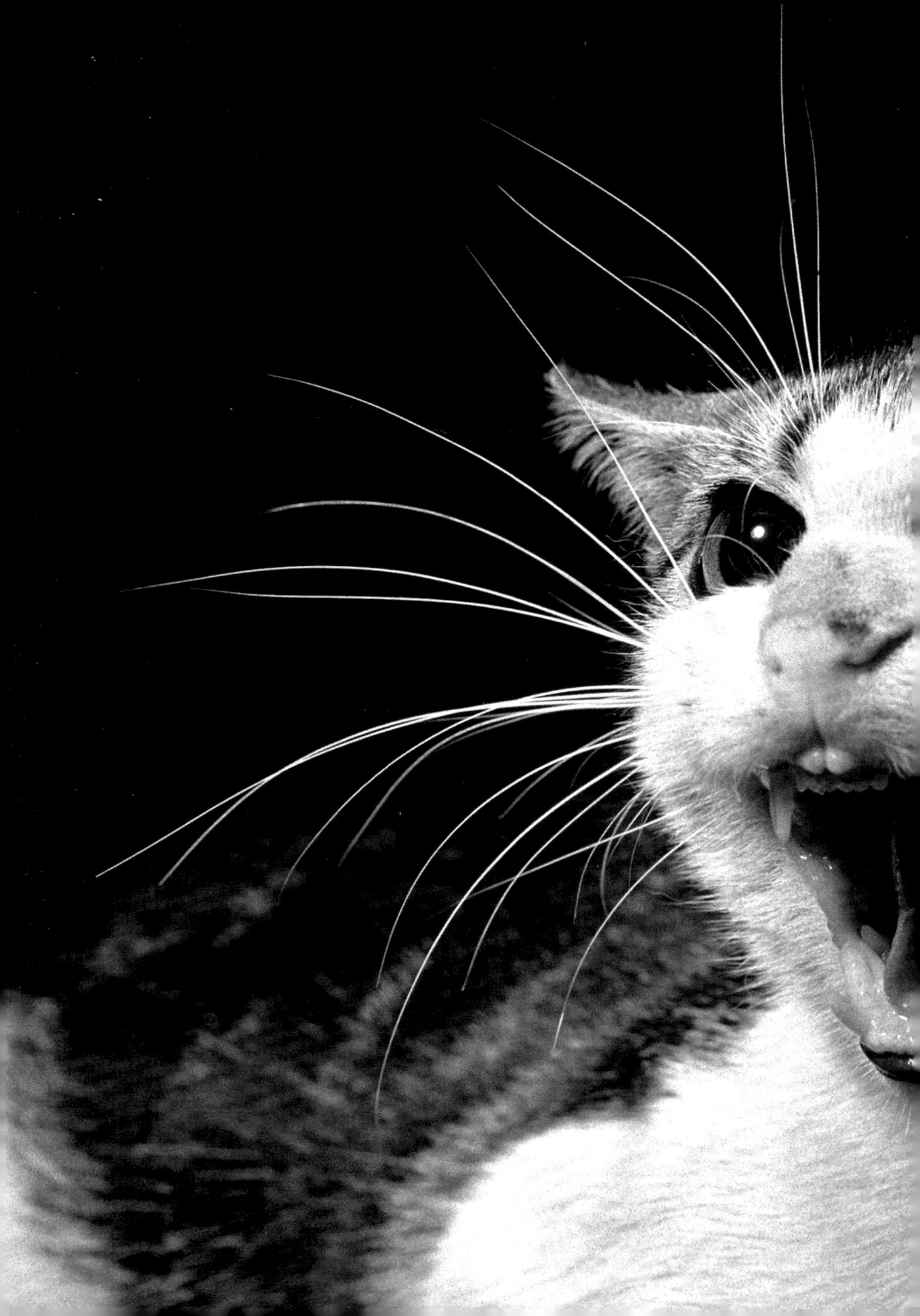

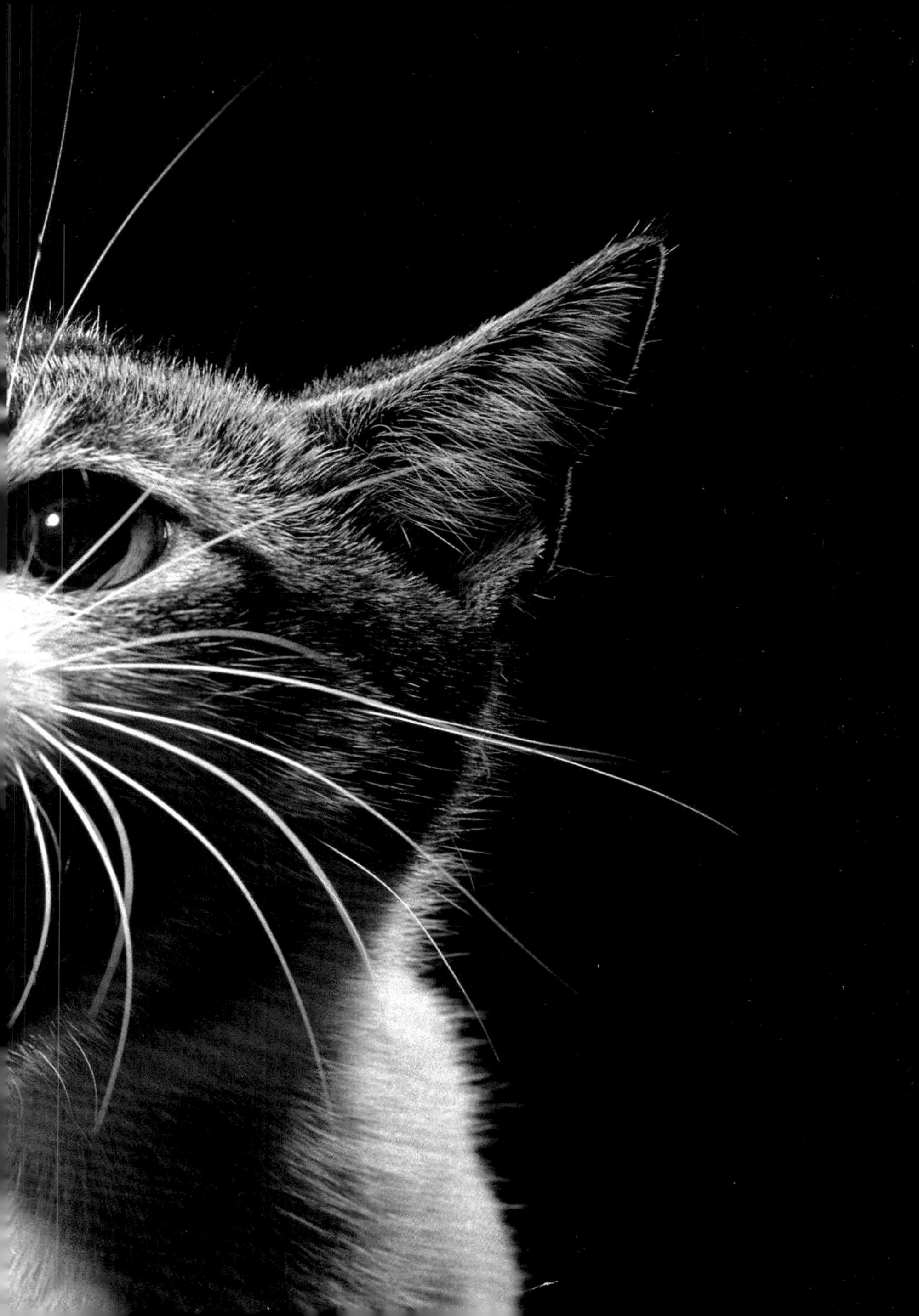

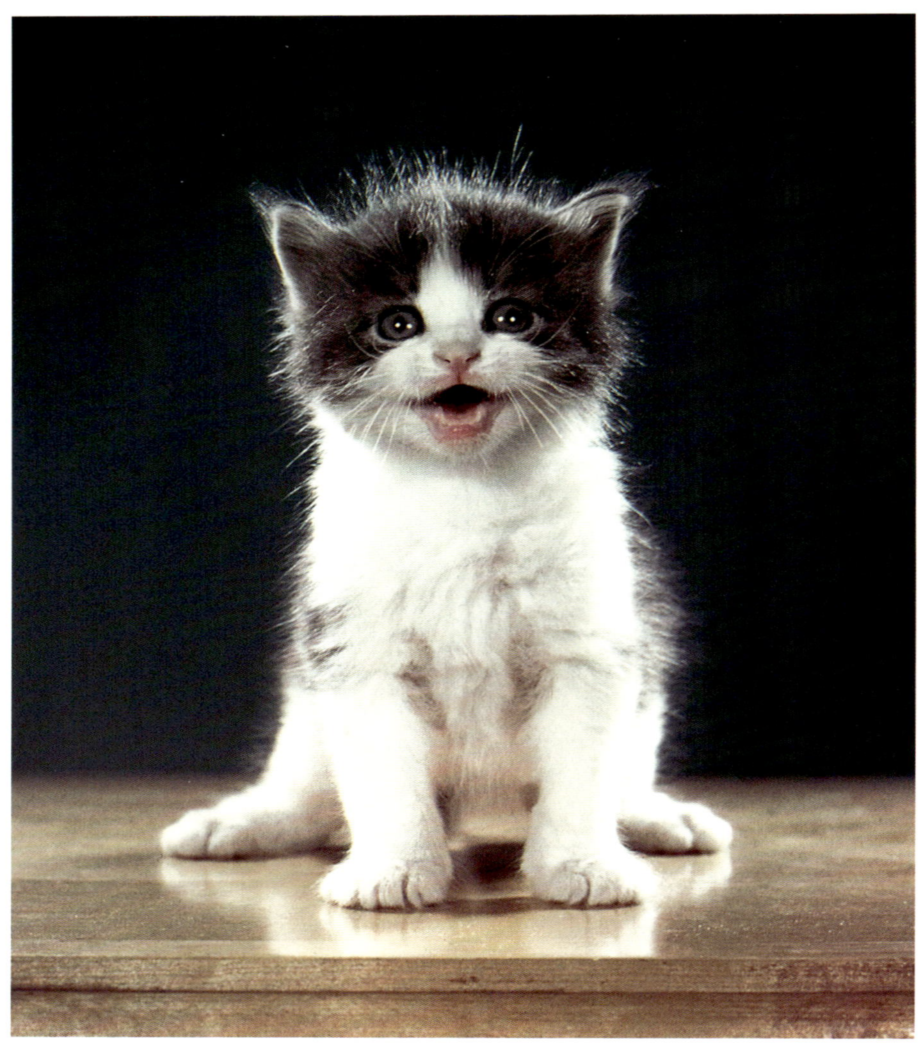

Previous: Domestic shorthair, Queens, 1950.

Domestic shorthair kitten, Long Island, 1954.

Domestic shorthair kitten, Long Island, 1978.

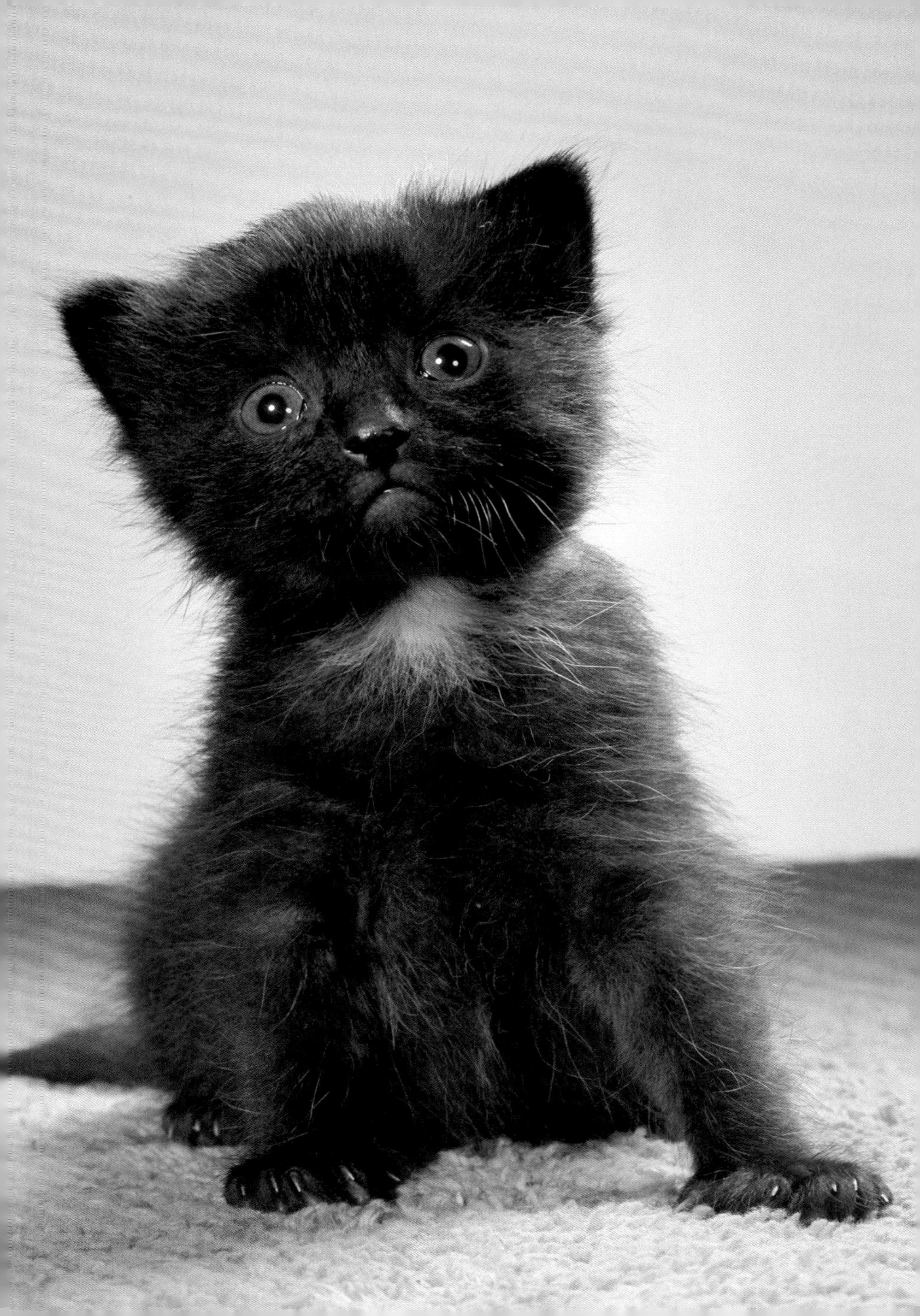

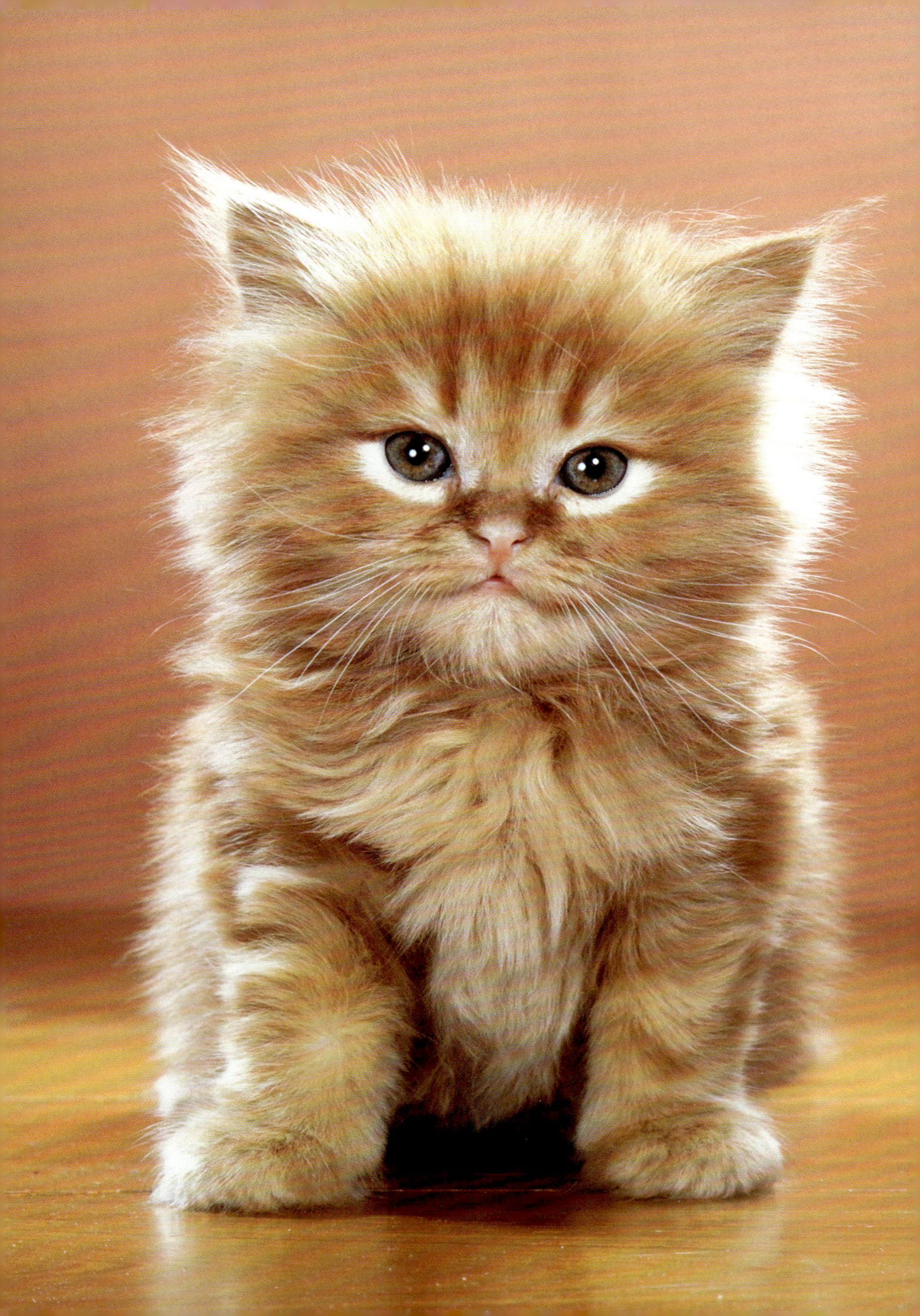

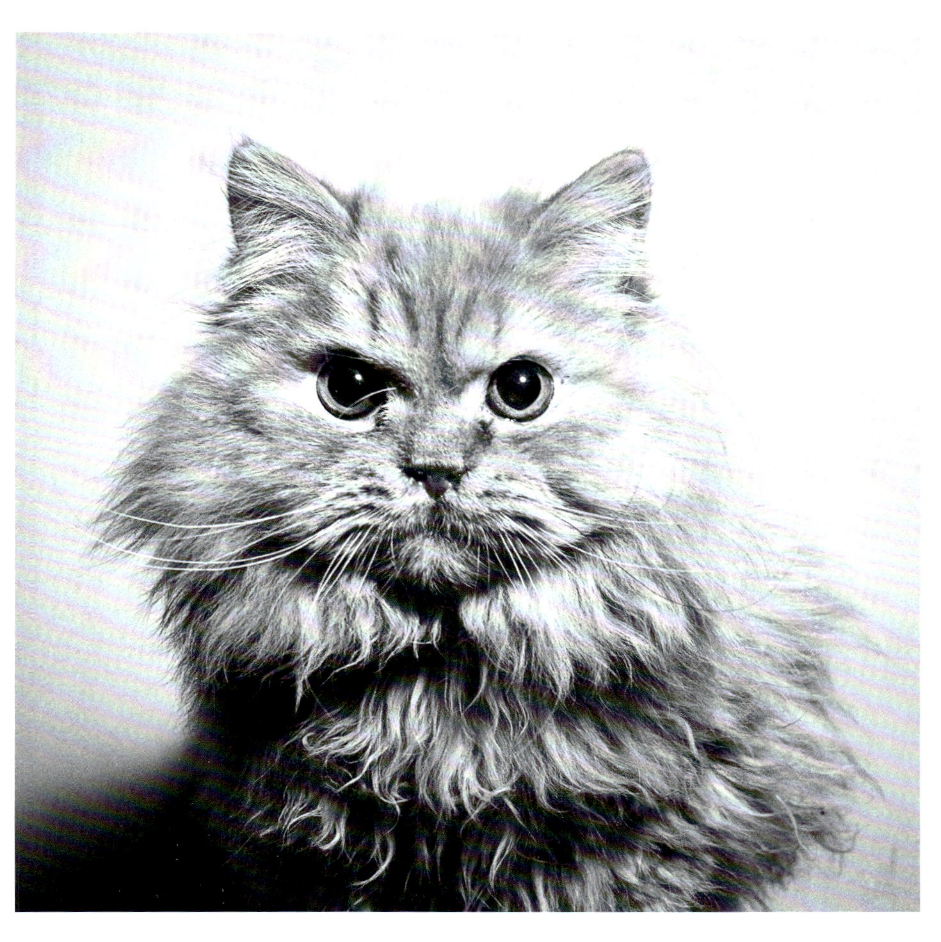

Persian kitten, New Jersey, 1962.

Persian kitten, Long Island, 1960.

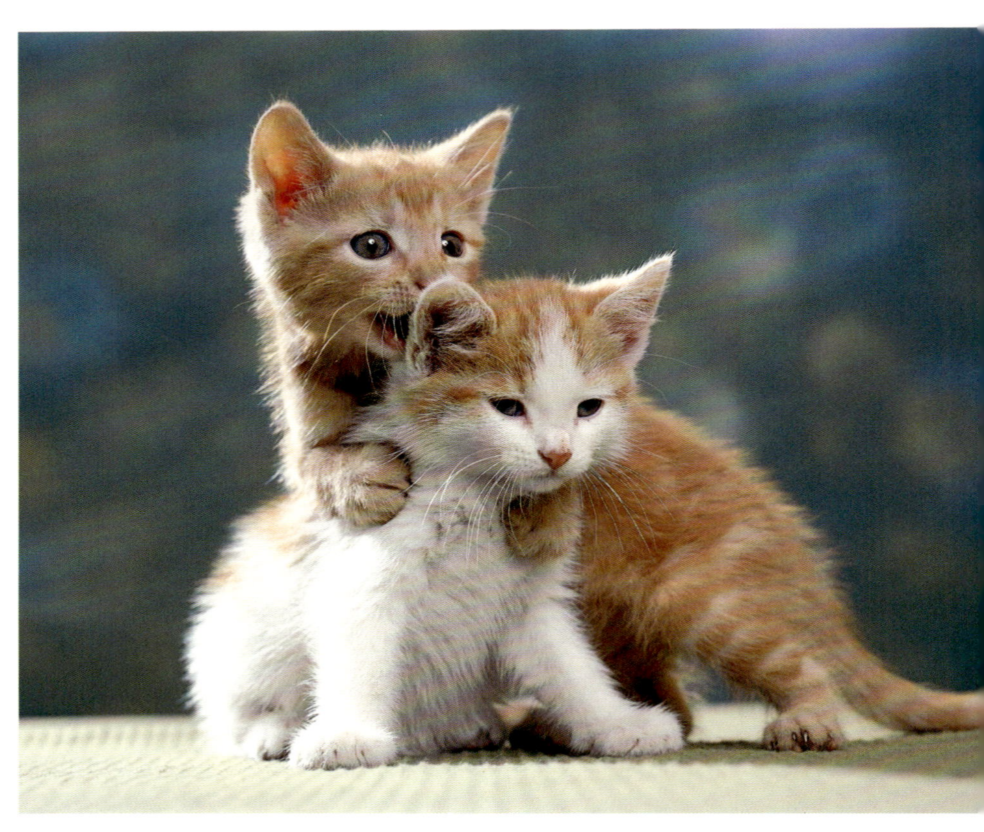

Domestic shorthairs, New Jersey, 1979.

Domestic shorthairs, Long Island, 1952.

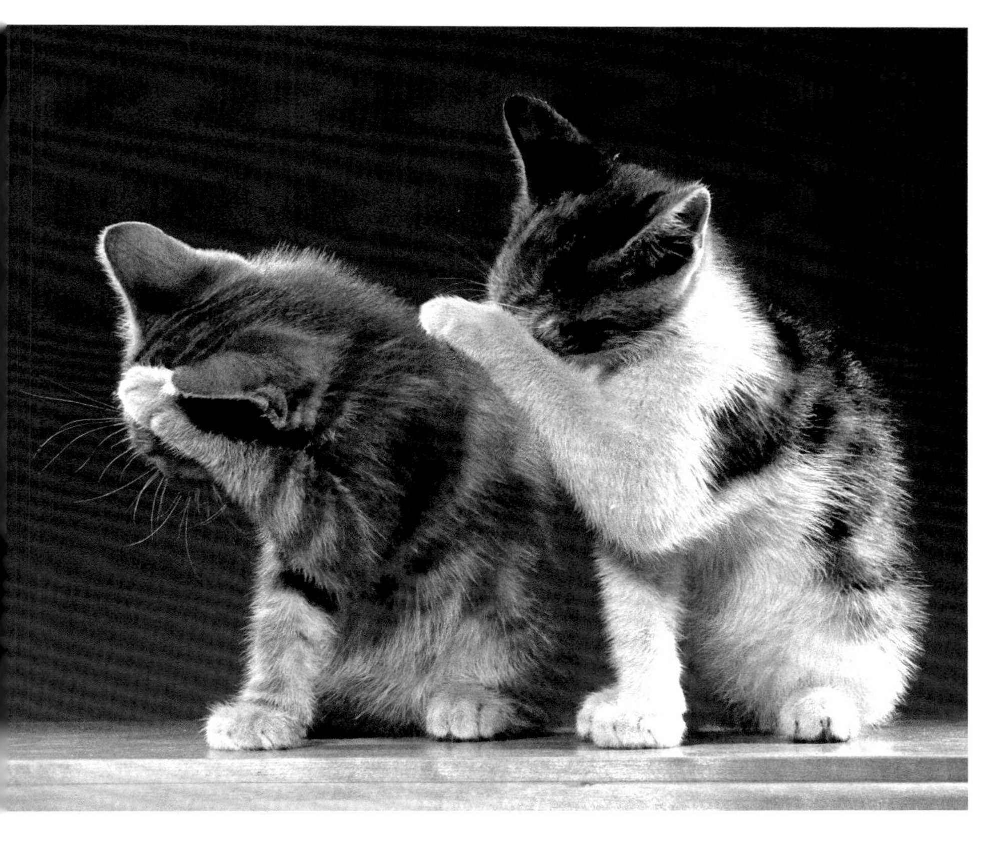

Following: Domestic shorthair mother
and kitten, New Jersey, 1965.

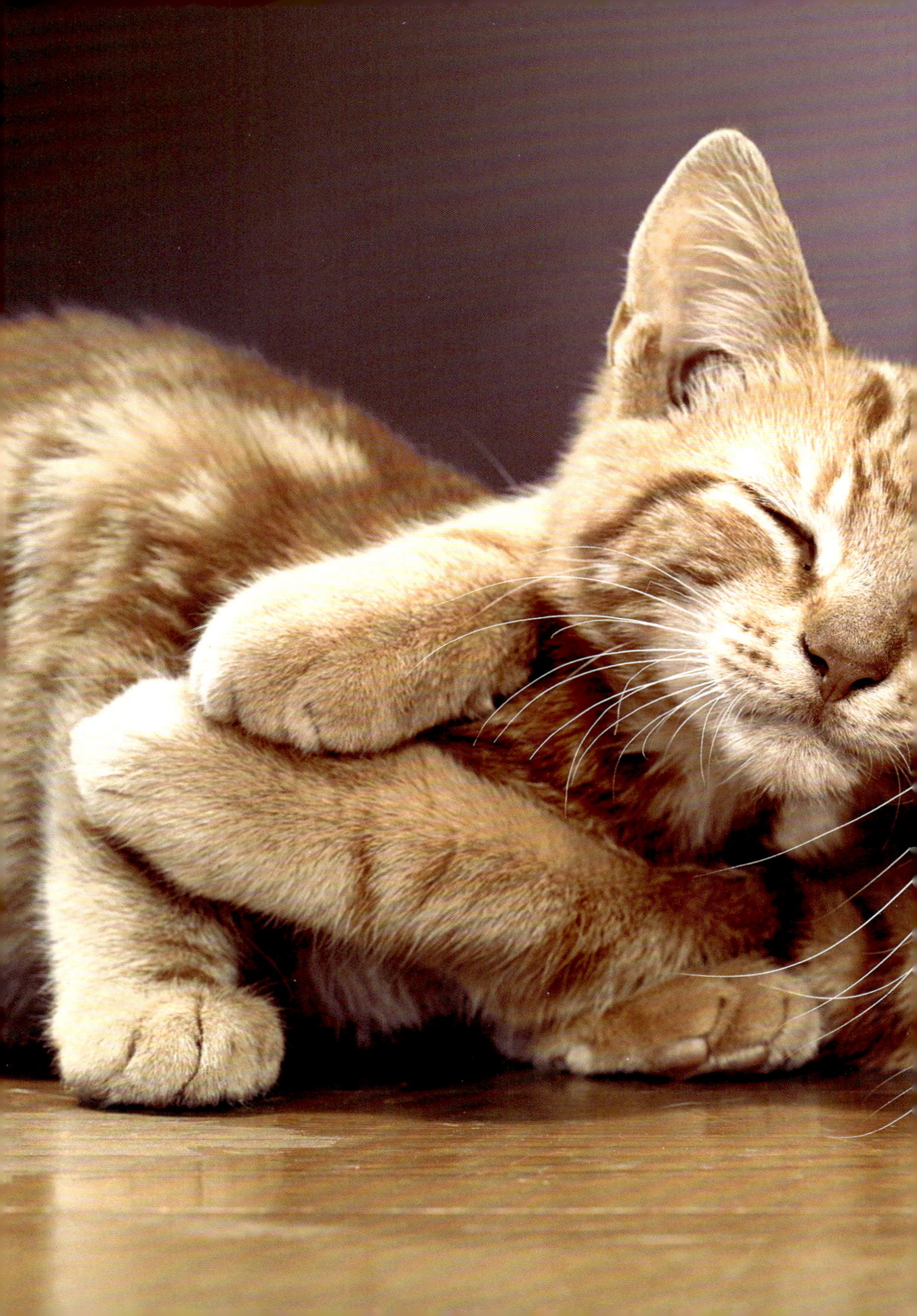

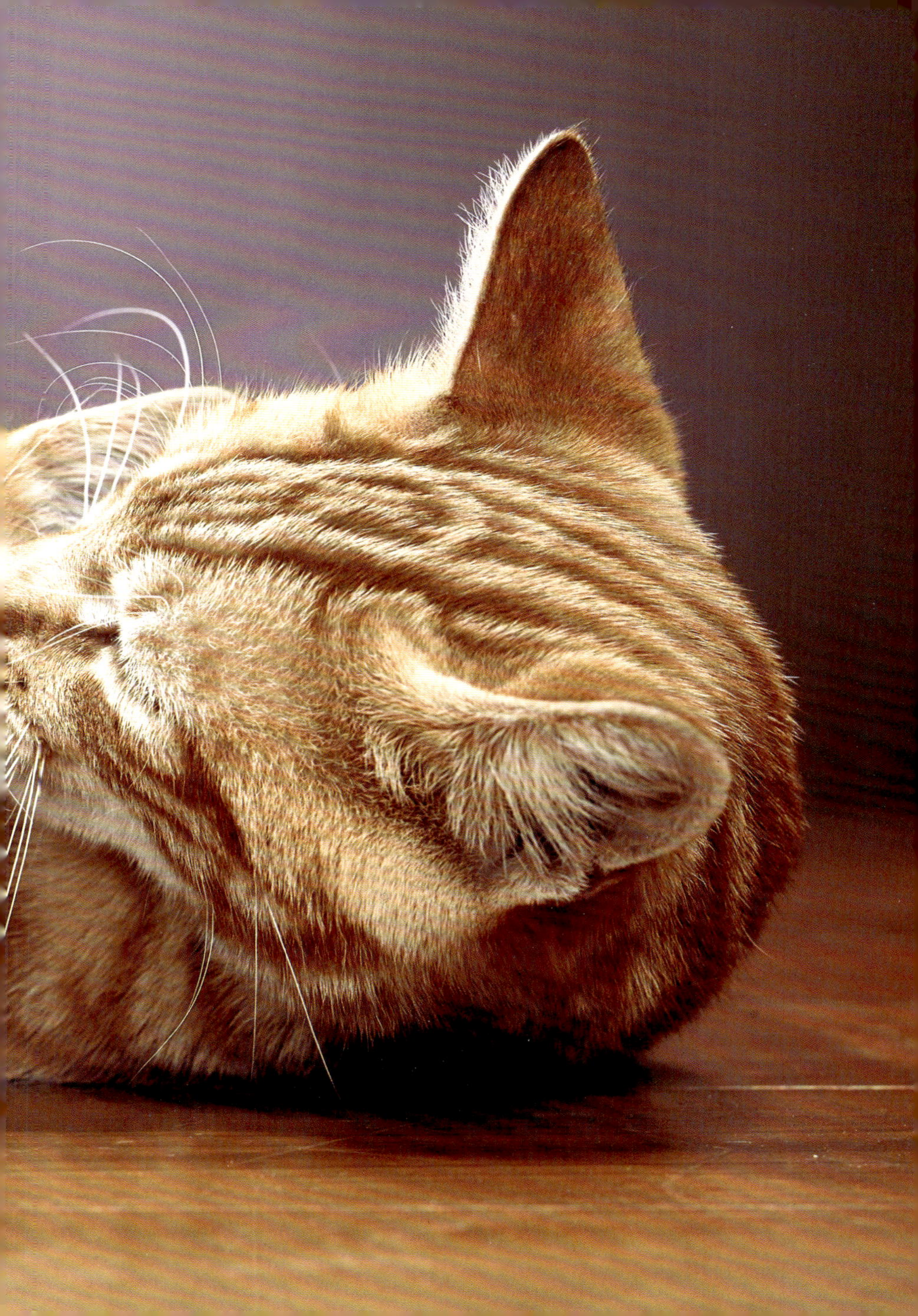

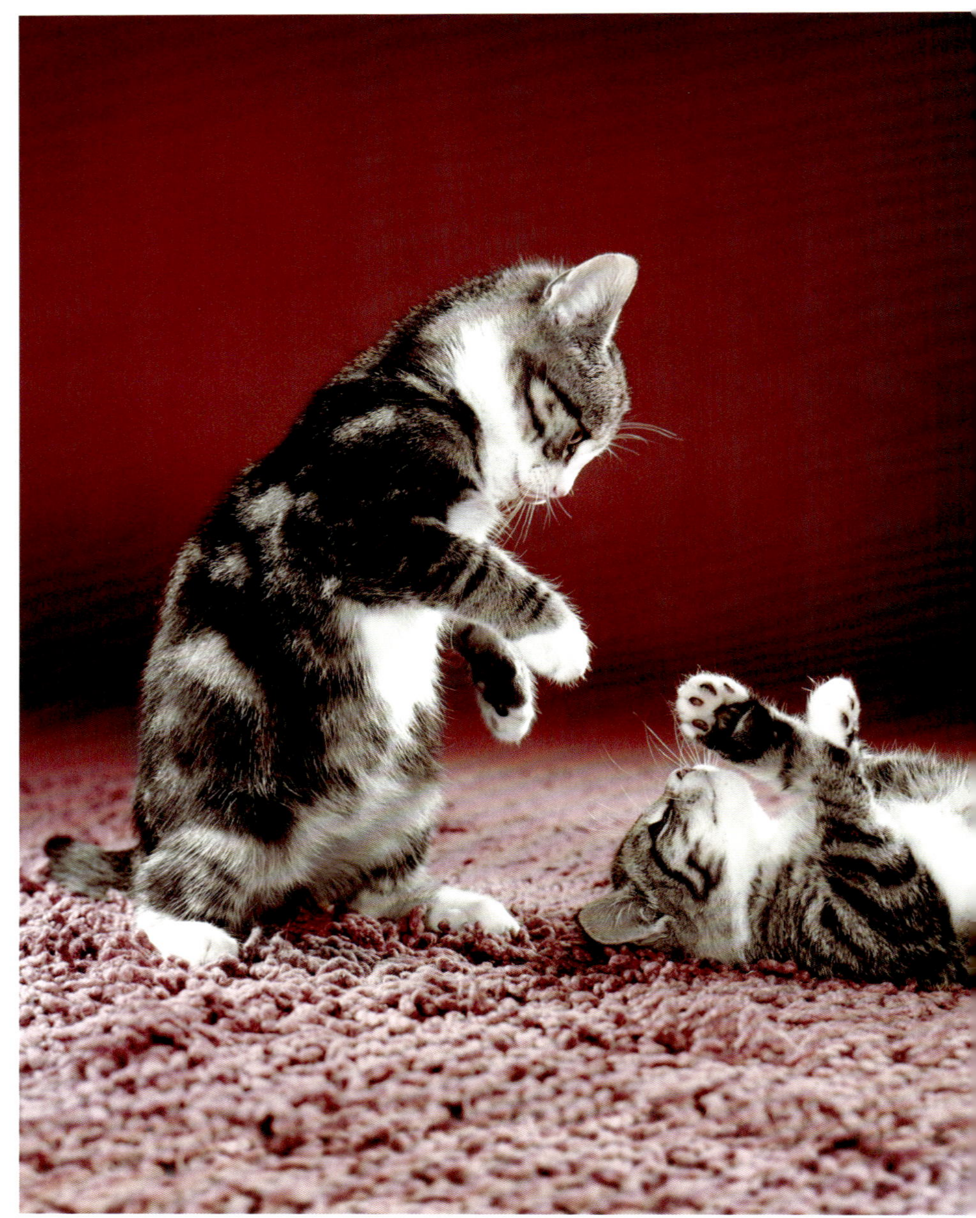

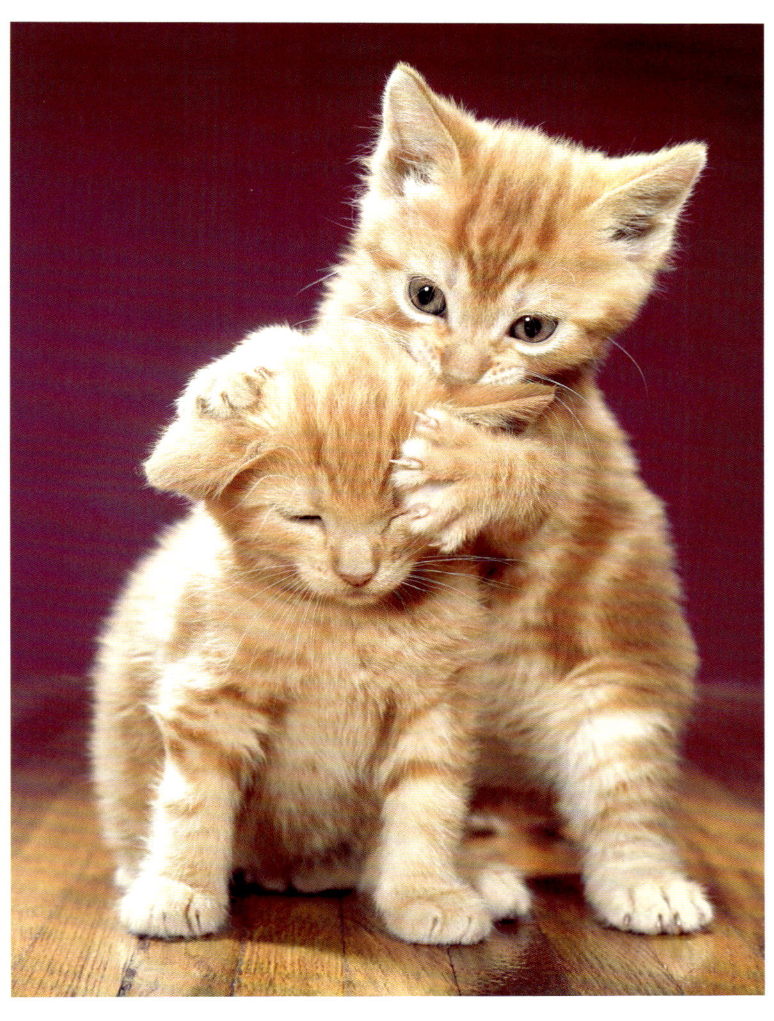

Domestic shorthairs, Long Island, 1955.

Domestic shorthairs, New Jersey, 1968.

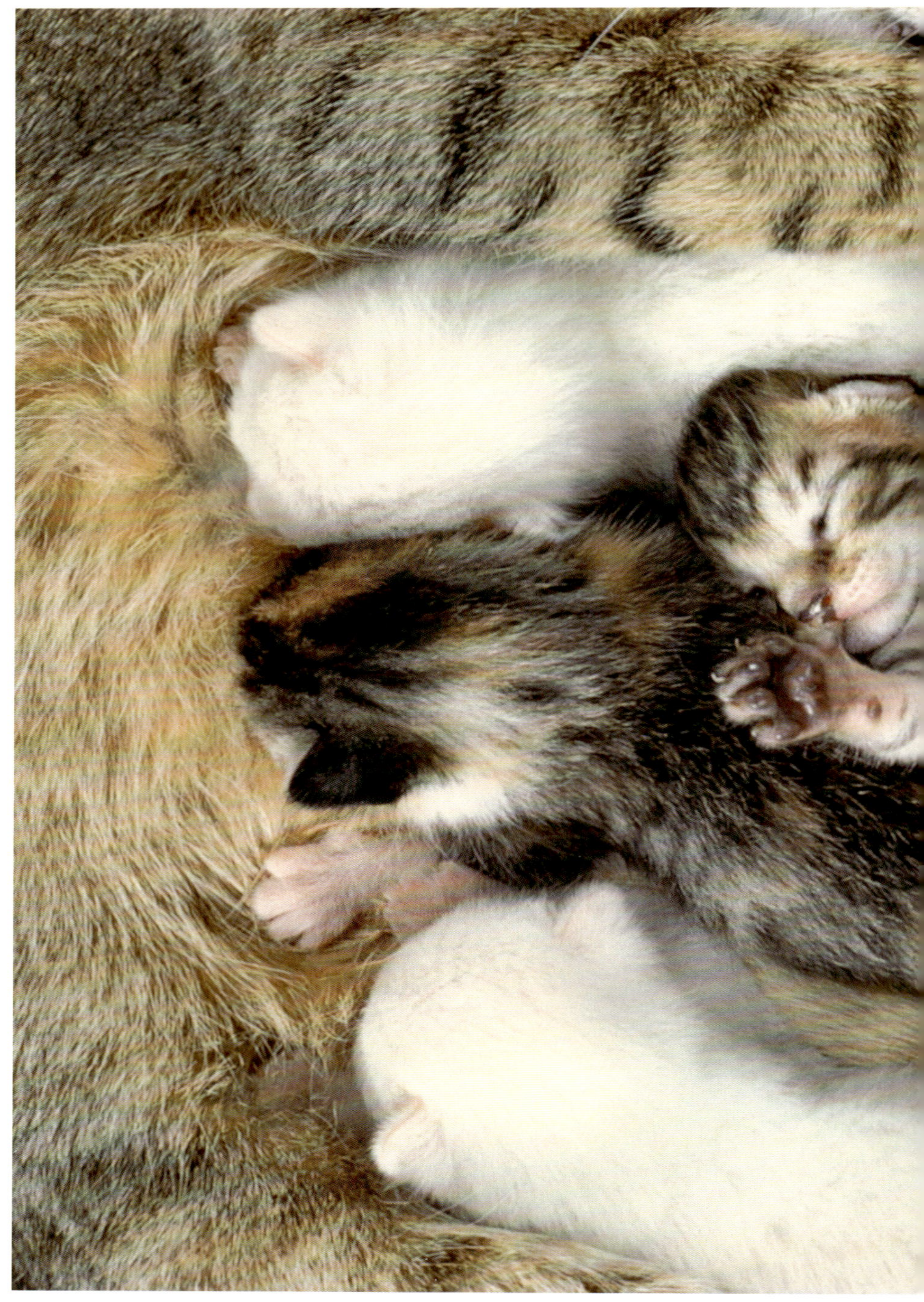

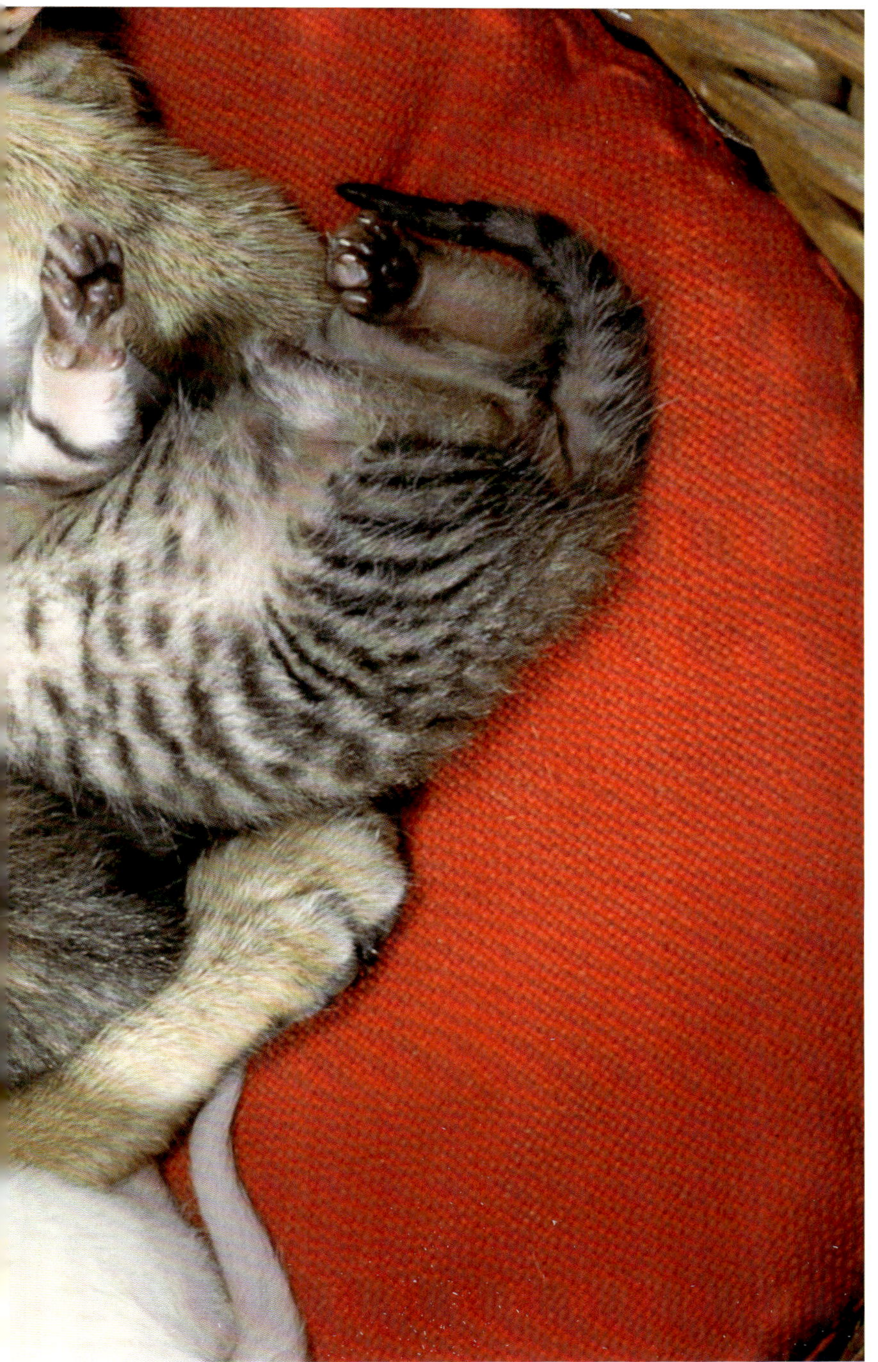

Previous: Domestic shorthair
and kittens, New Jersey, 1979.

Domestic shorthair and kitten,
Long Island, 1956.

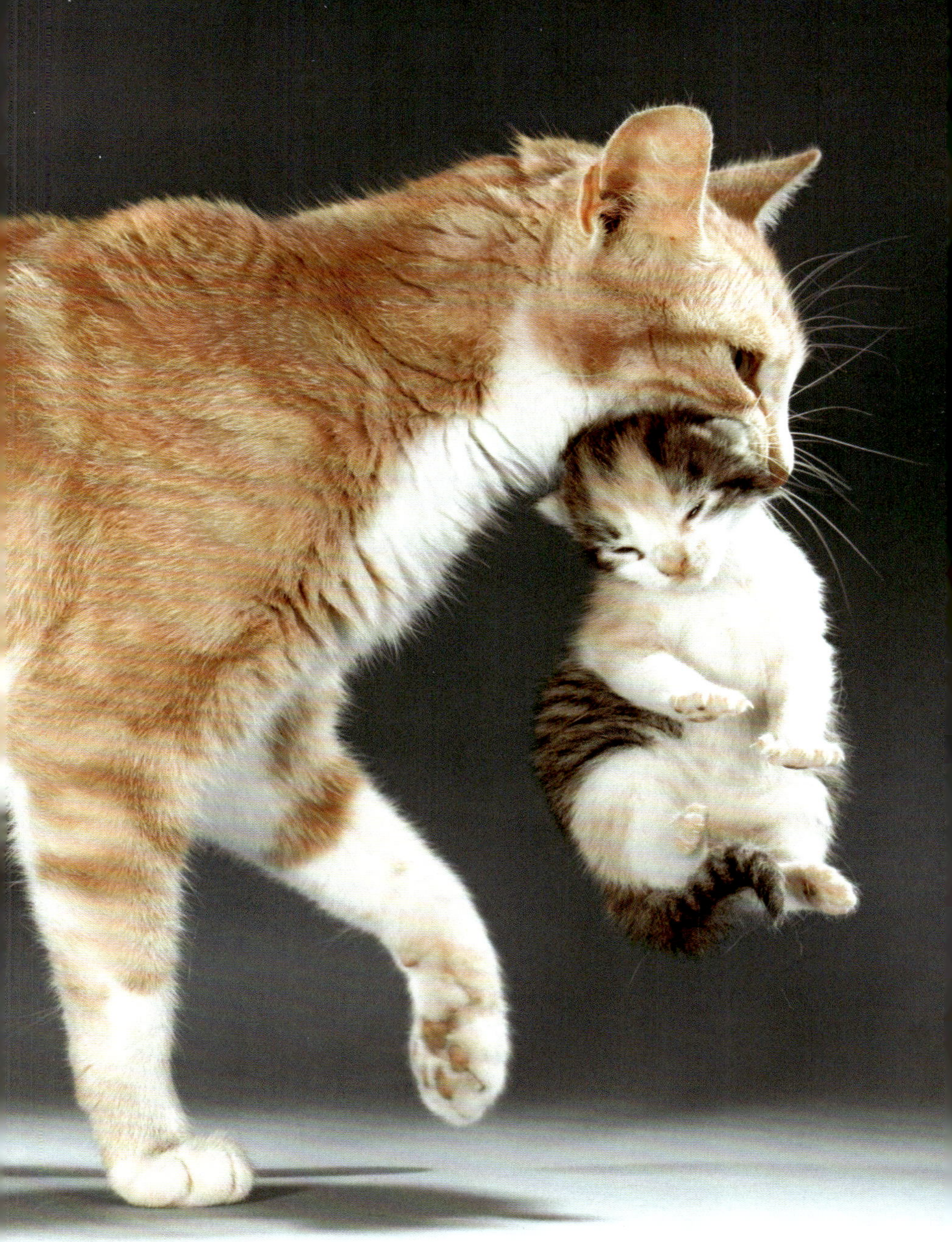

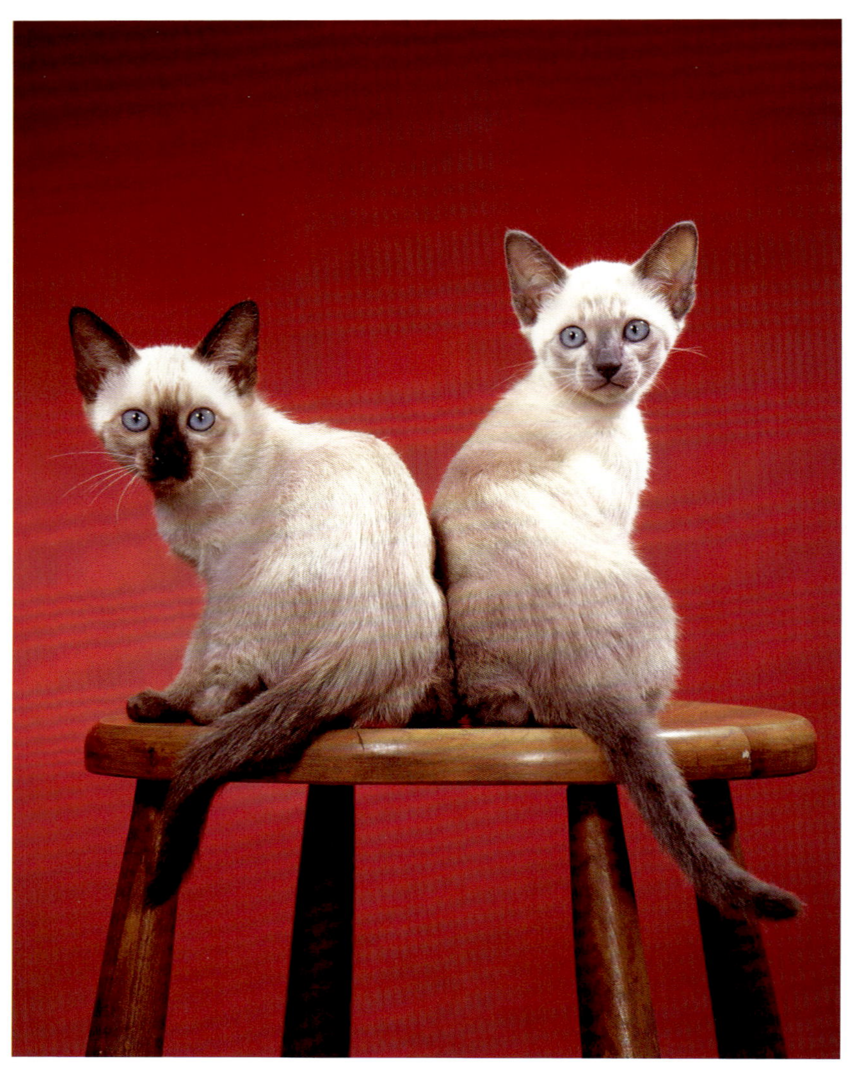

Siamese, New Jersey, 1963.

Domestic shorthair, Long Island, 1959.

Following: Siamese kittens, New Jersey, 1962.

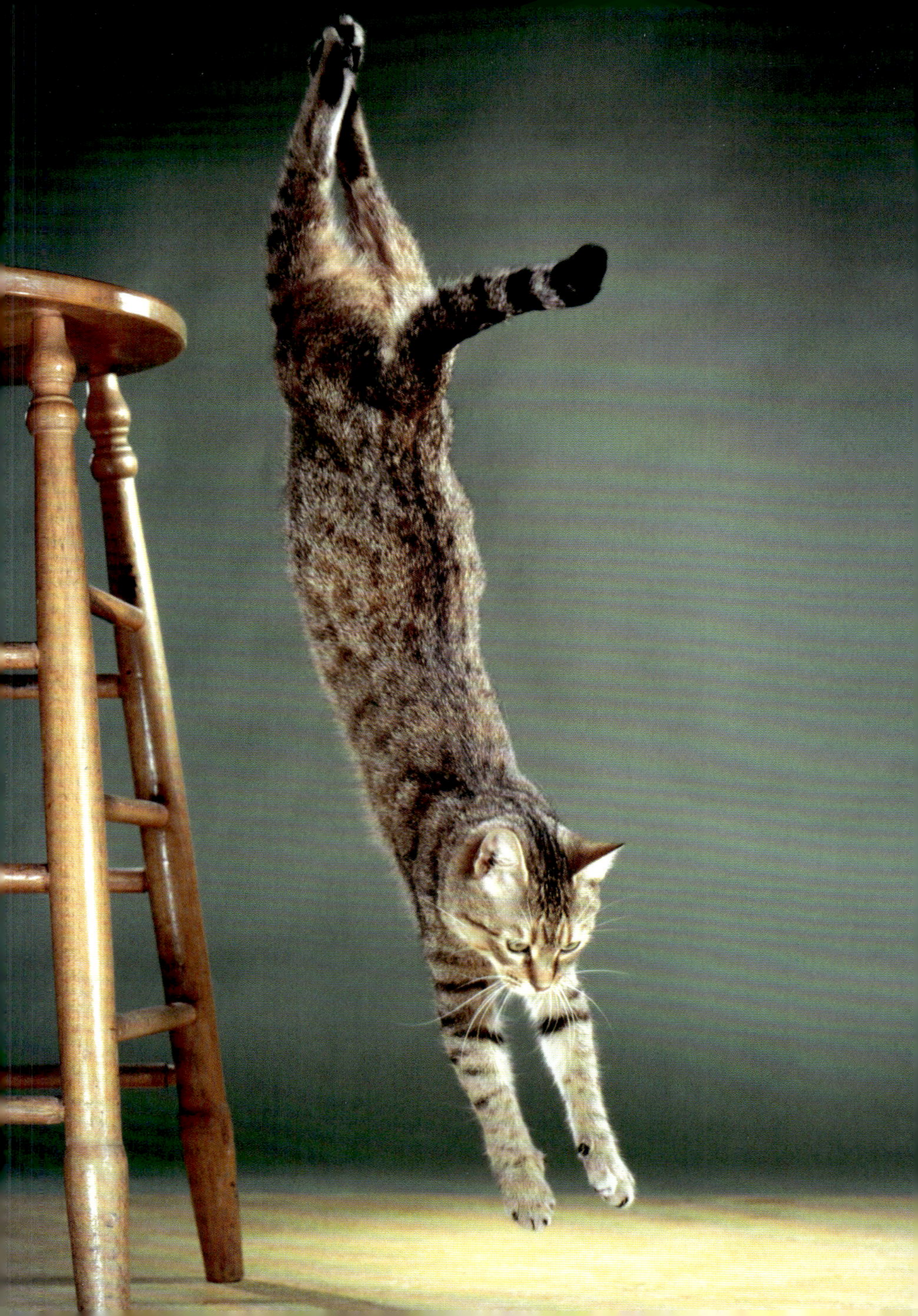

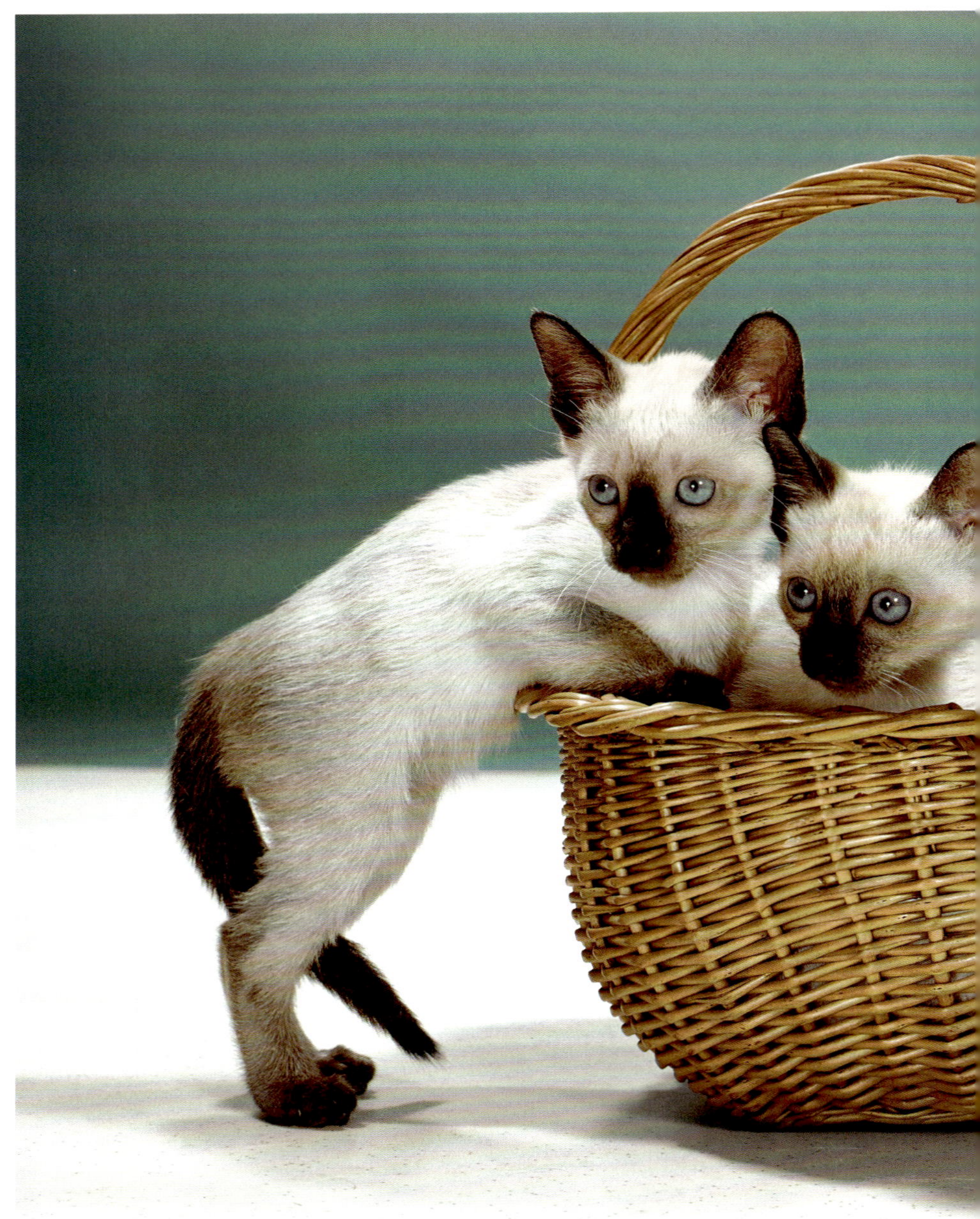

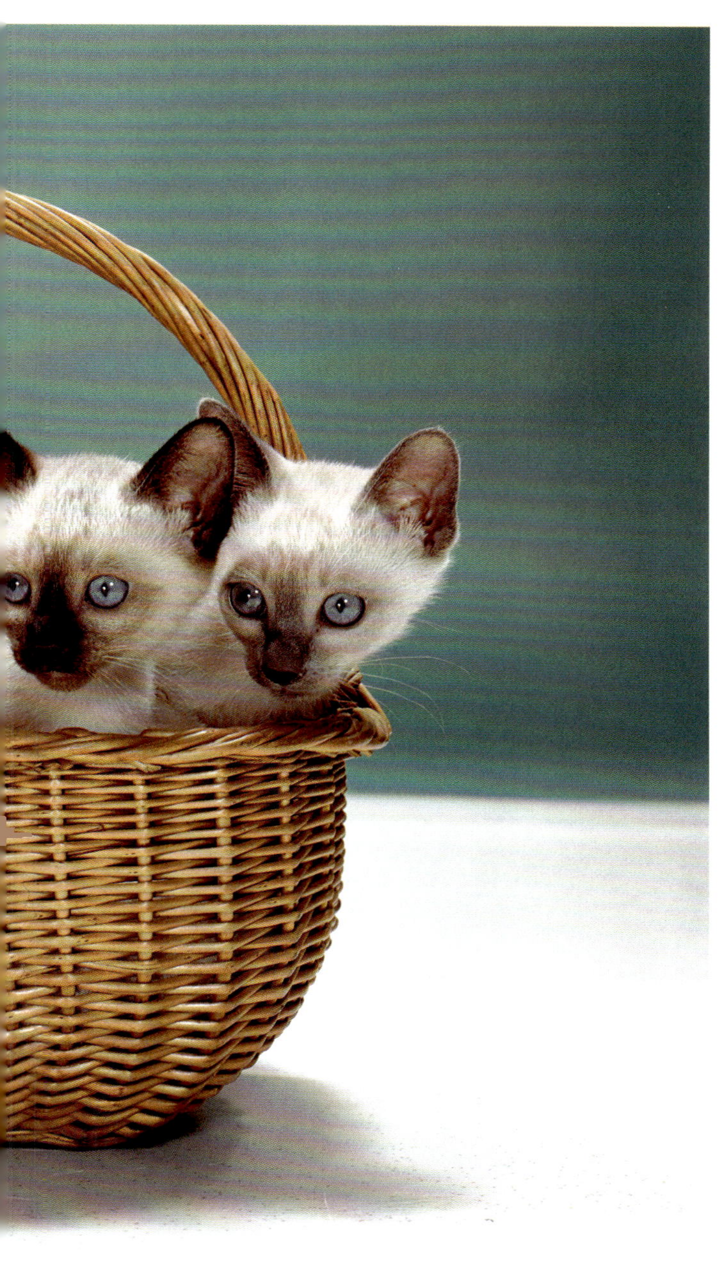

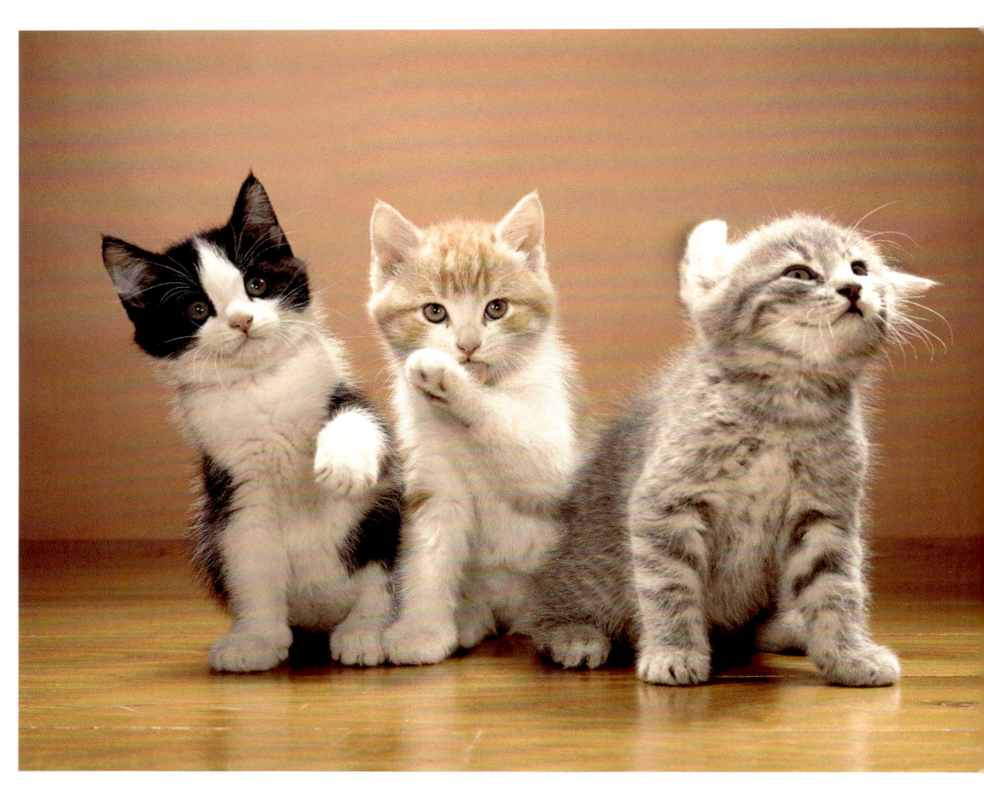

Domestic shorthairs, New Jersey, 1962.

Persian, Domestic shorthair, and
Siamese kittens, New Jersey, 1963.

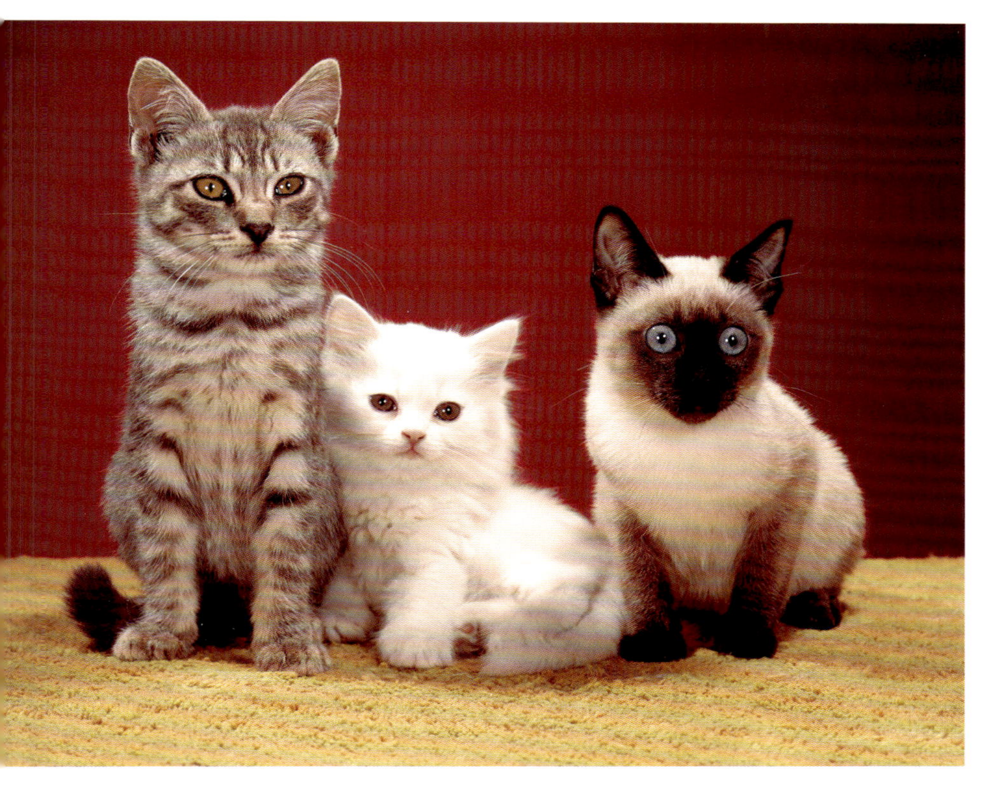

Following: Domestic shorthair
mother and kitten, New Jersey, 1966.

Pages 80–81: Domestic shorthairs,
New Jersey, 1974.

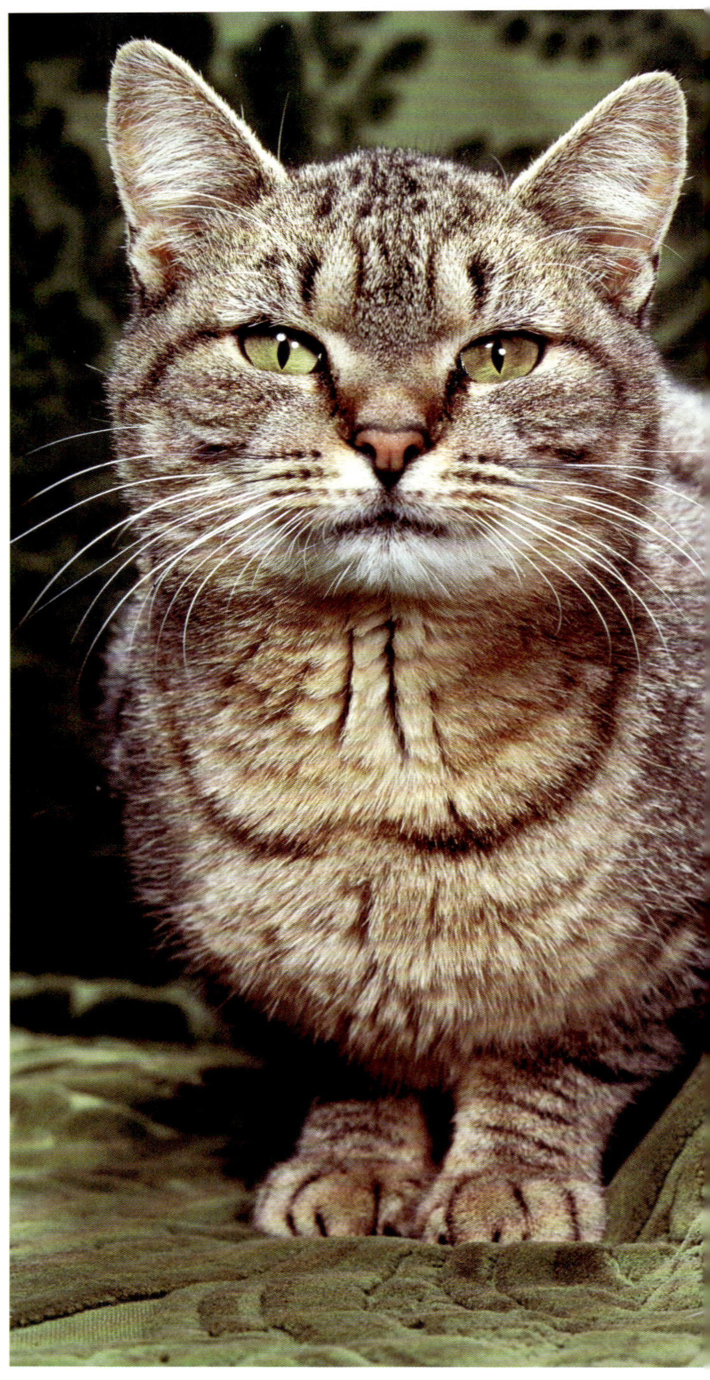

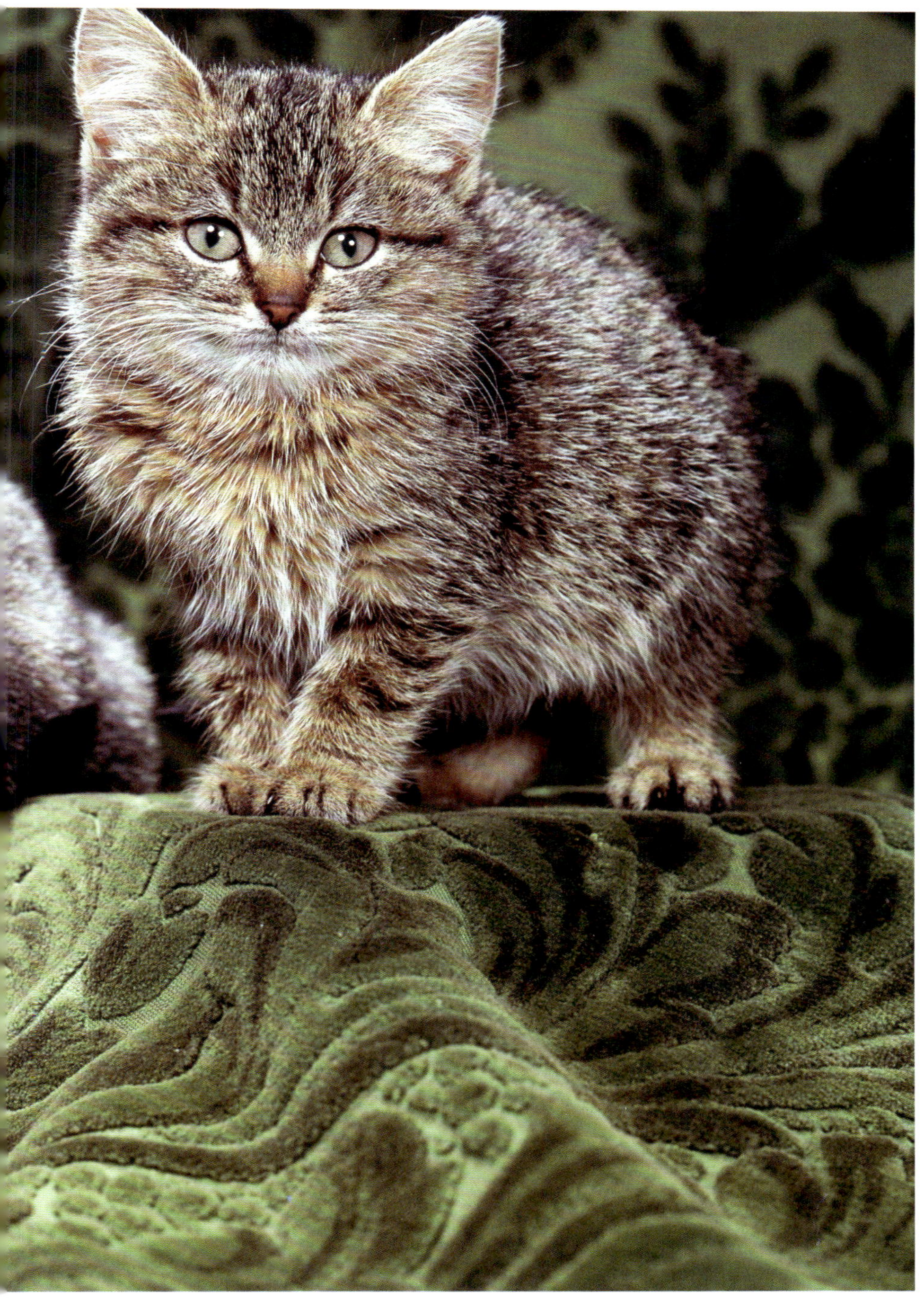

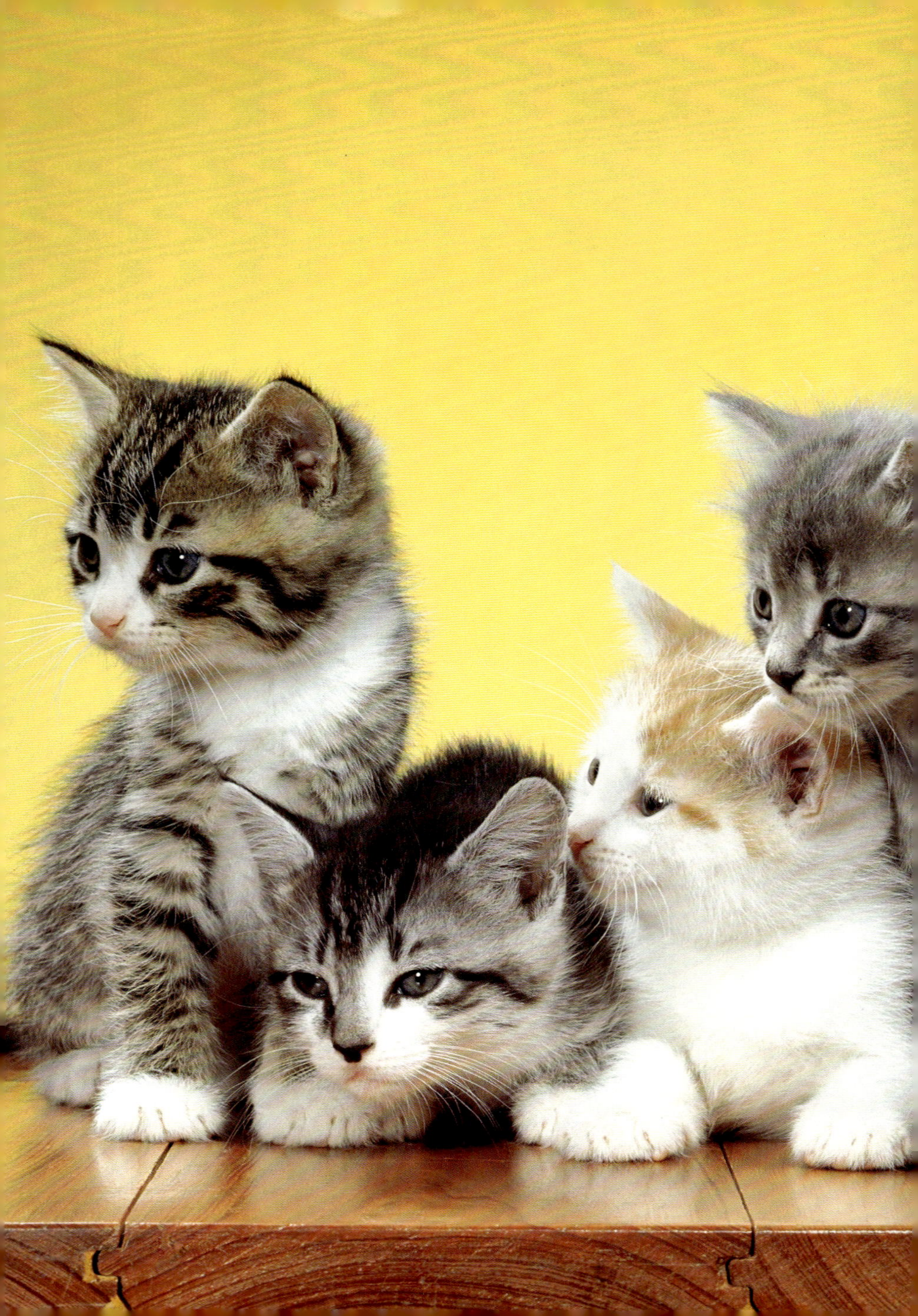

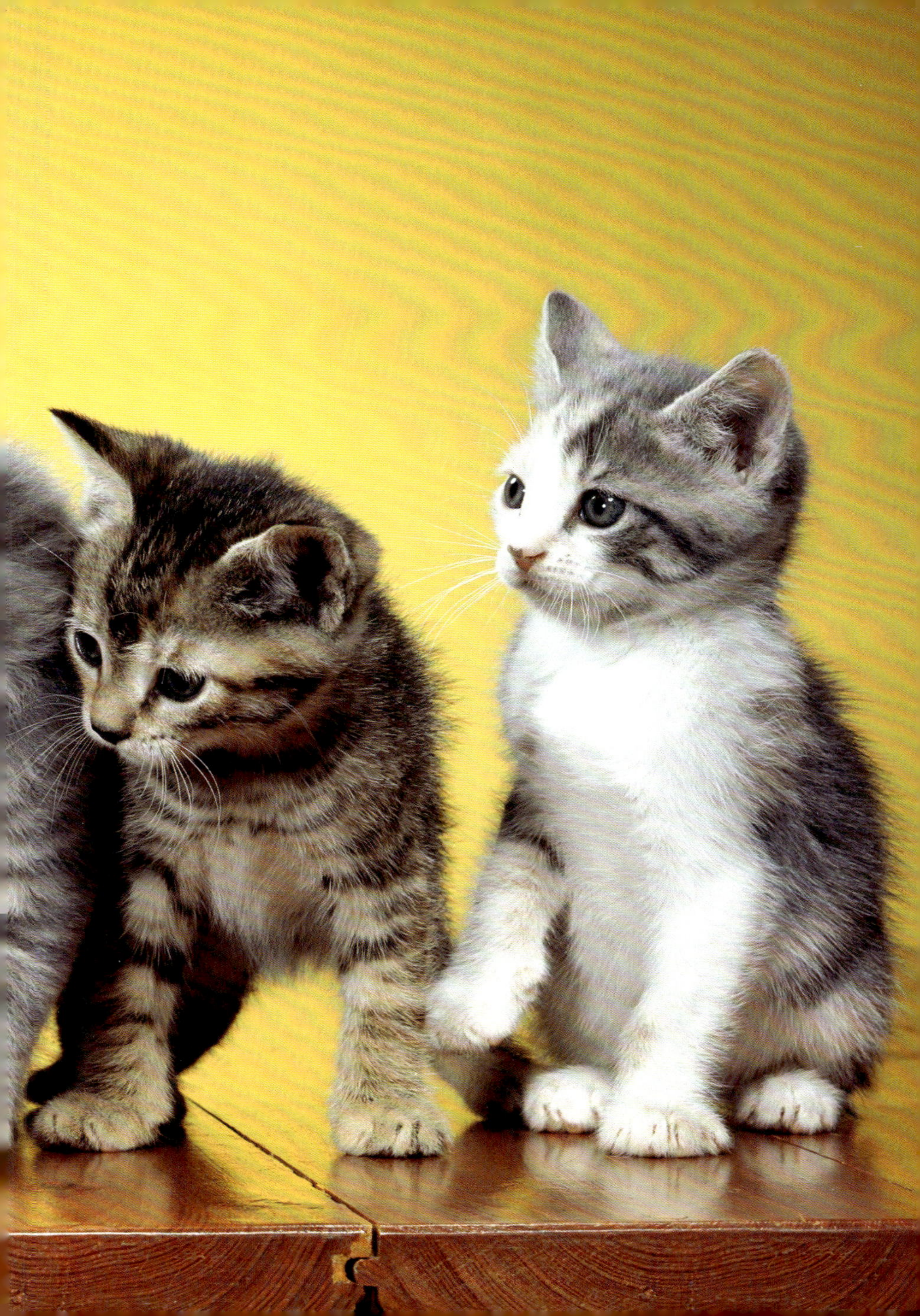

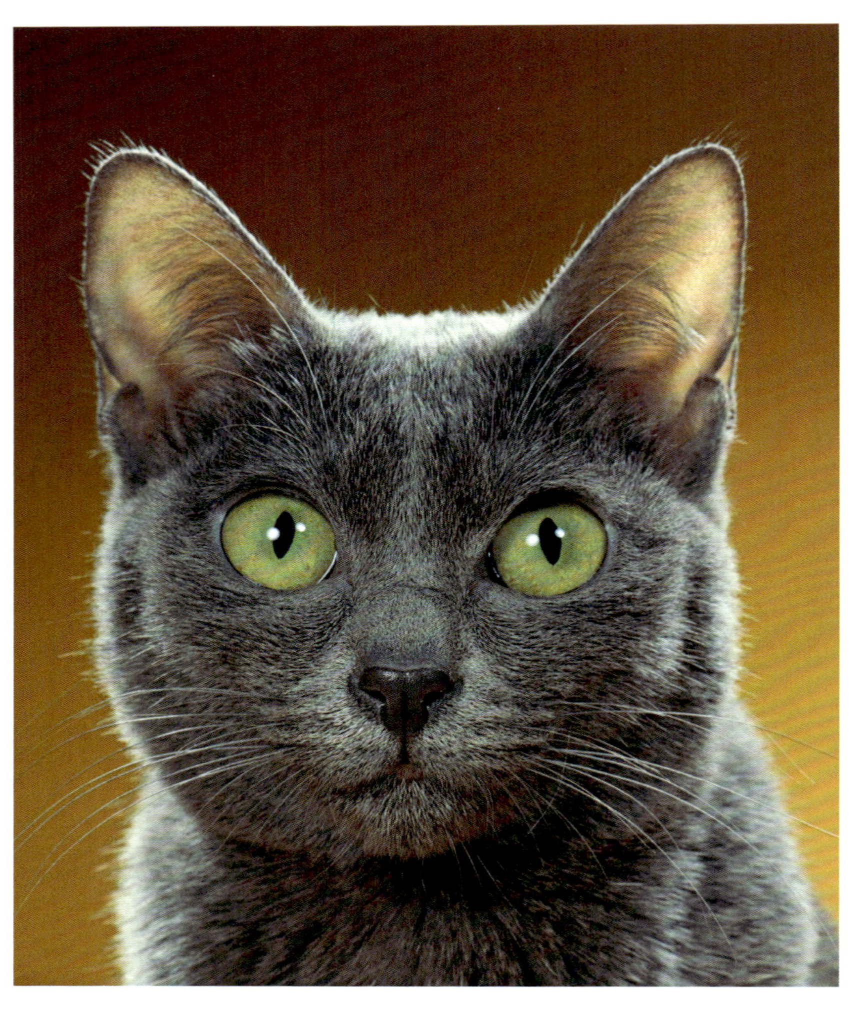

Korat, New Jersey, 1984.

Loco, Queens, 1951.

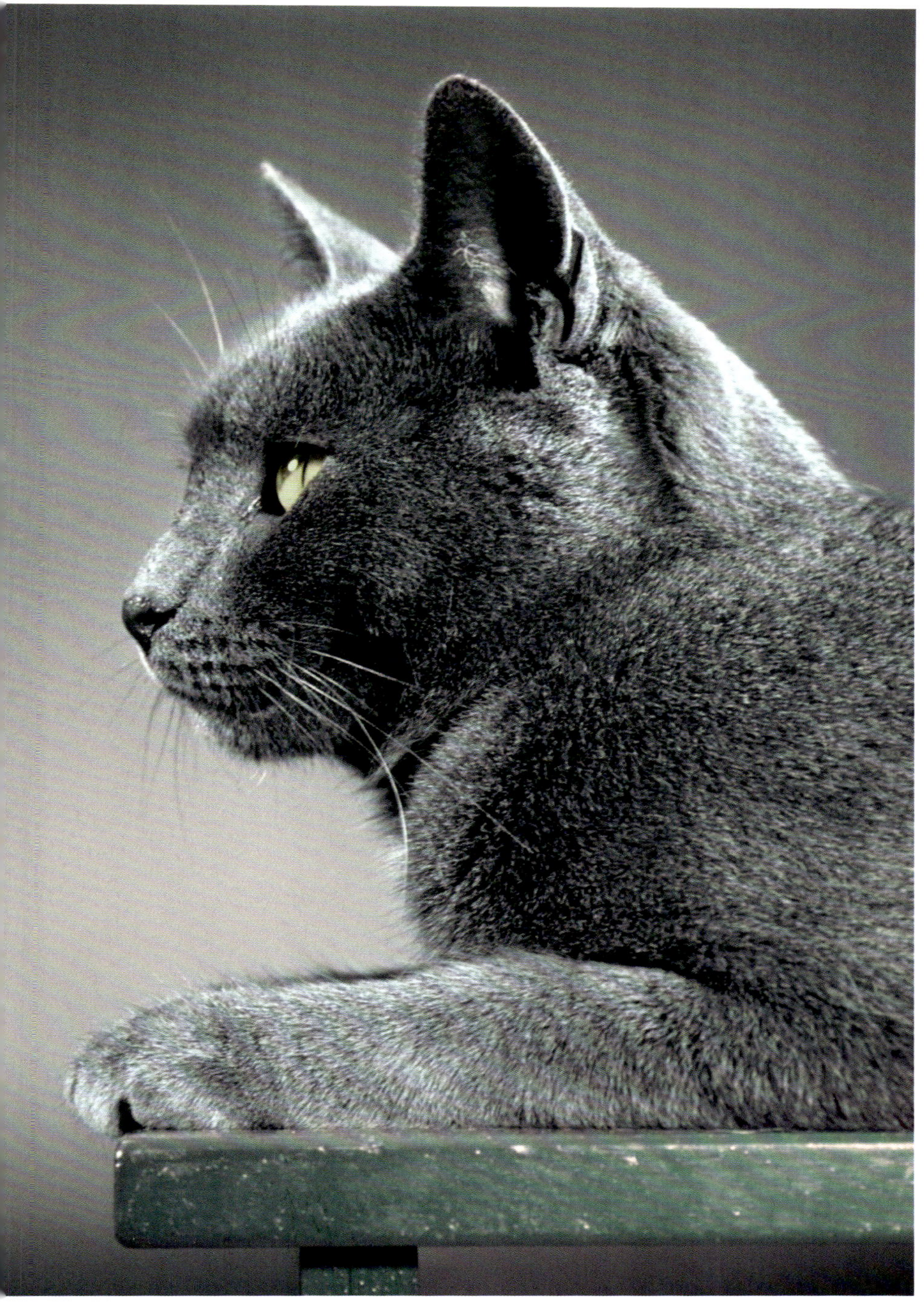

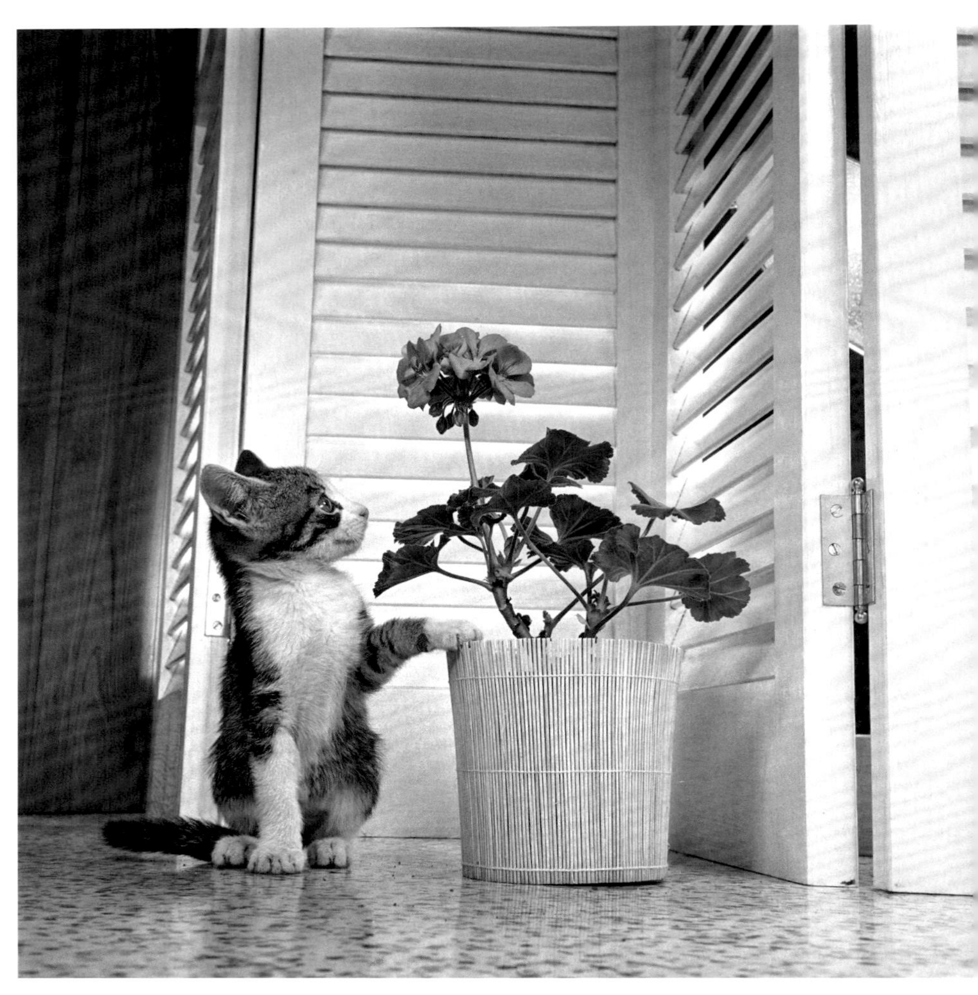

Domestic shorthair, Long Island, 1960.
Domestic shorthair, New Jersey, 1968.

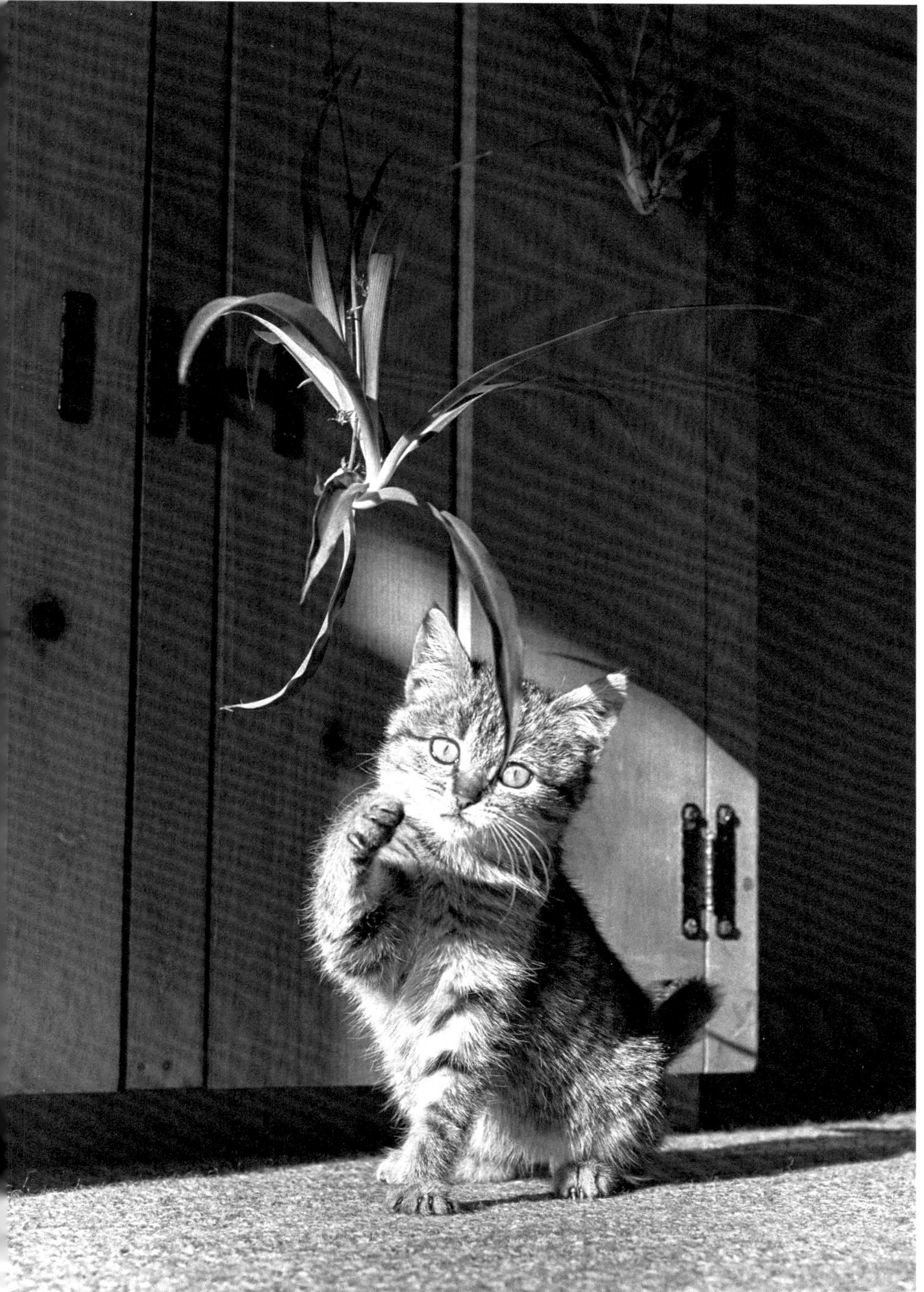

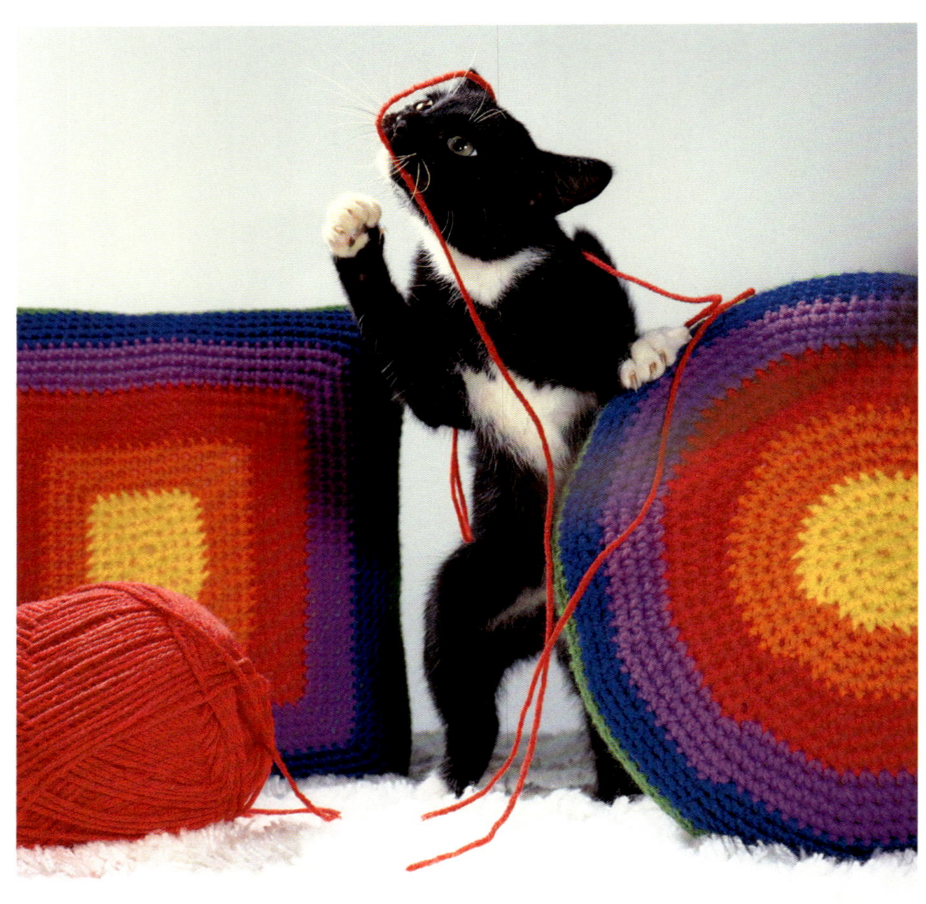

Domestic shorthair, New Jersey, 1982.

Red-point Siamese, New Jersey, 1987.

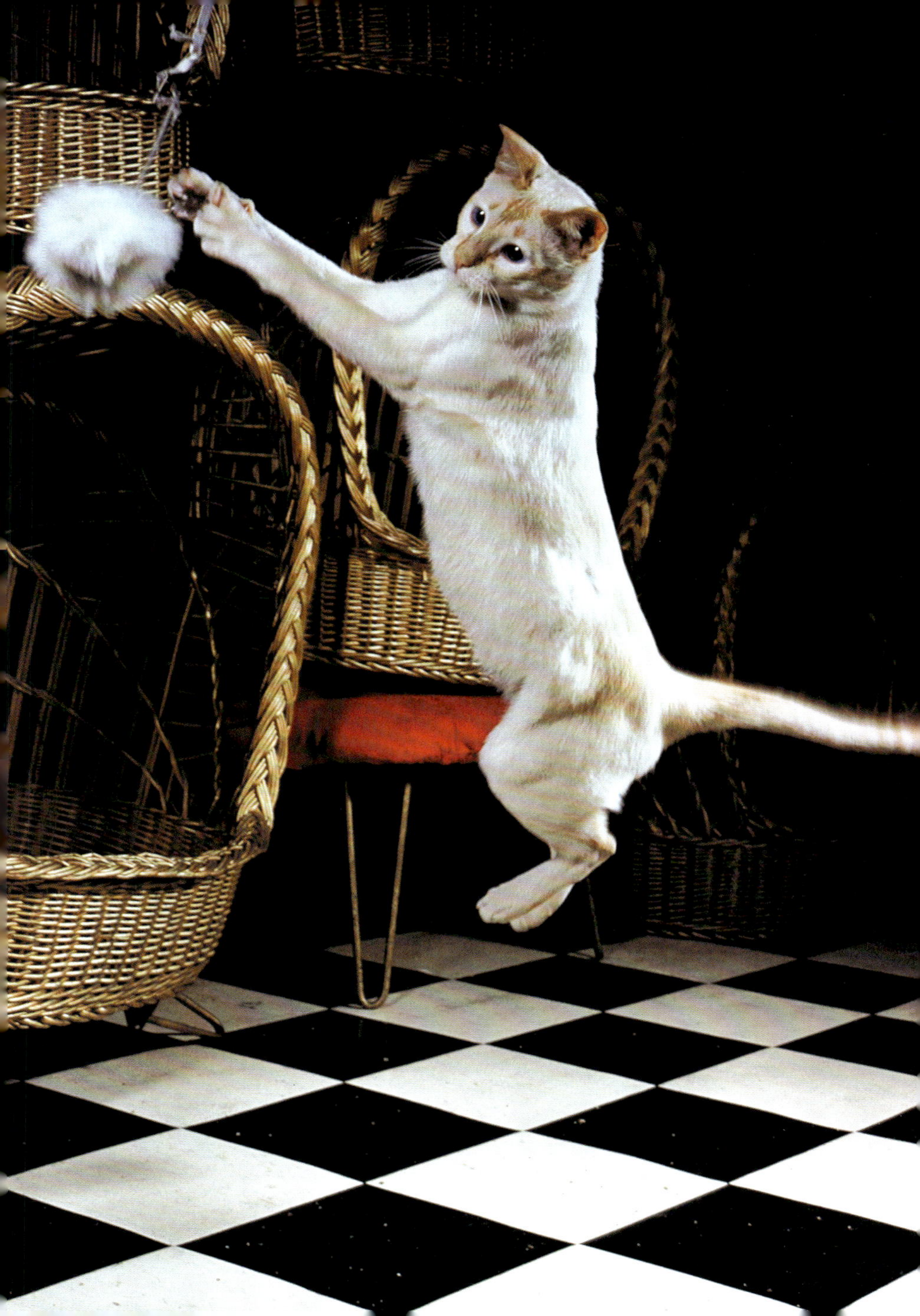

Loco and tabby, Queens, 1950.

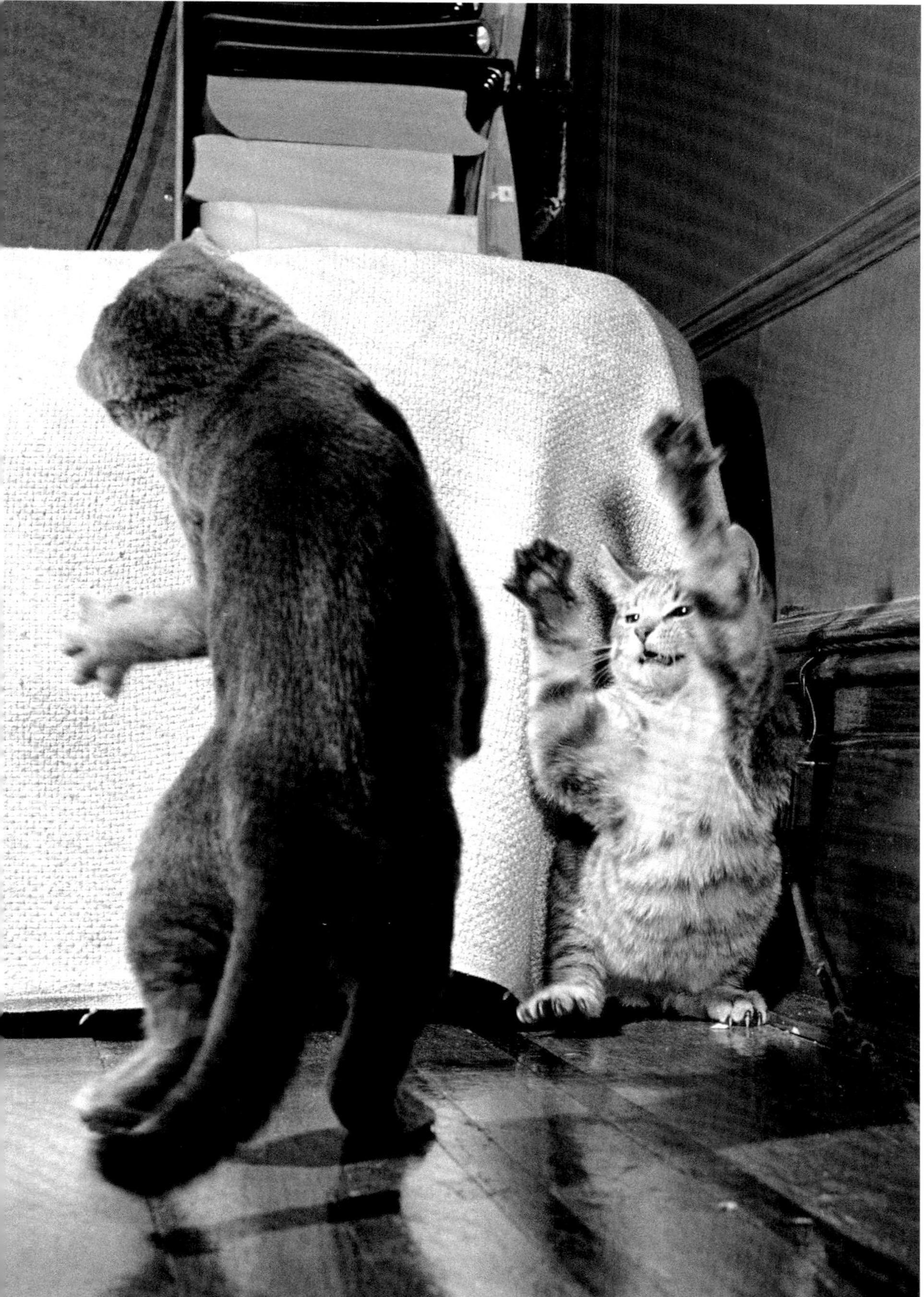

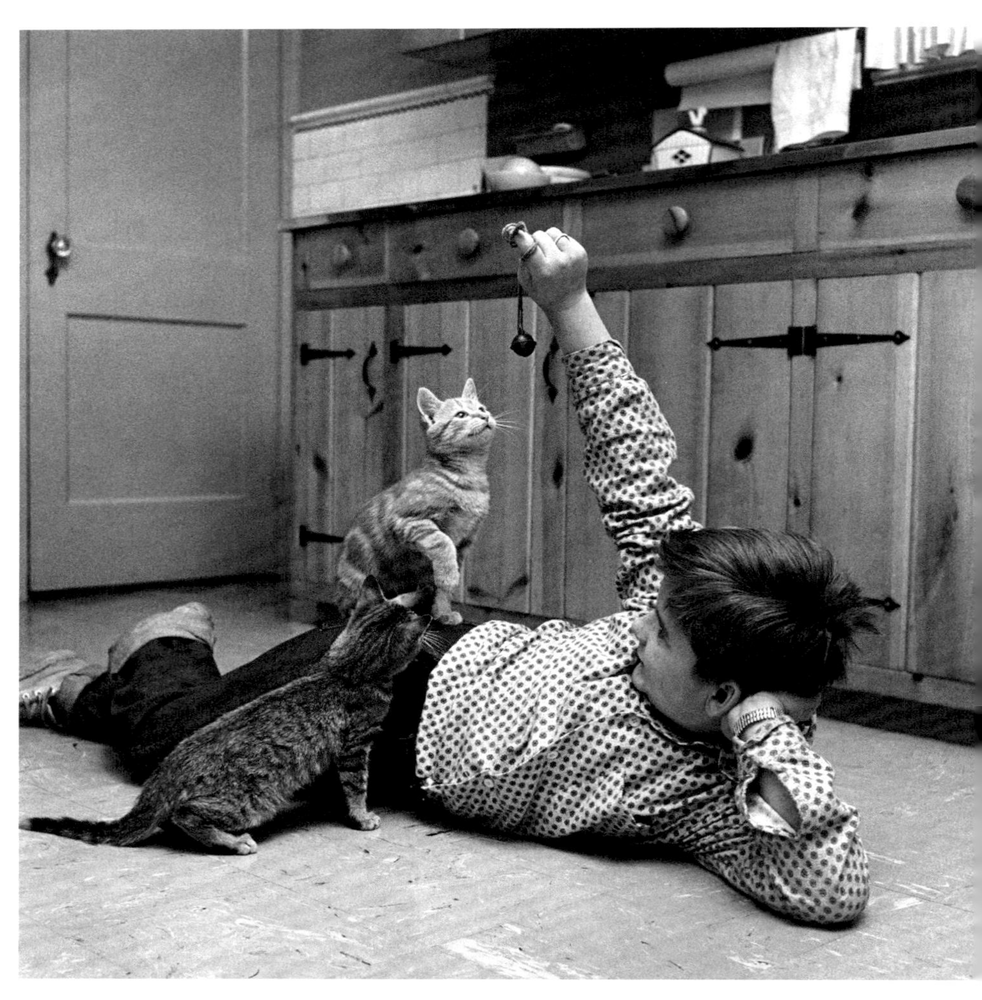

Son Enrico with family kittens,
Long Island, 1960.

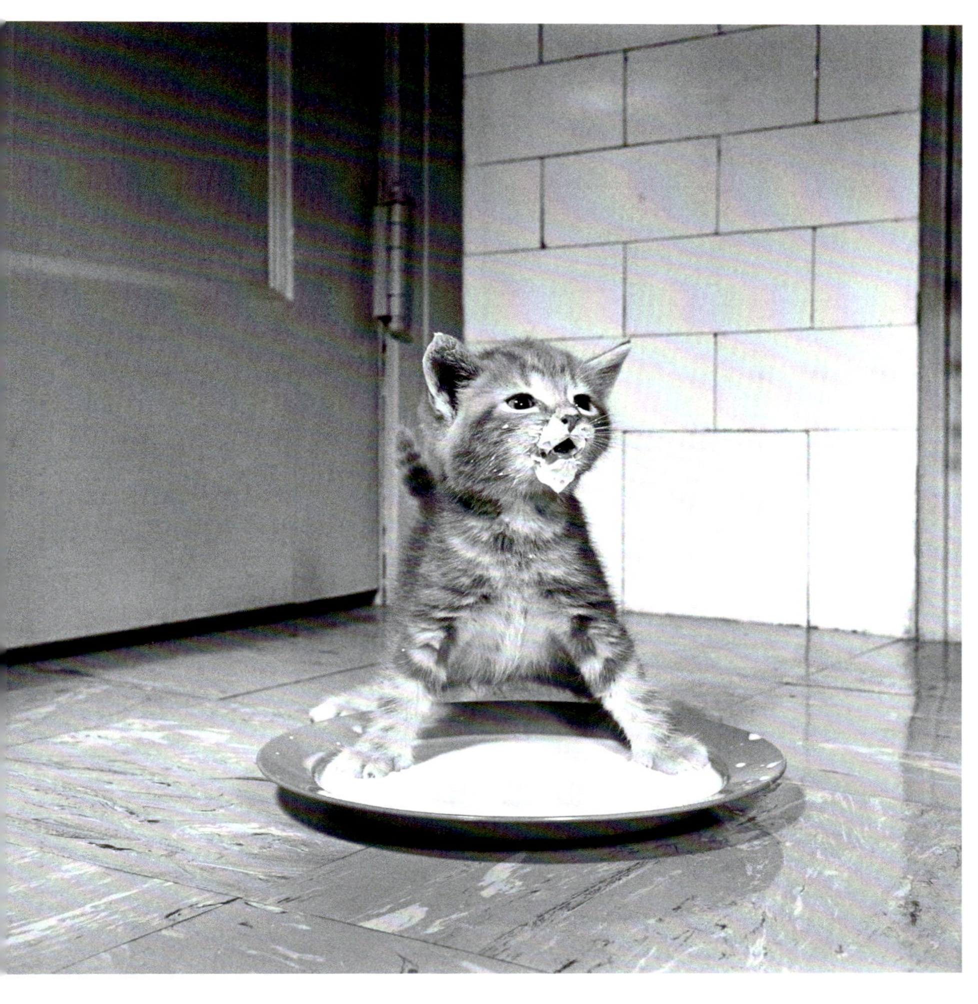

Domestic shorthair, Long Island, 1955.

Following: Daughter Chiara and Persian, New Jersey, 1961.

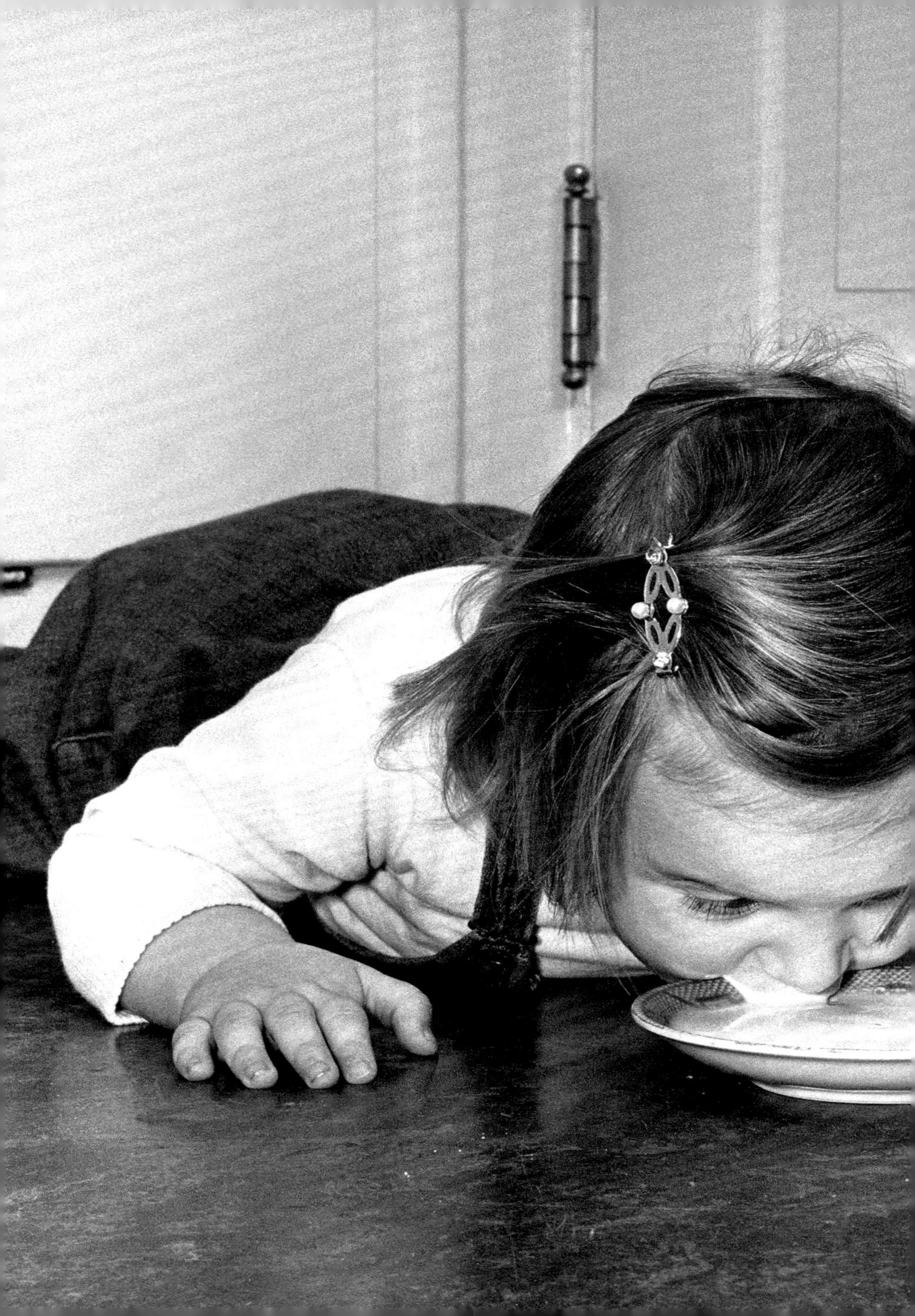

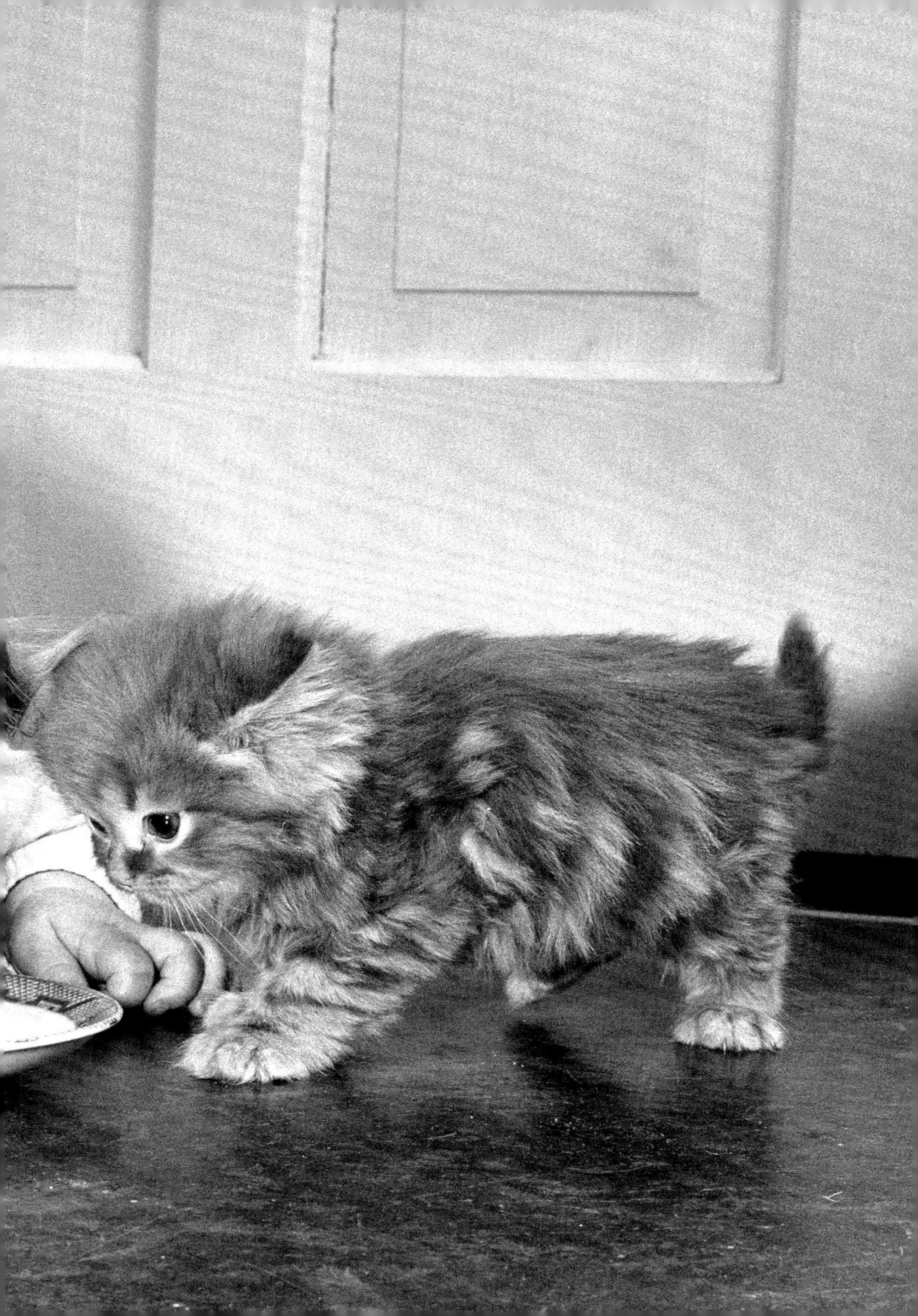

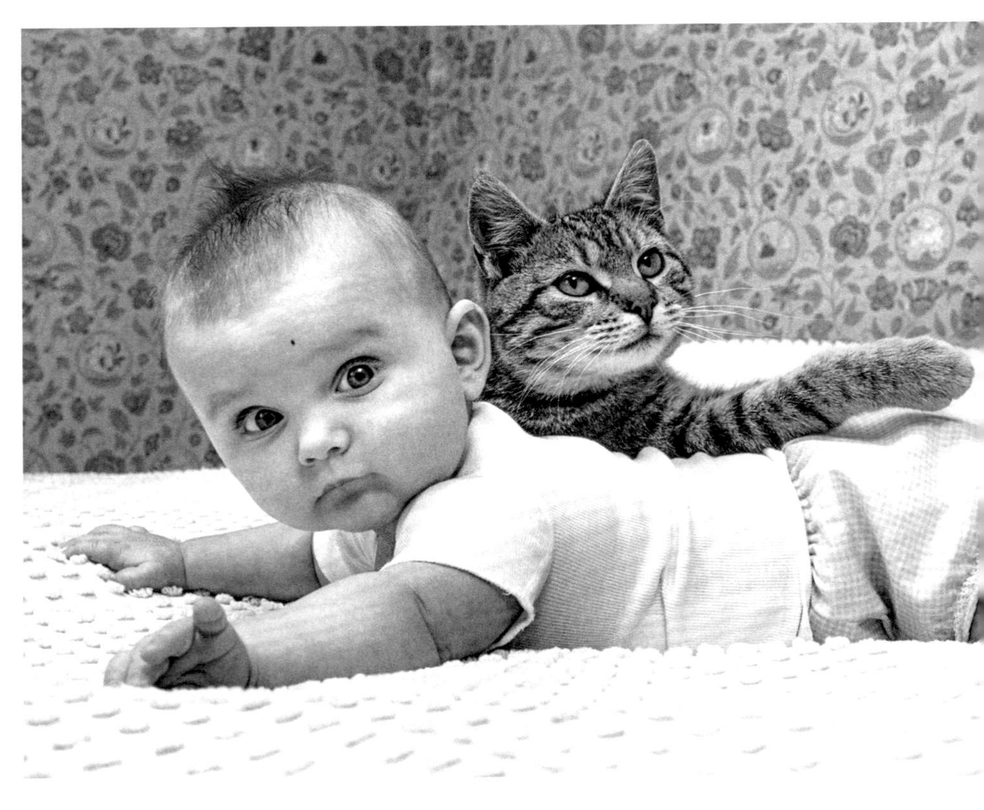

Daughter Chiara and Tiger,
Long Island, 1960.

Son Sam and Tom, Domestic
shorthair, Long Island, 1957.

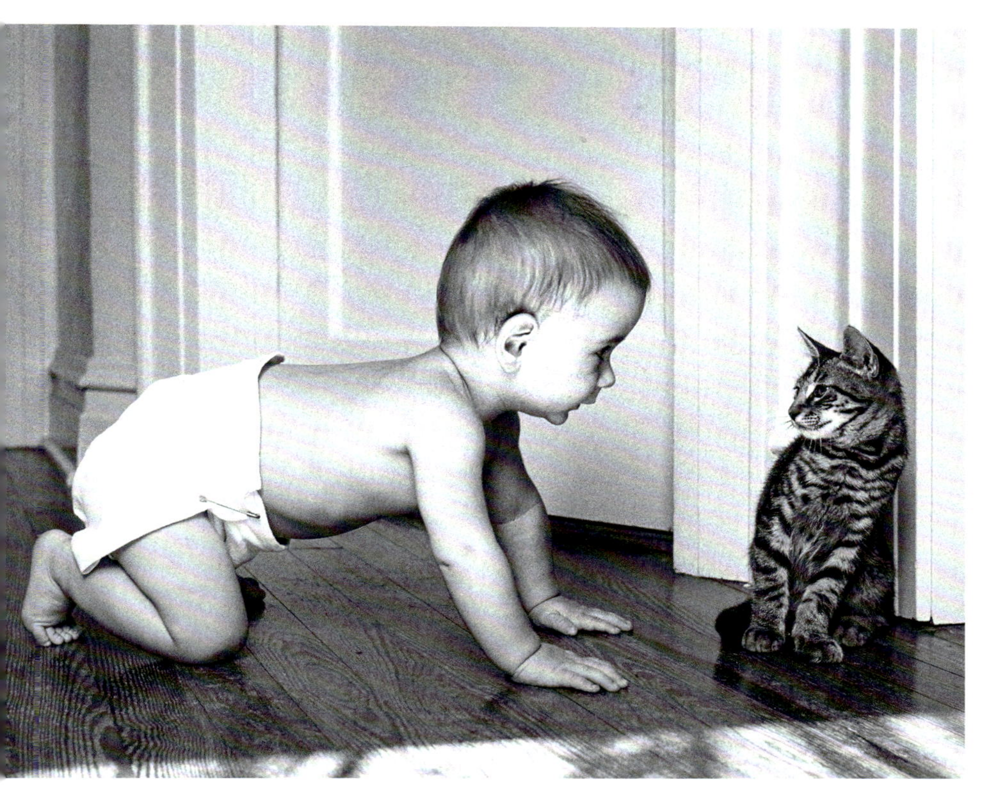

Following: Domestic shorthair,
New Jersey, 1964.

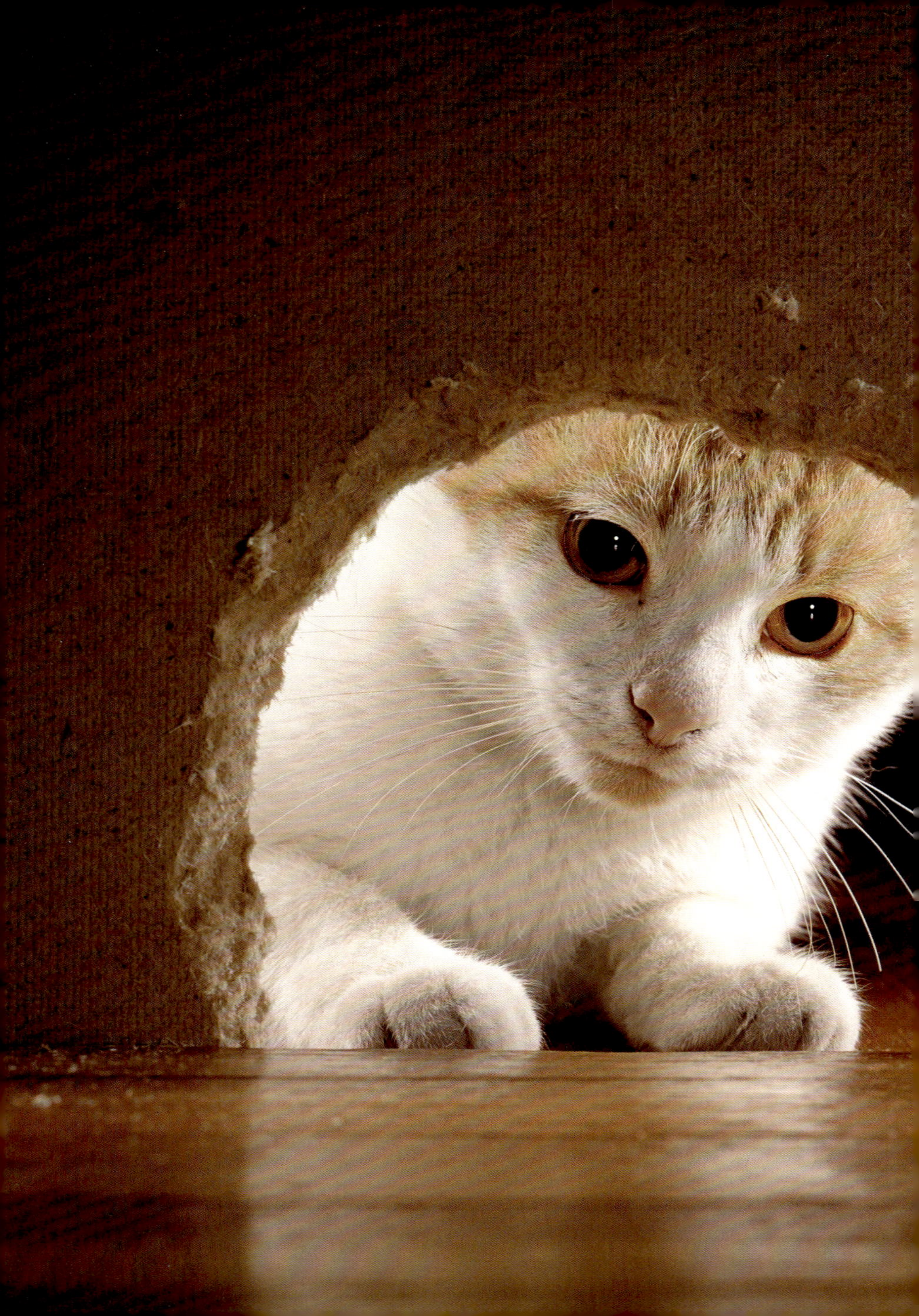

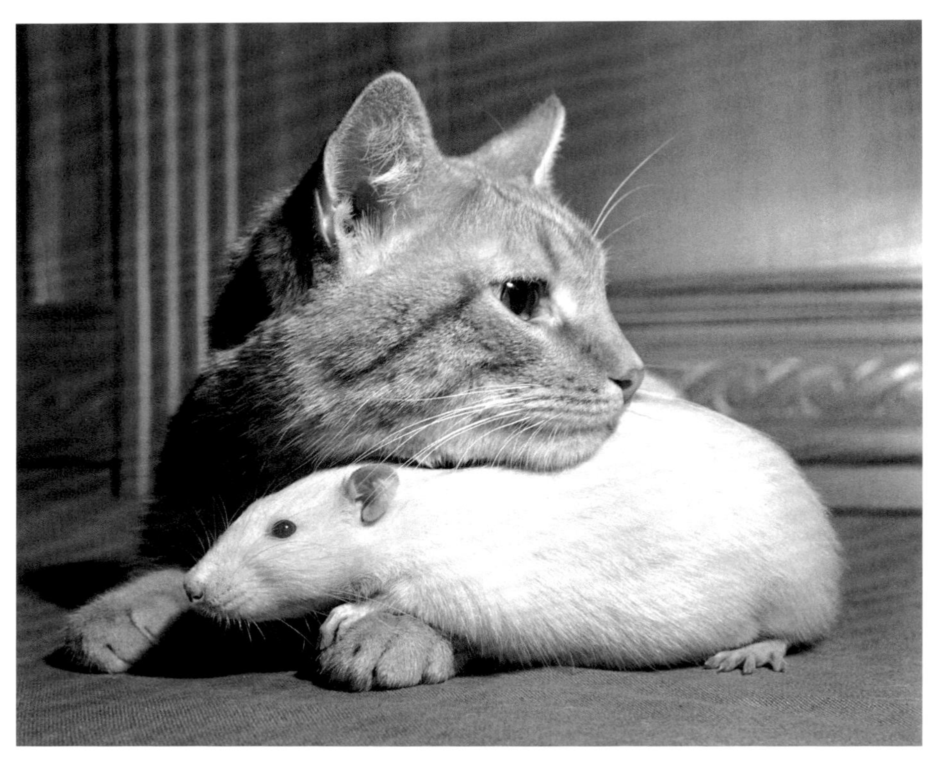

Domestic shorthair and rat, Queens, 1949.

Domestic shorthair and goldfish, New Jersey, 1976.

Following: Domestic shorthair and beagle, New Jersey, 1966.

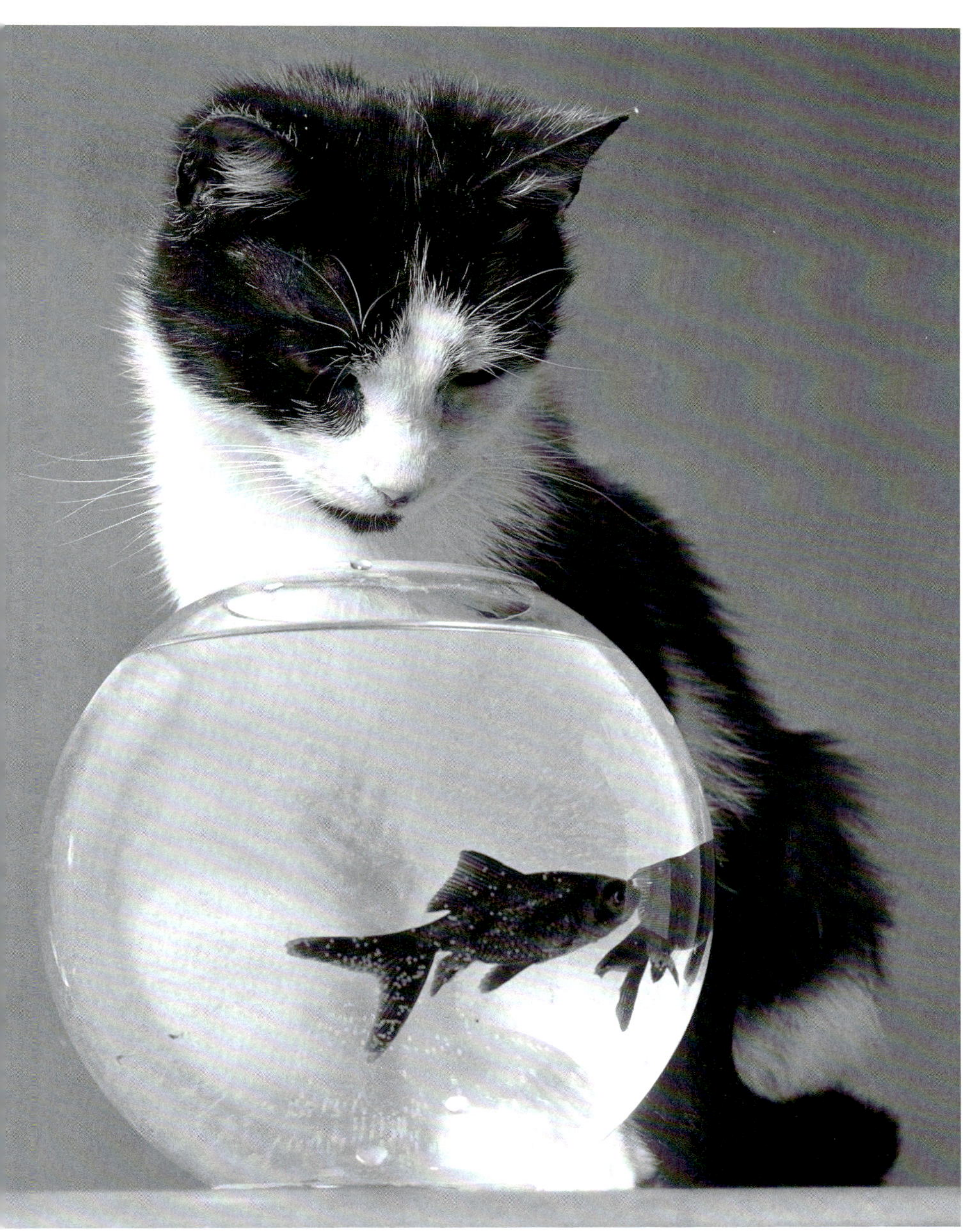

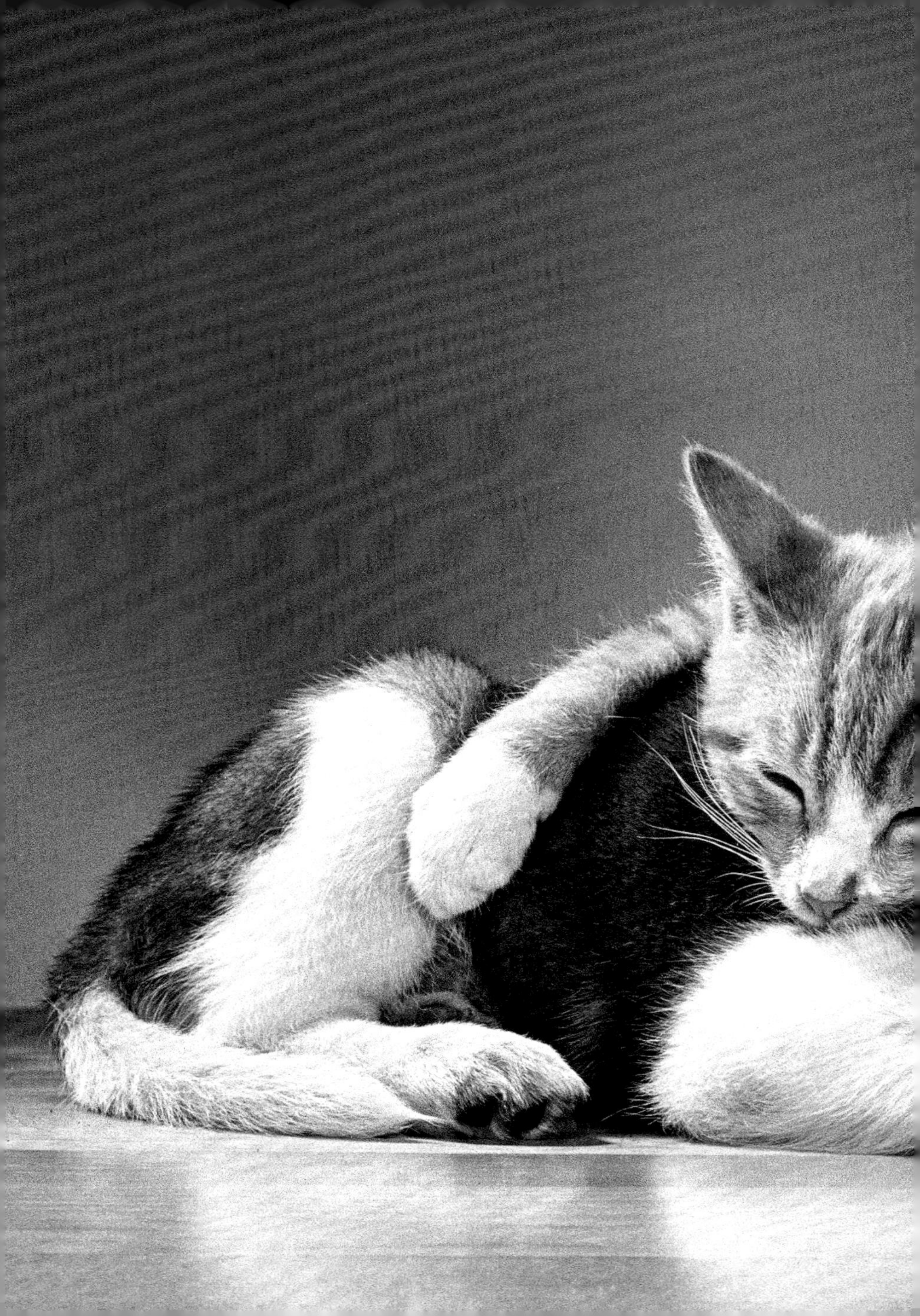

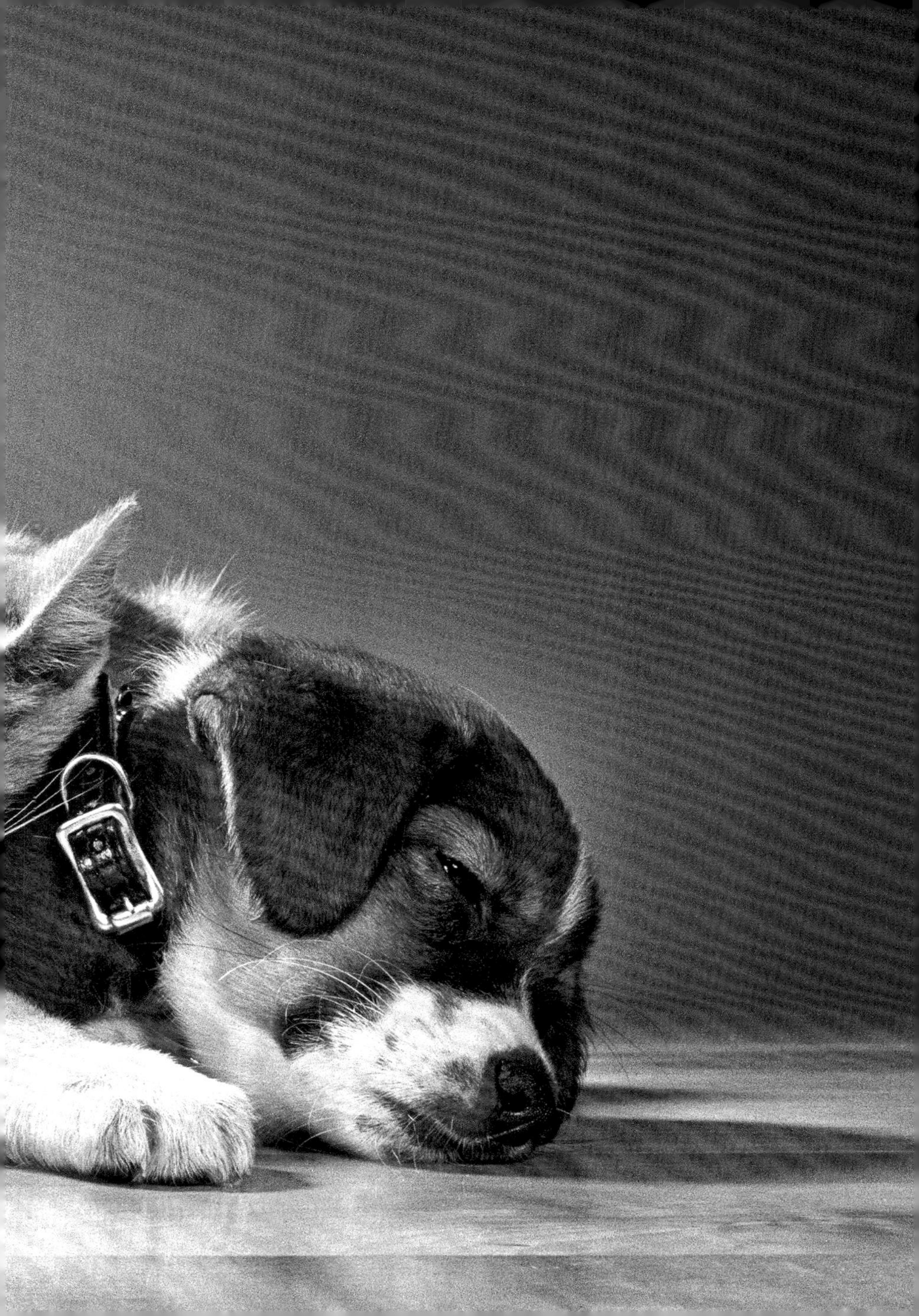

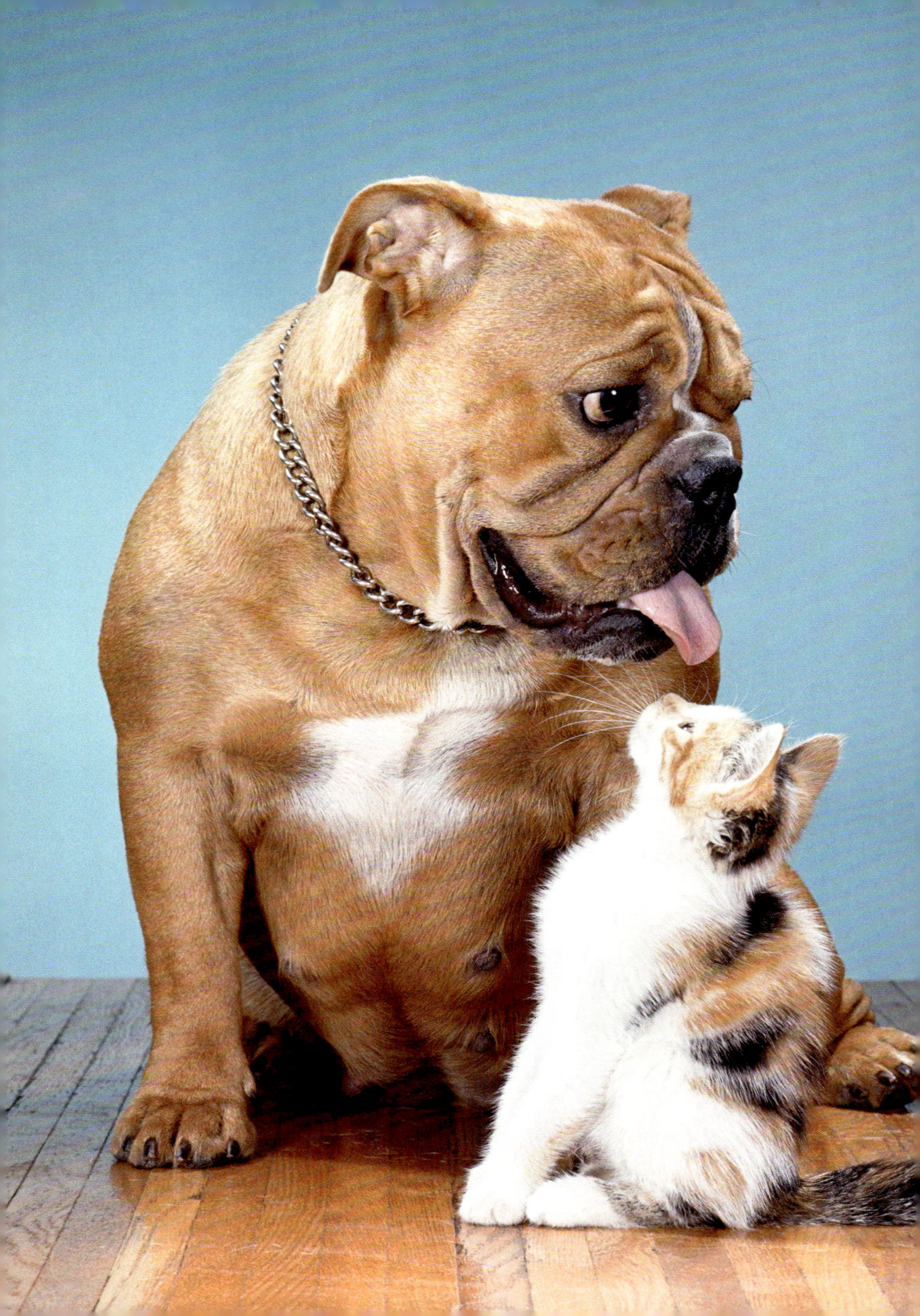

Domestic shorthair kitten and
bulldog, New Jersey, 1972.

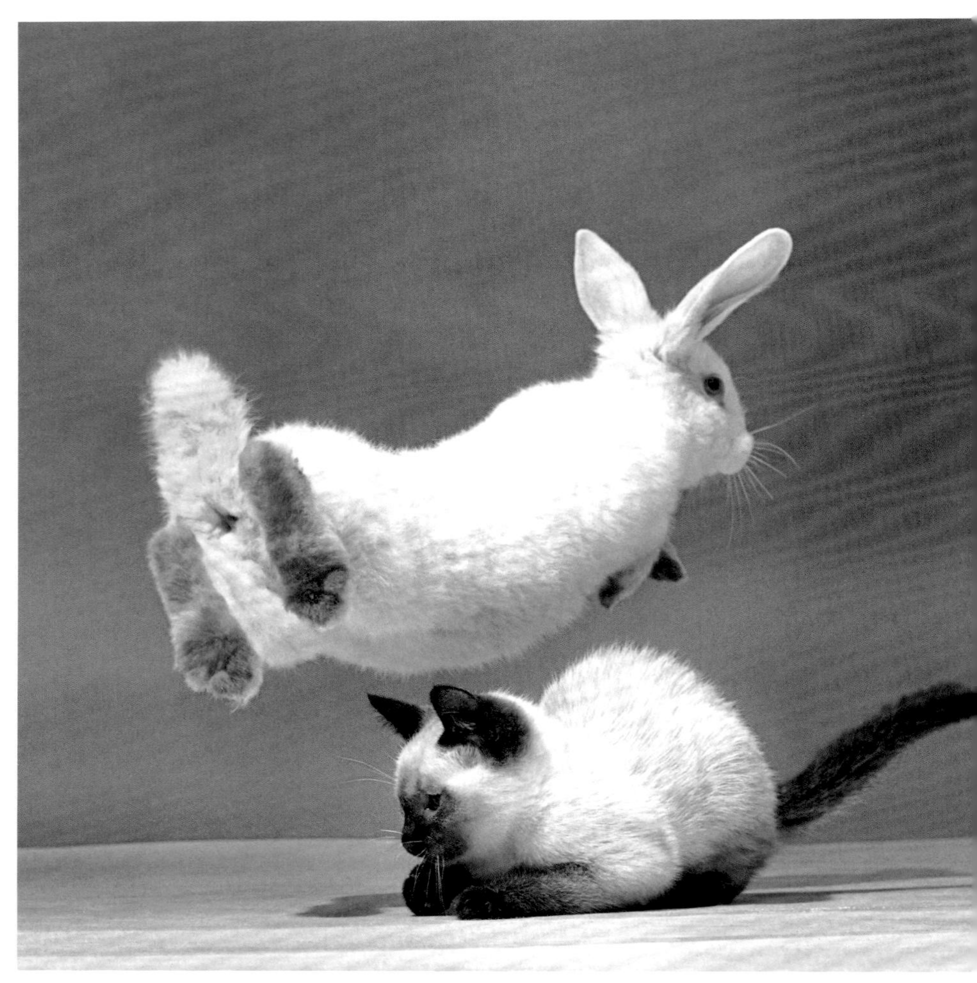

"If you know your subjects well, you also know what
they will and will not do in a given situation. But you
often have to wait a very long time for them to do it."
Siamese and rabbit, New Jersey, 1960.

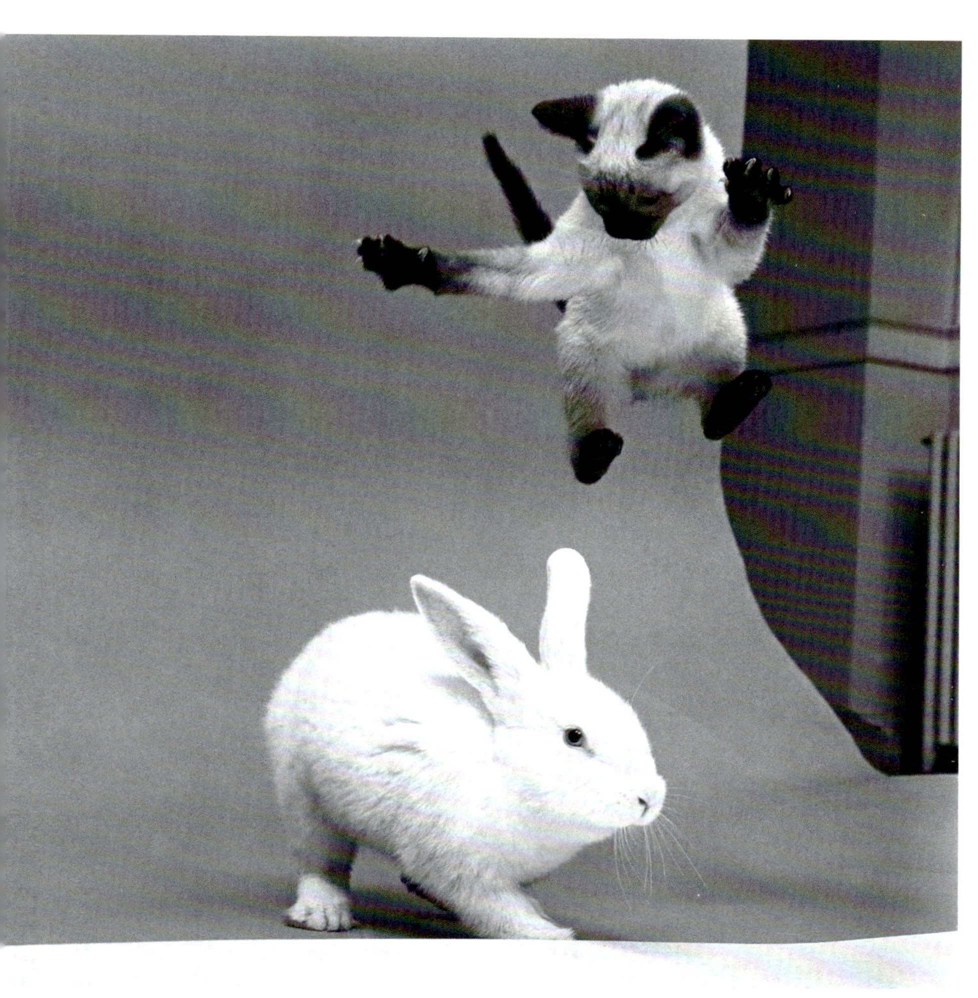

Following: Domestic shorthairs,
New Jersey, 1976.

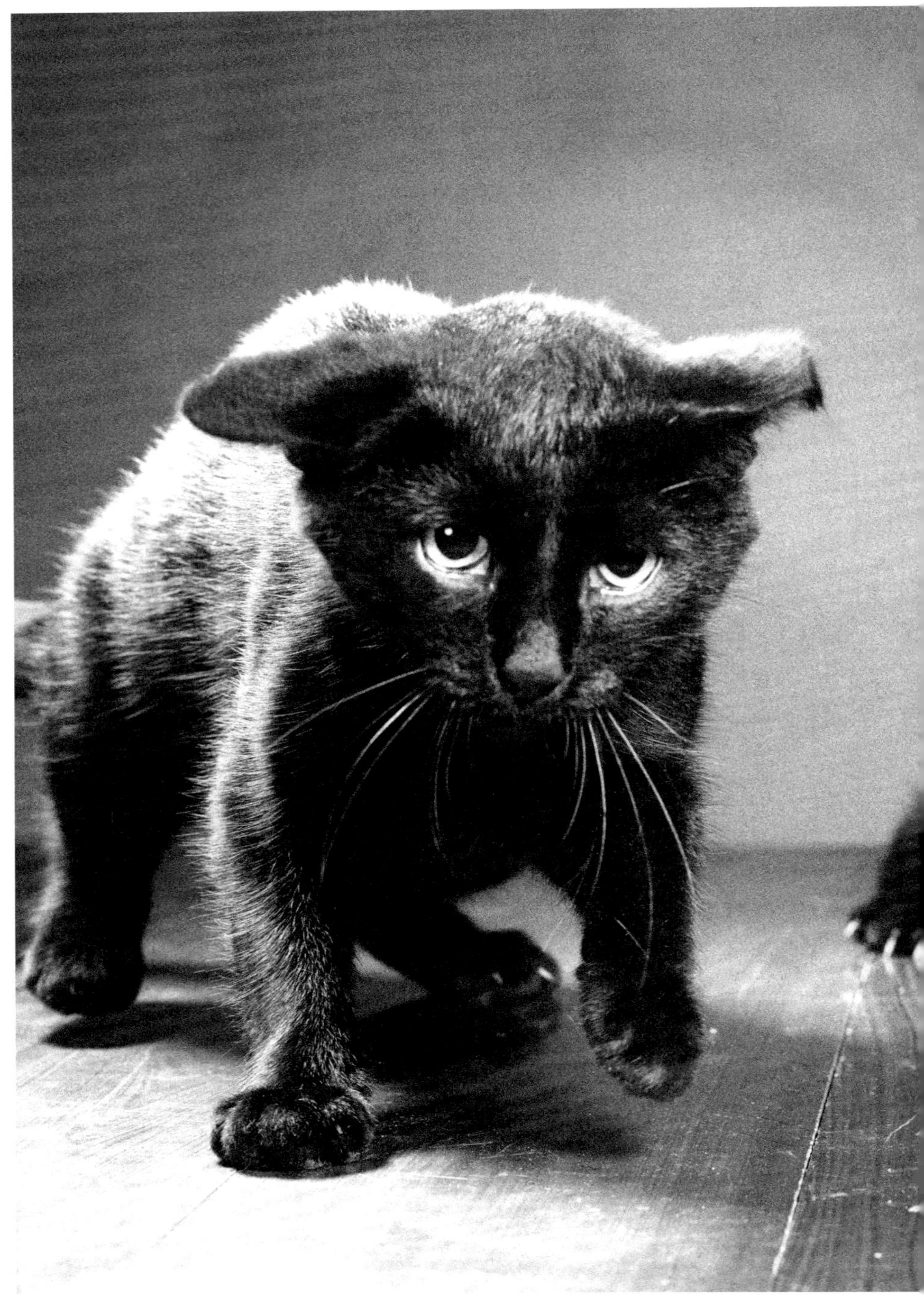

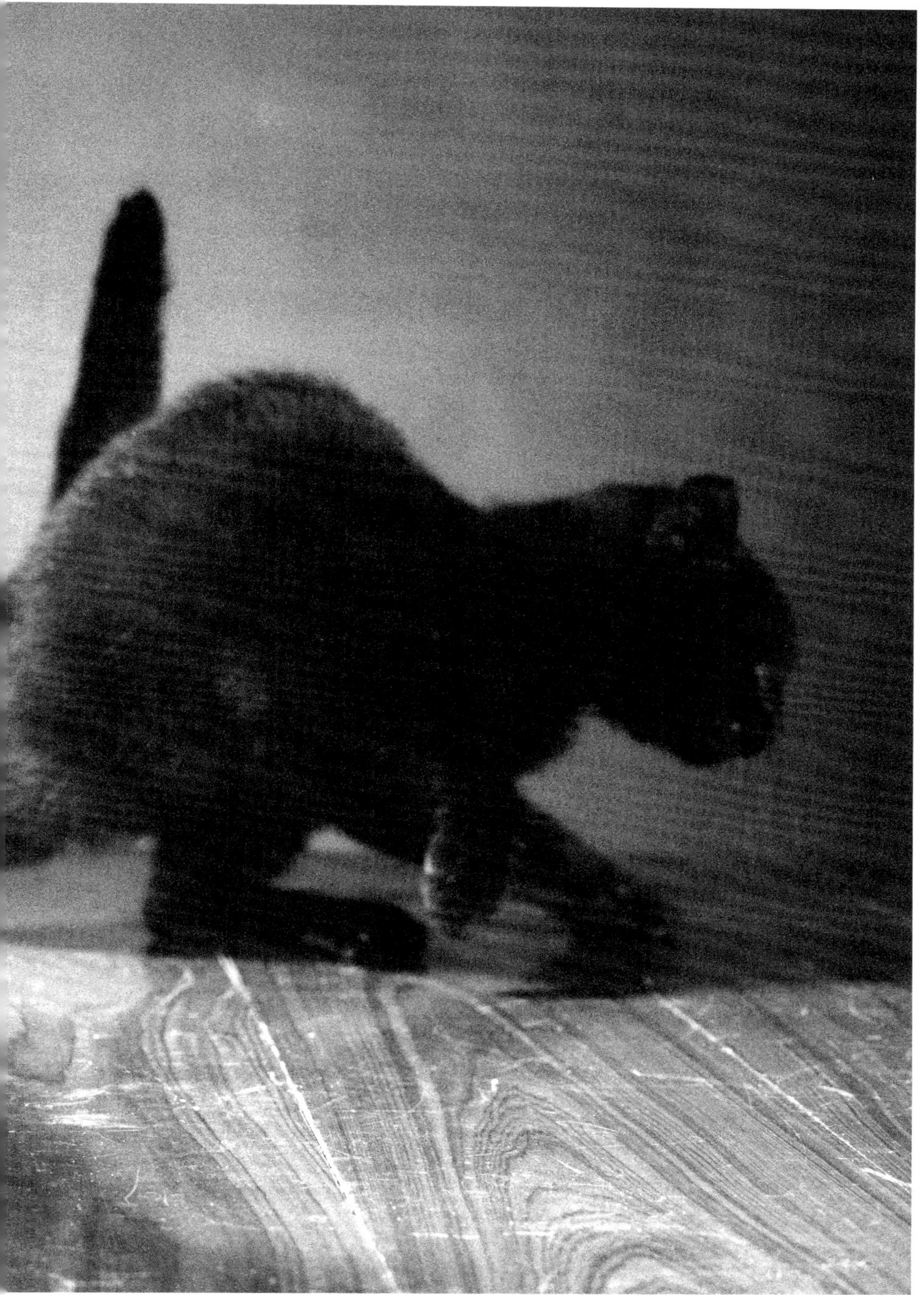

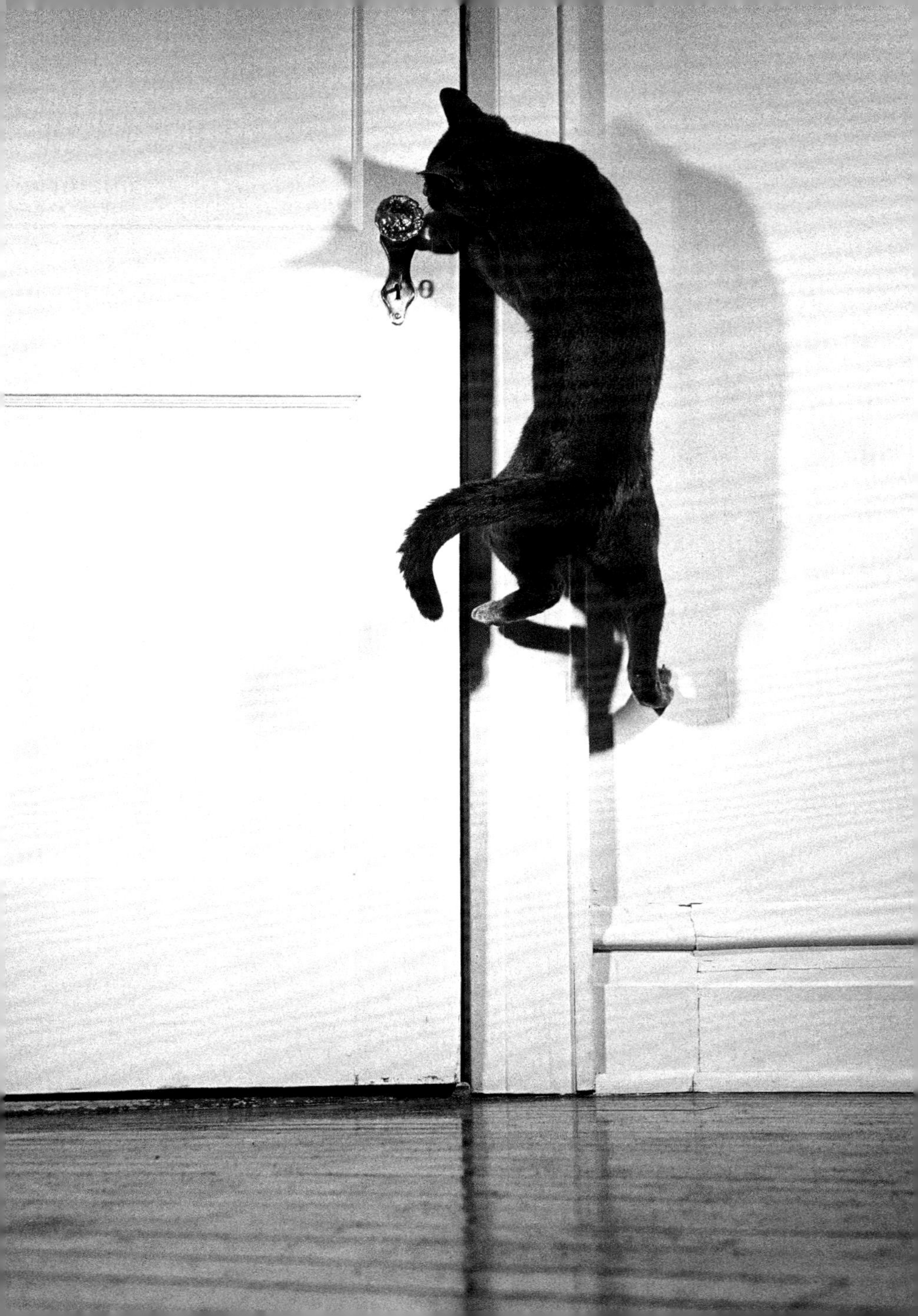

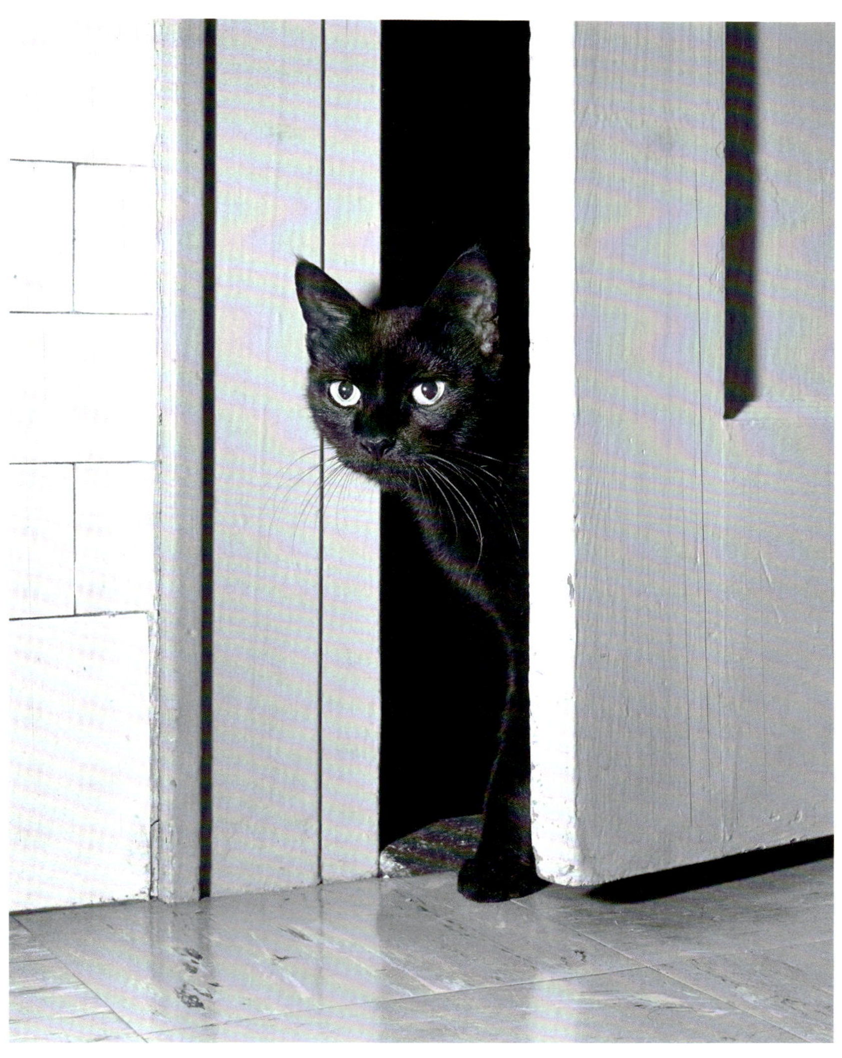

Loco, Queens, 1951.

Domestic shorthair, Long Island, 1958.

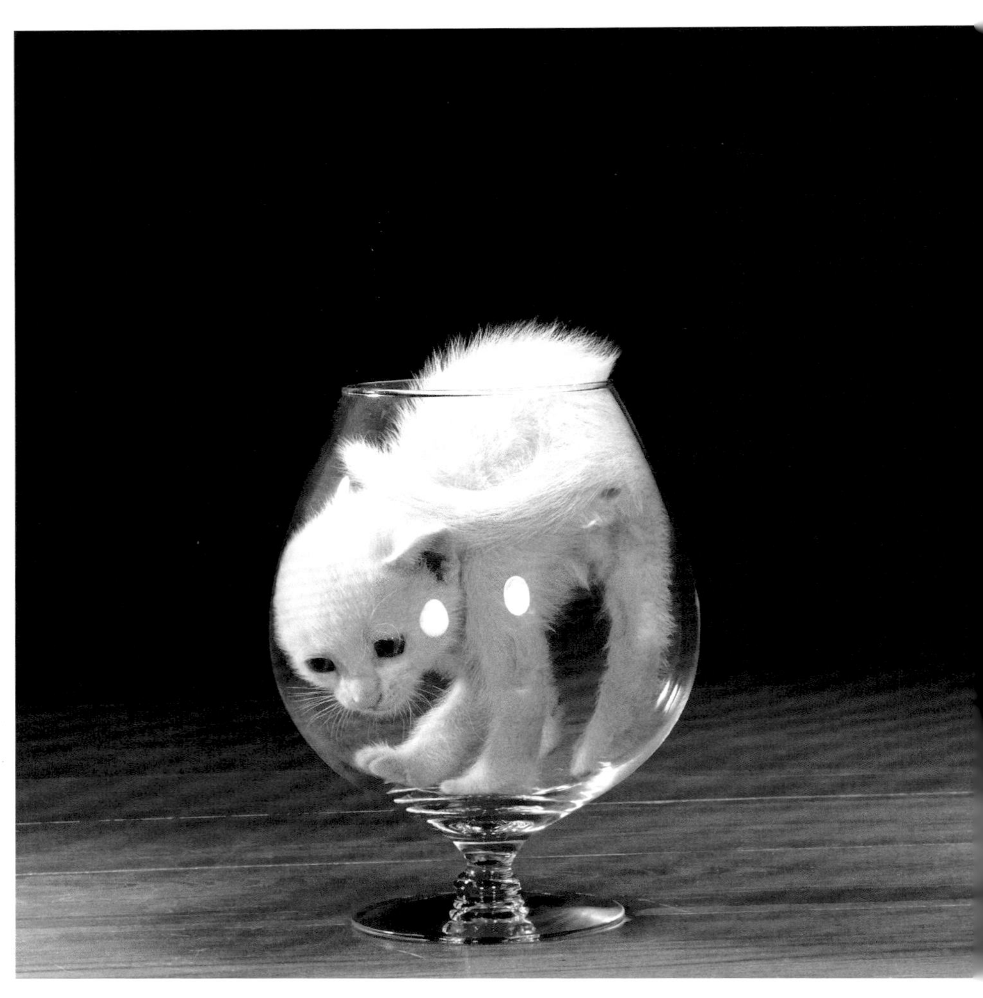

Domestic shorthair, New Jersey, 1960.

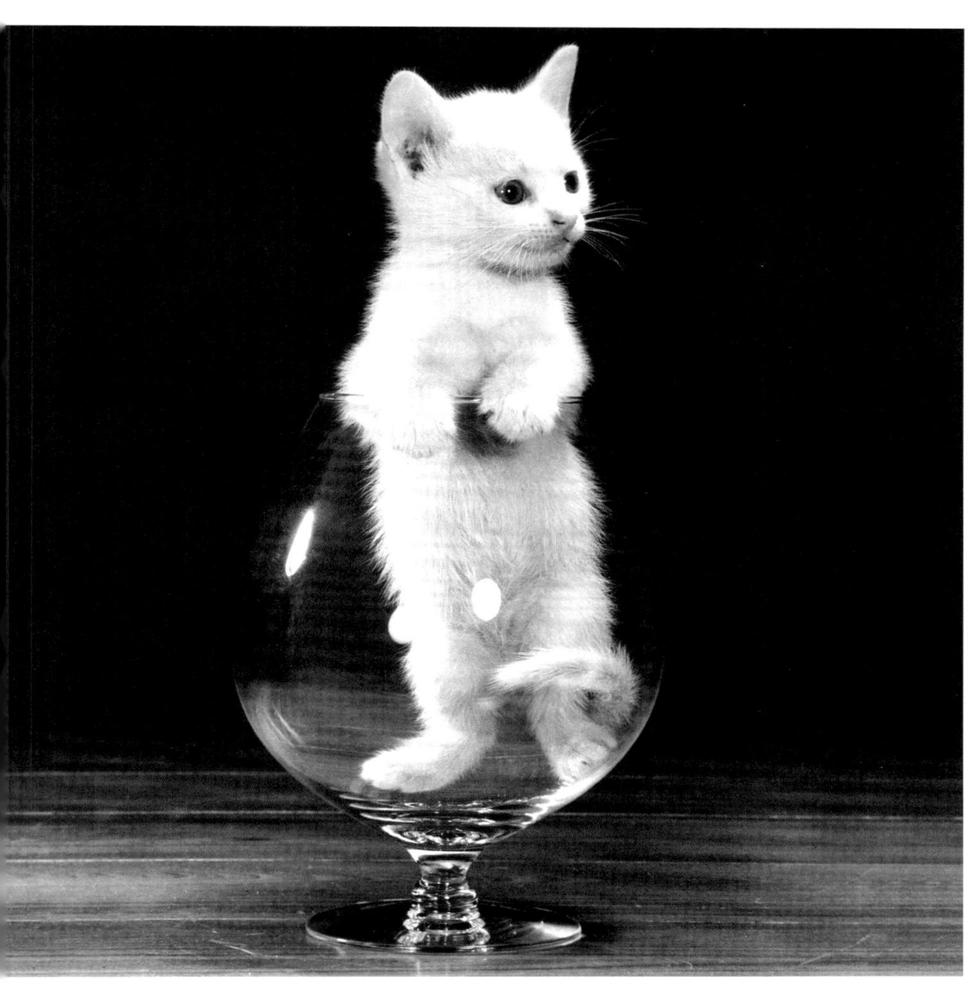

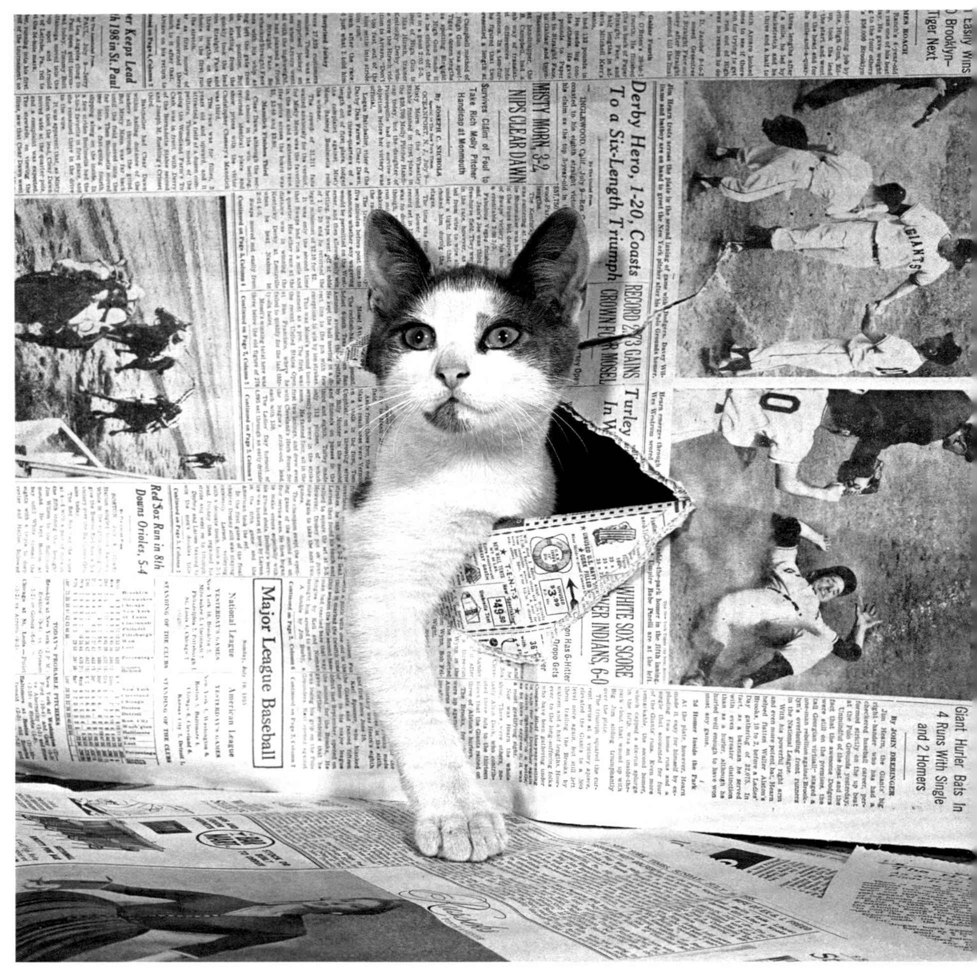

Domestic shorthair, Long Island, 1955.

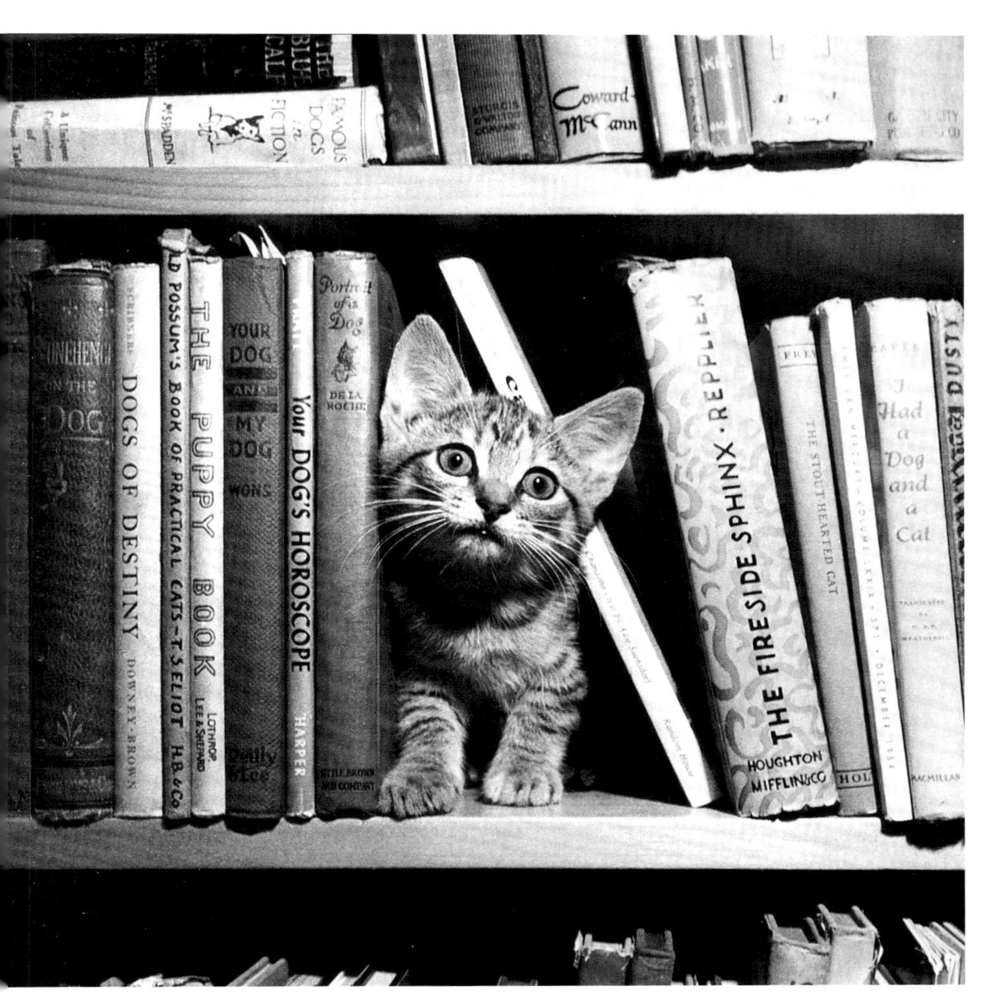

Domestic shorthair, Long Island, 1957.

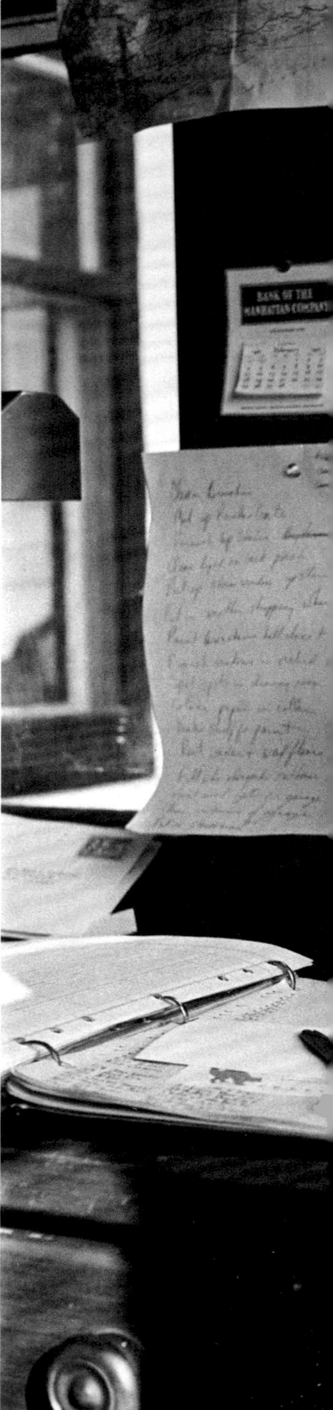

Loco, Long Island, 1951.

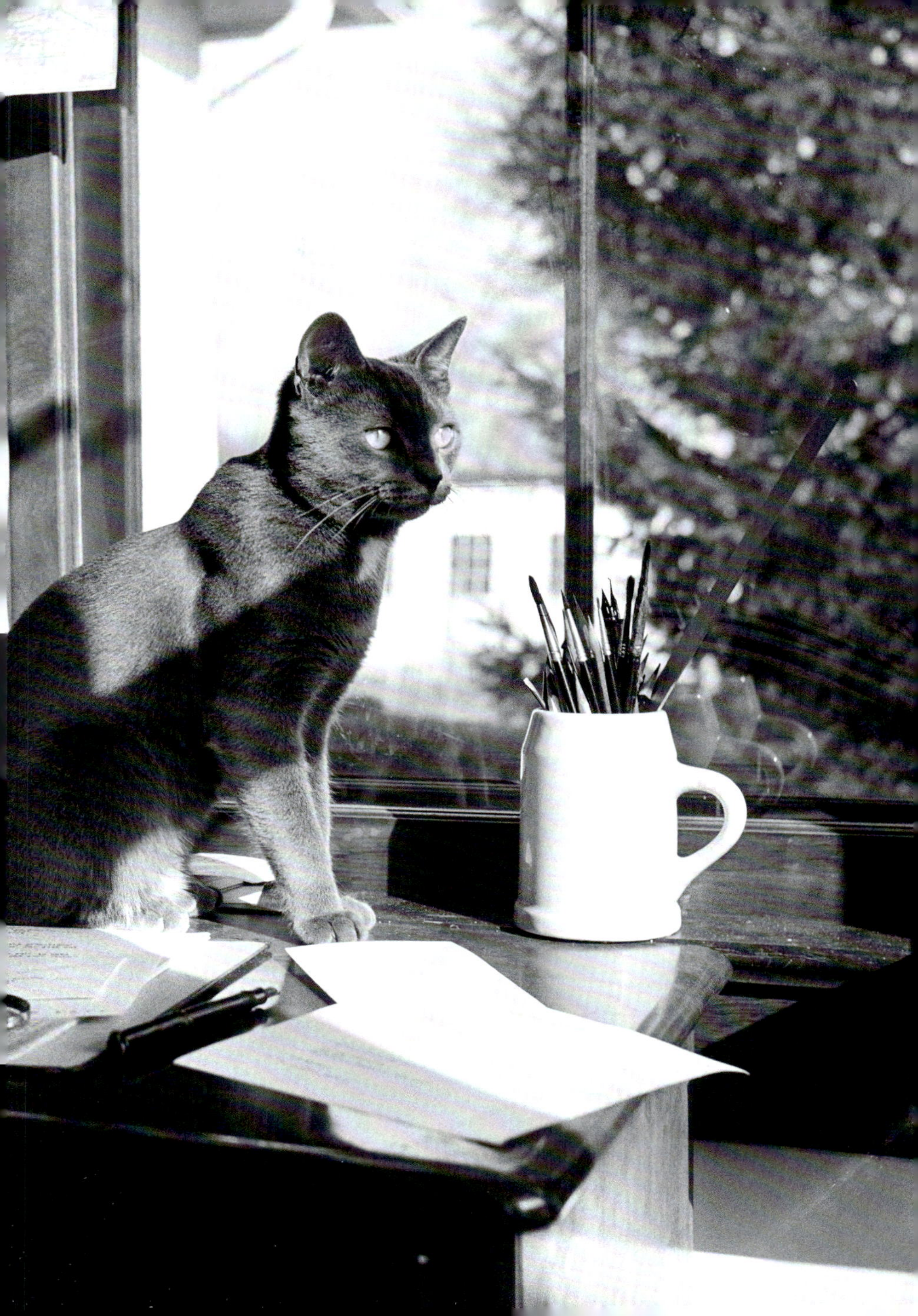

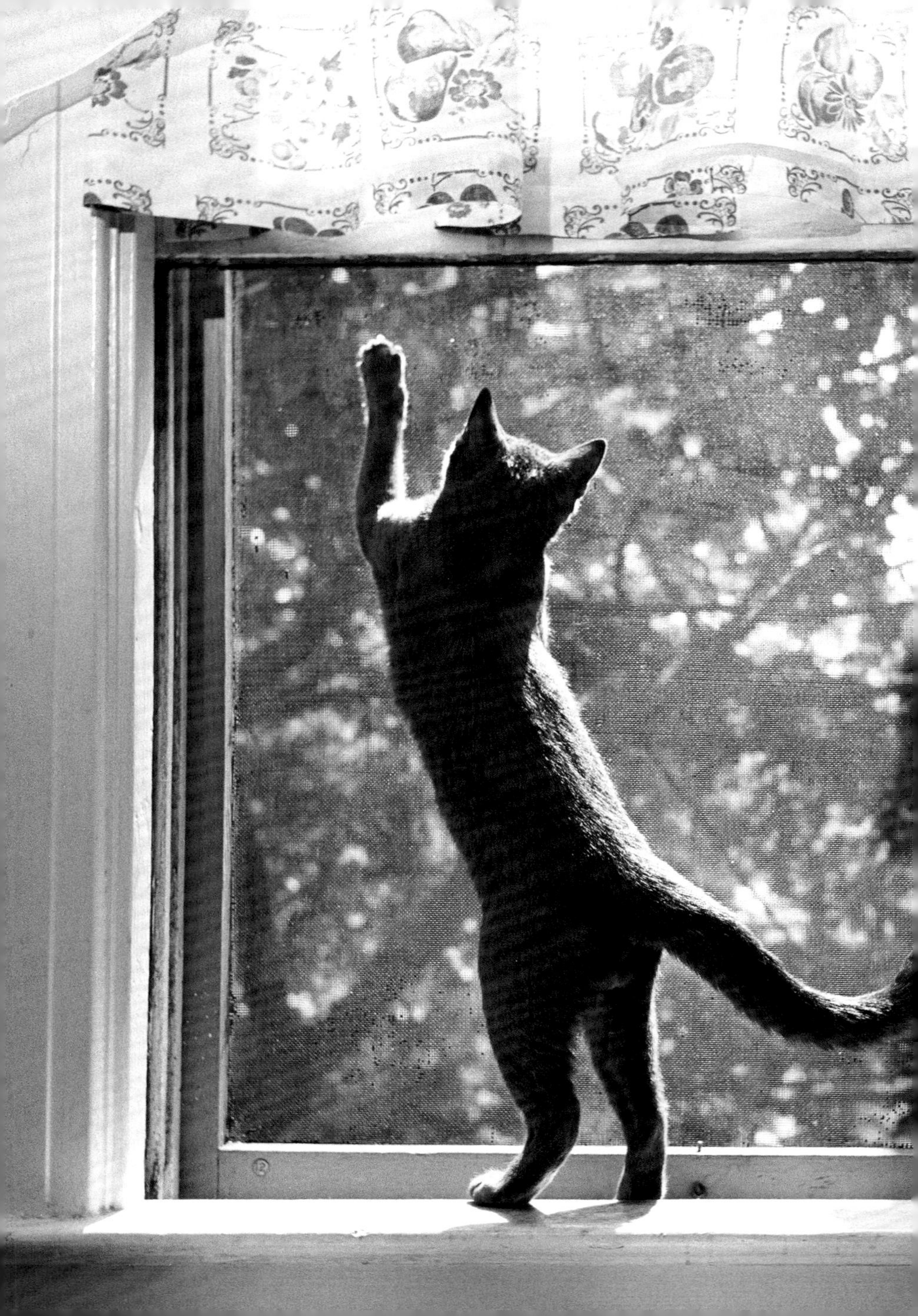

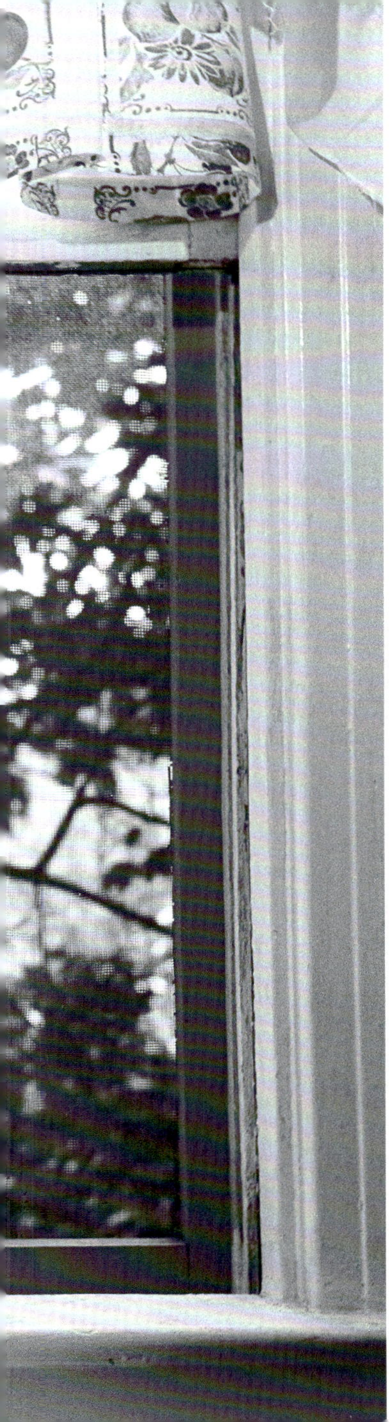

Loco, Queens, 1950.

Following: Domestic shorthair mother
and kitten, Long Island, 1958.

Pages 120–121:
Stray, New York City, 1972.

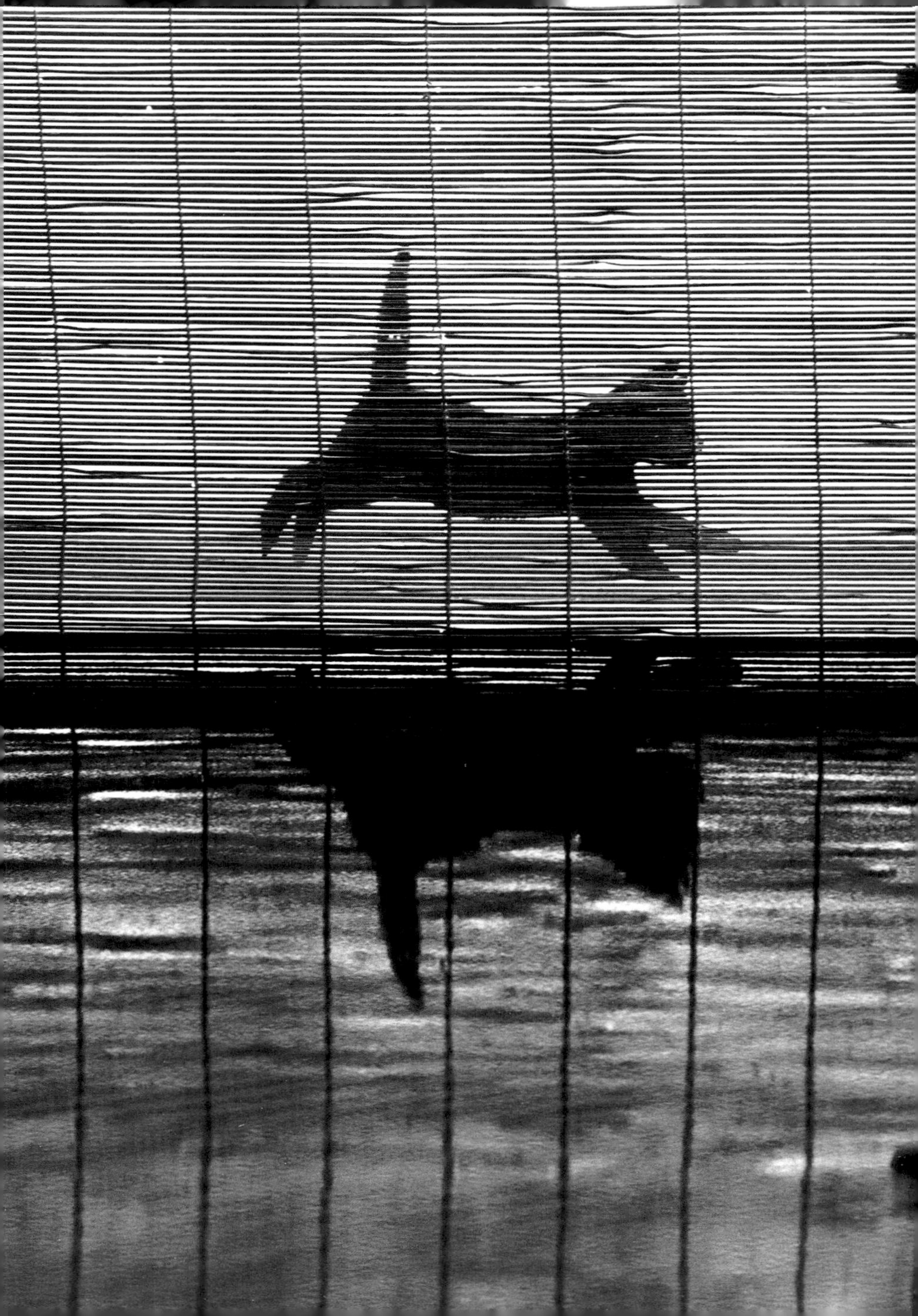

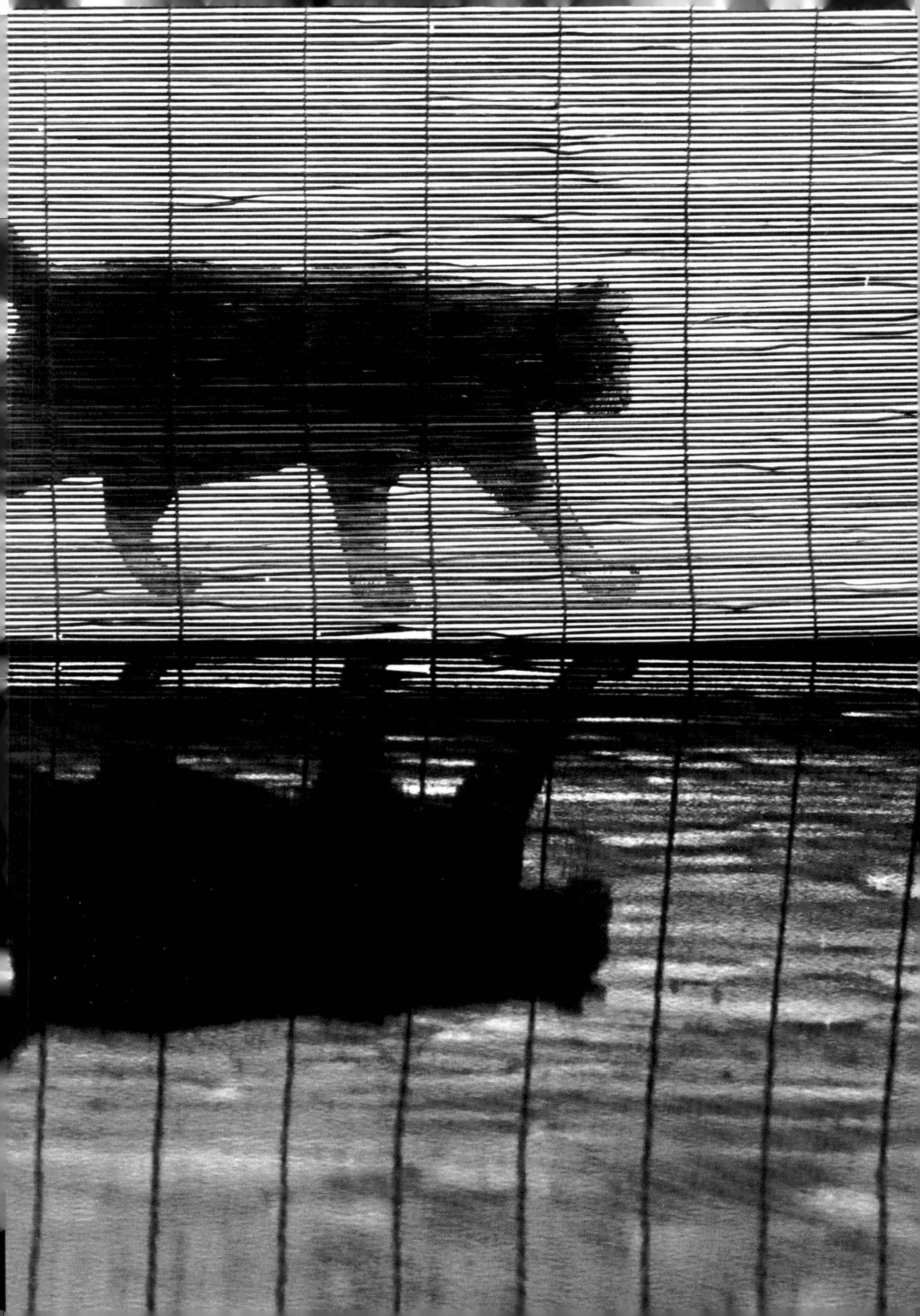

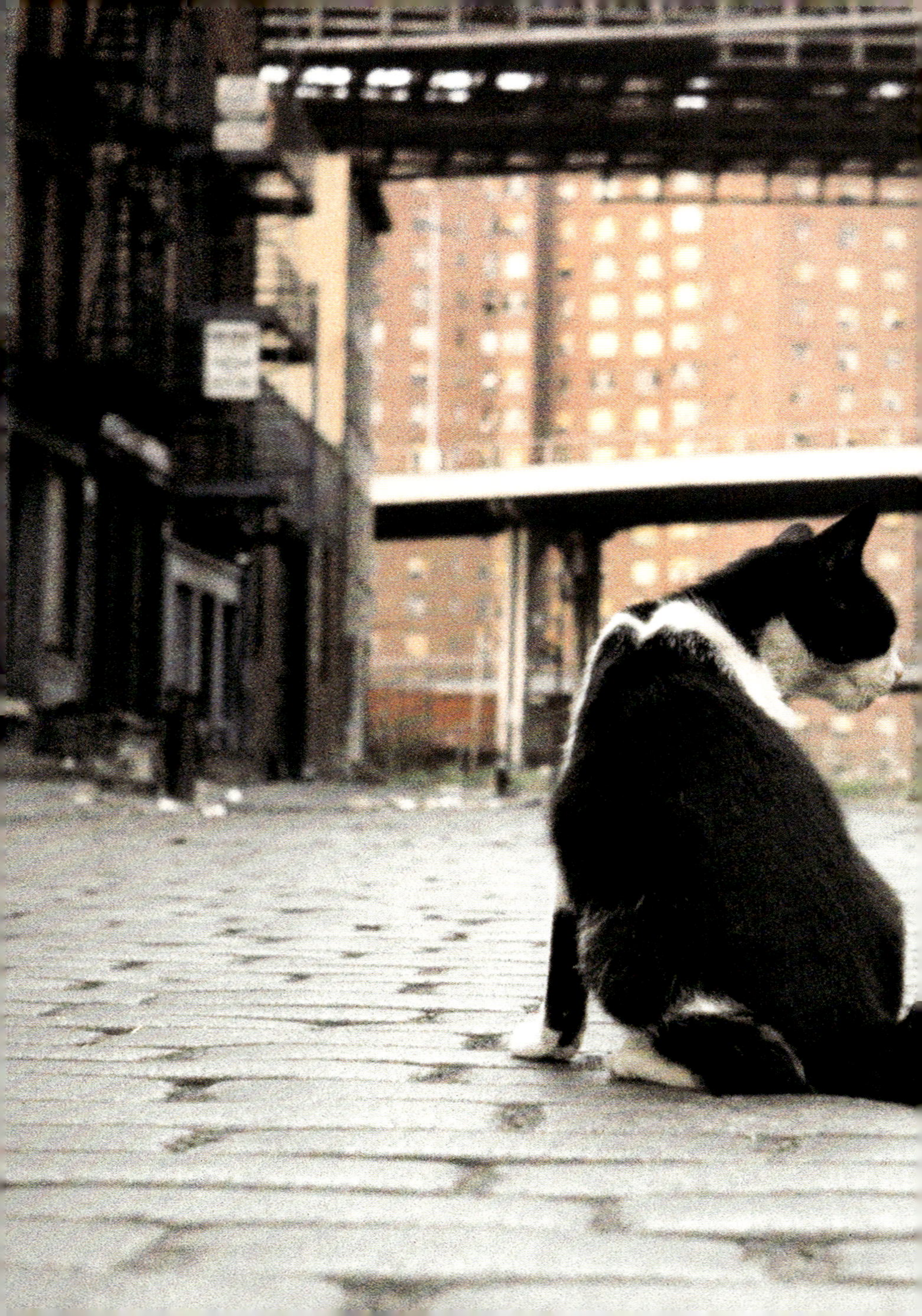

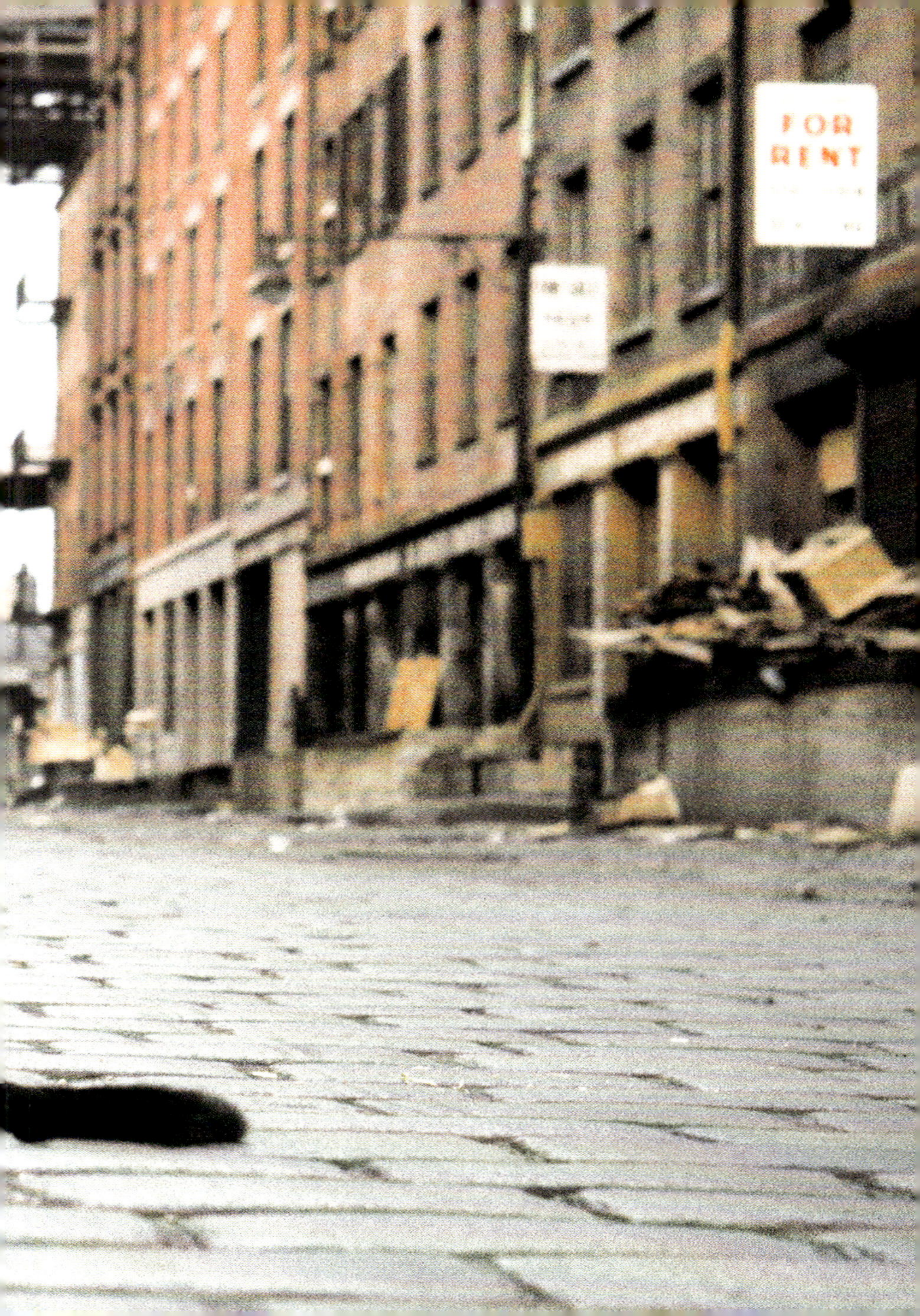

FOR
RENT

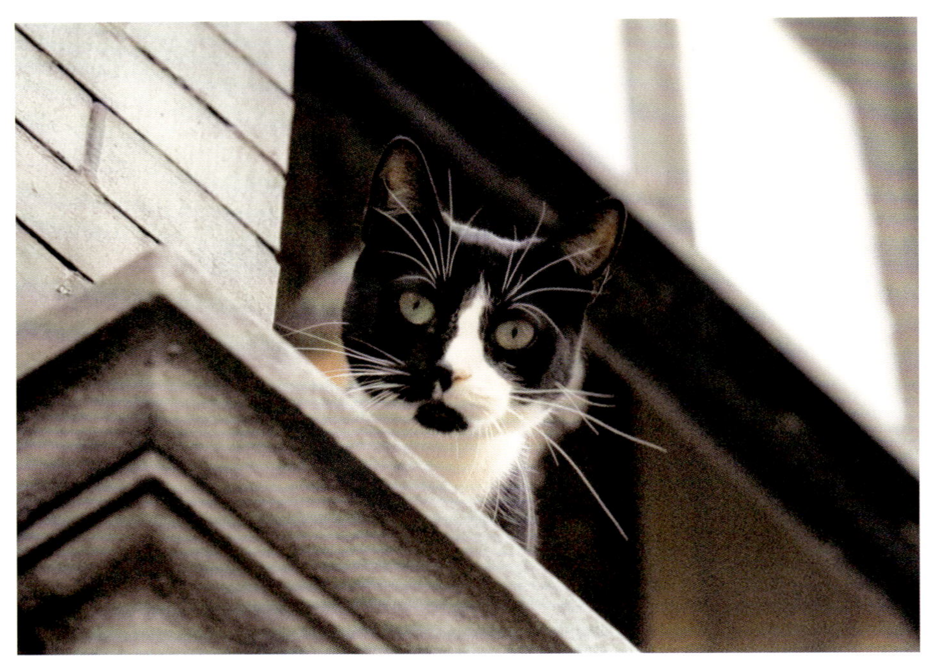

Domestic shorthair, New York City, 1963.

Stray, New York City, 1951.

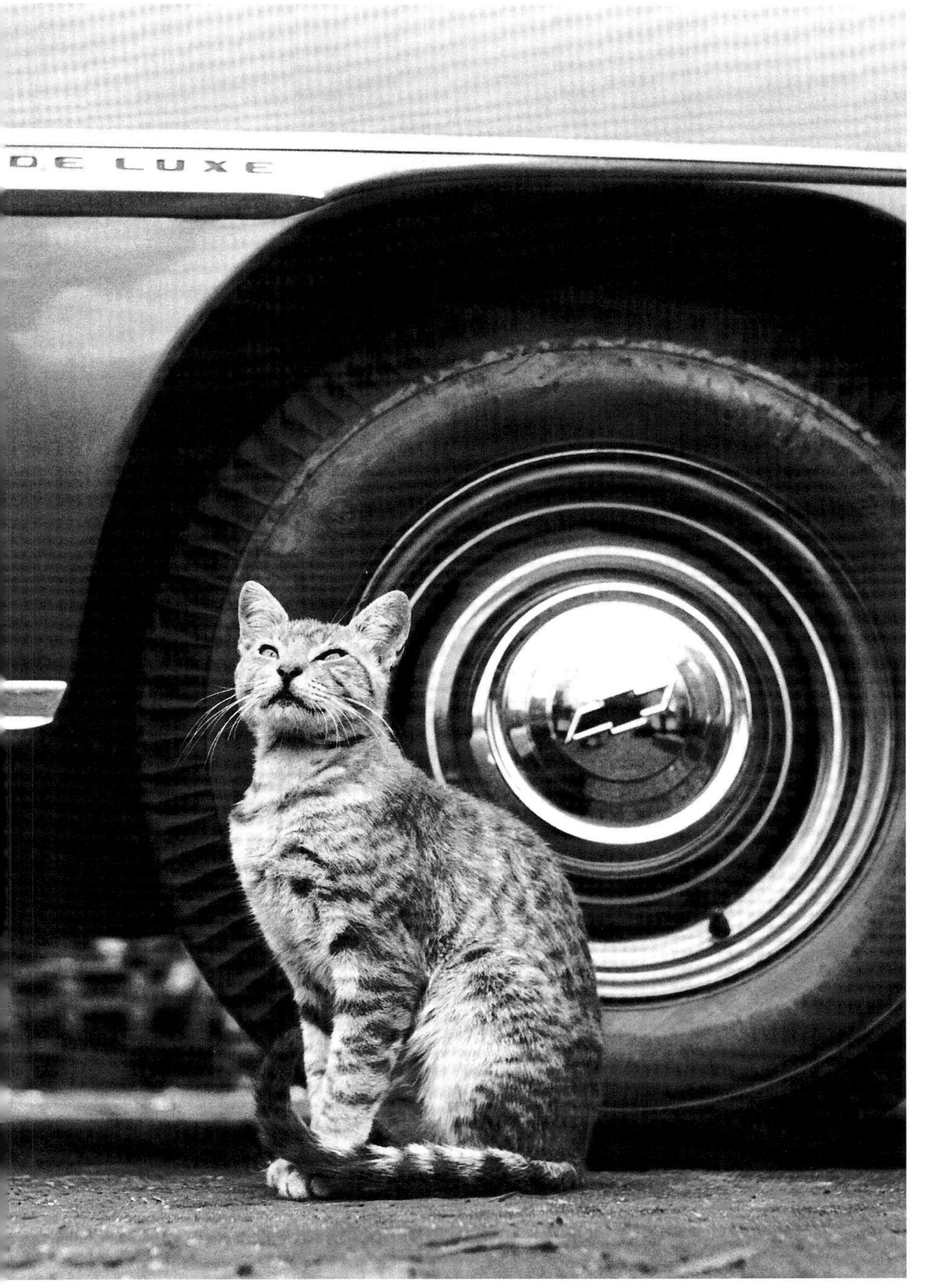
DE LUXE

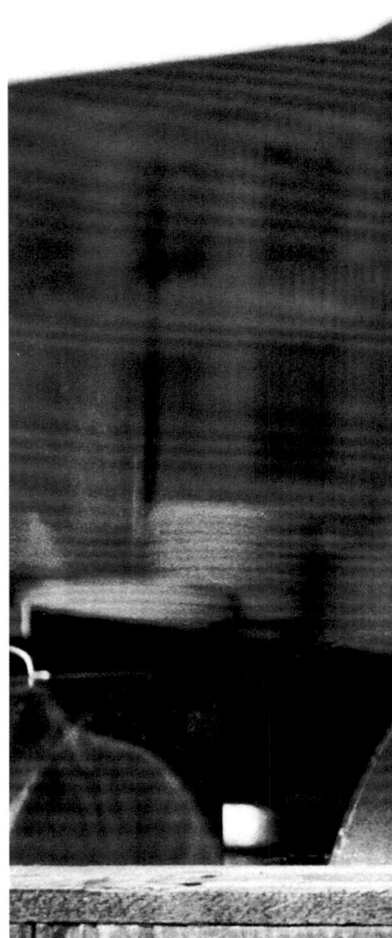
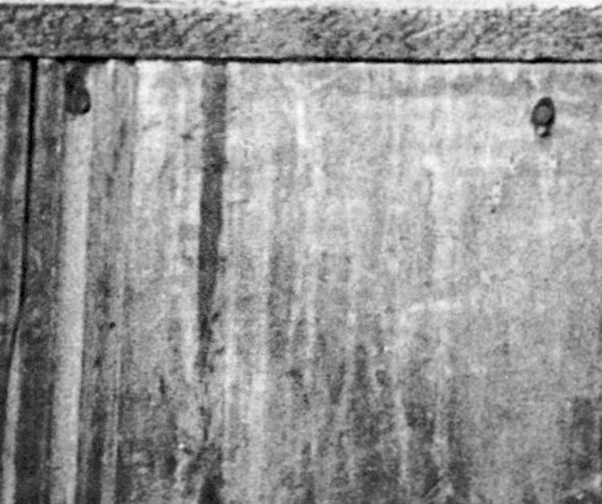

Domestic shorthair, New York City, 1950.

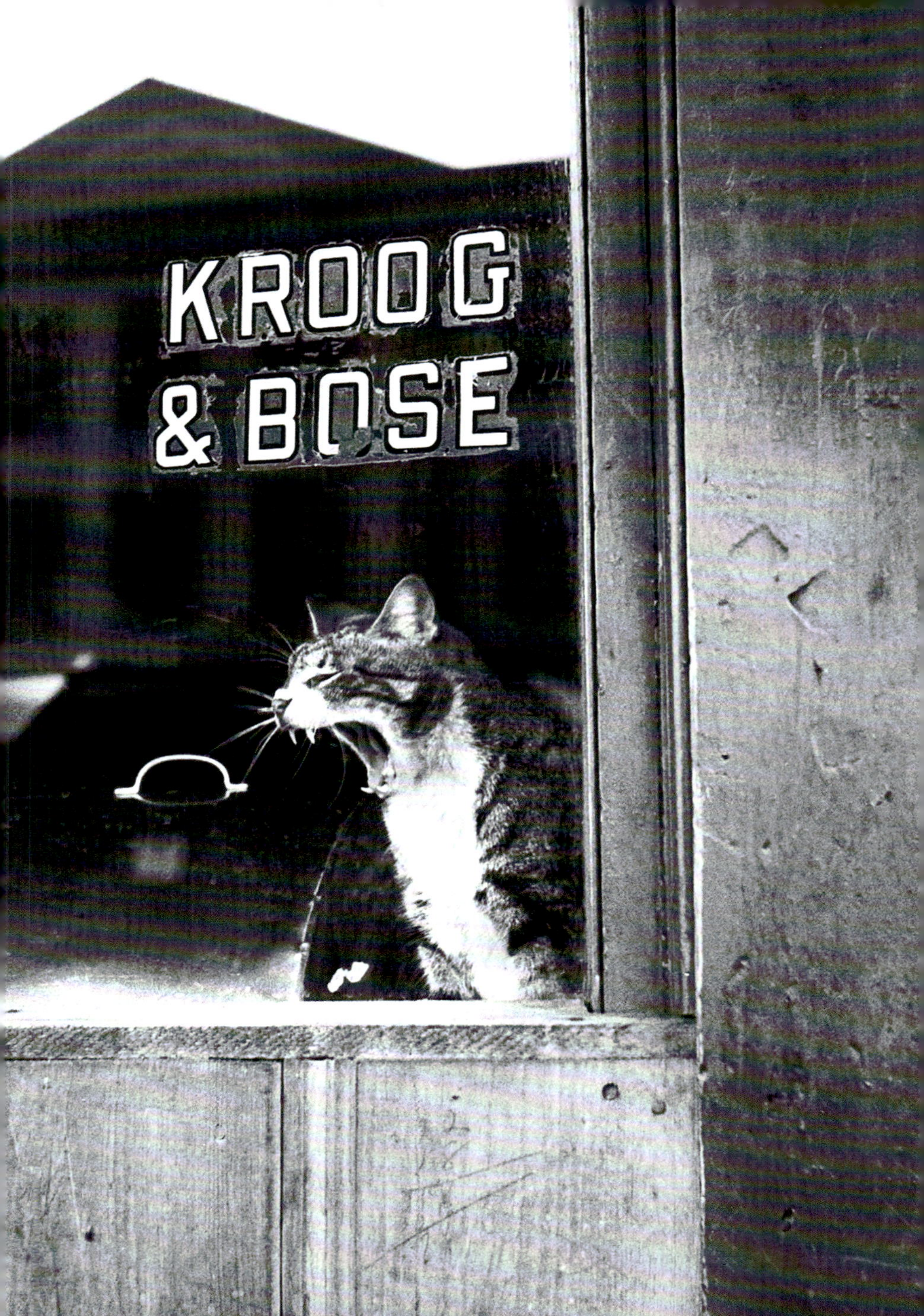

KROOG
& BOSE

Fabulous Felines pet store,
New York City, 1961.

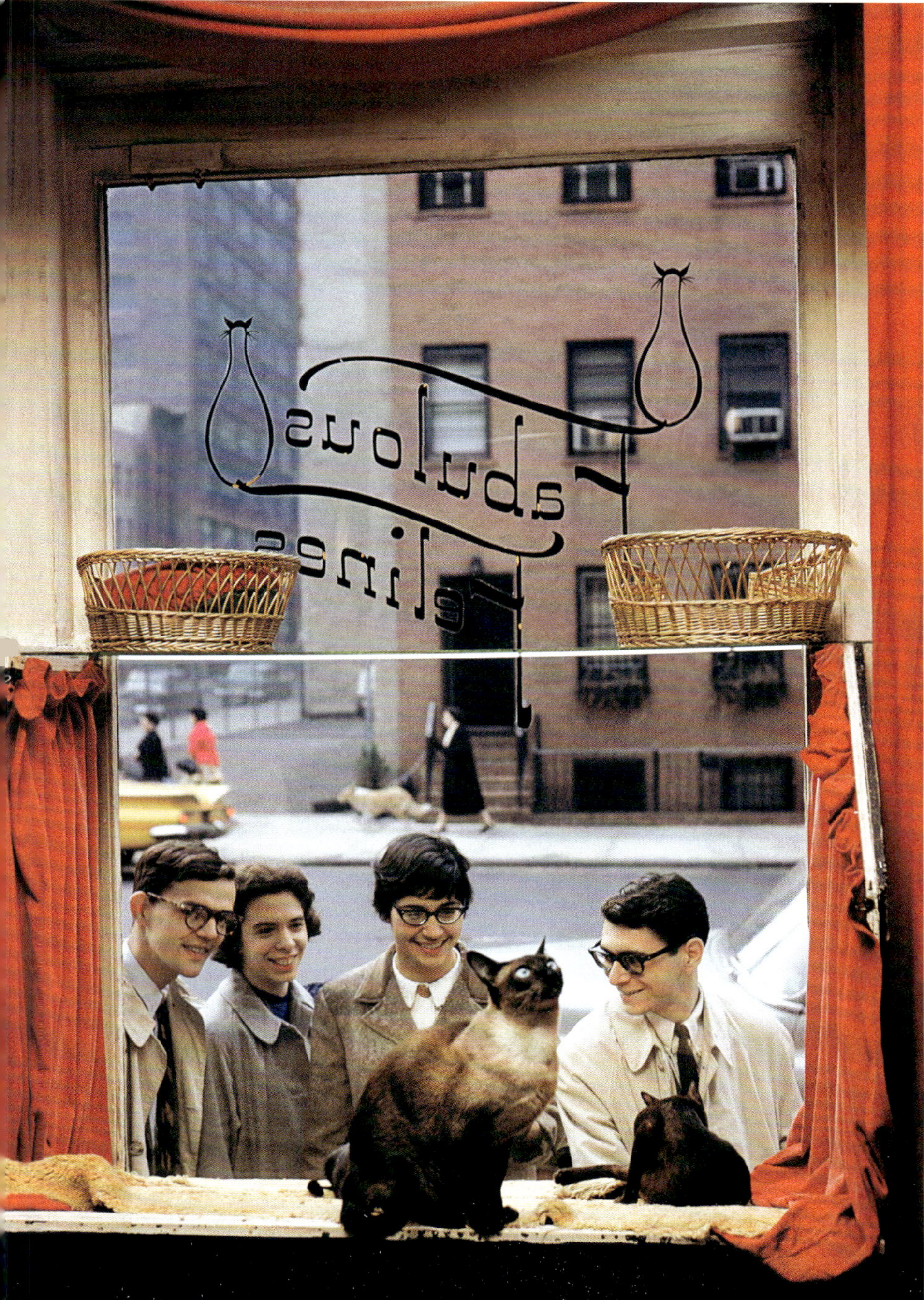

Fabulous
Felines

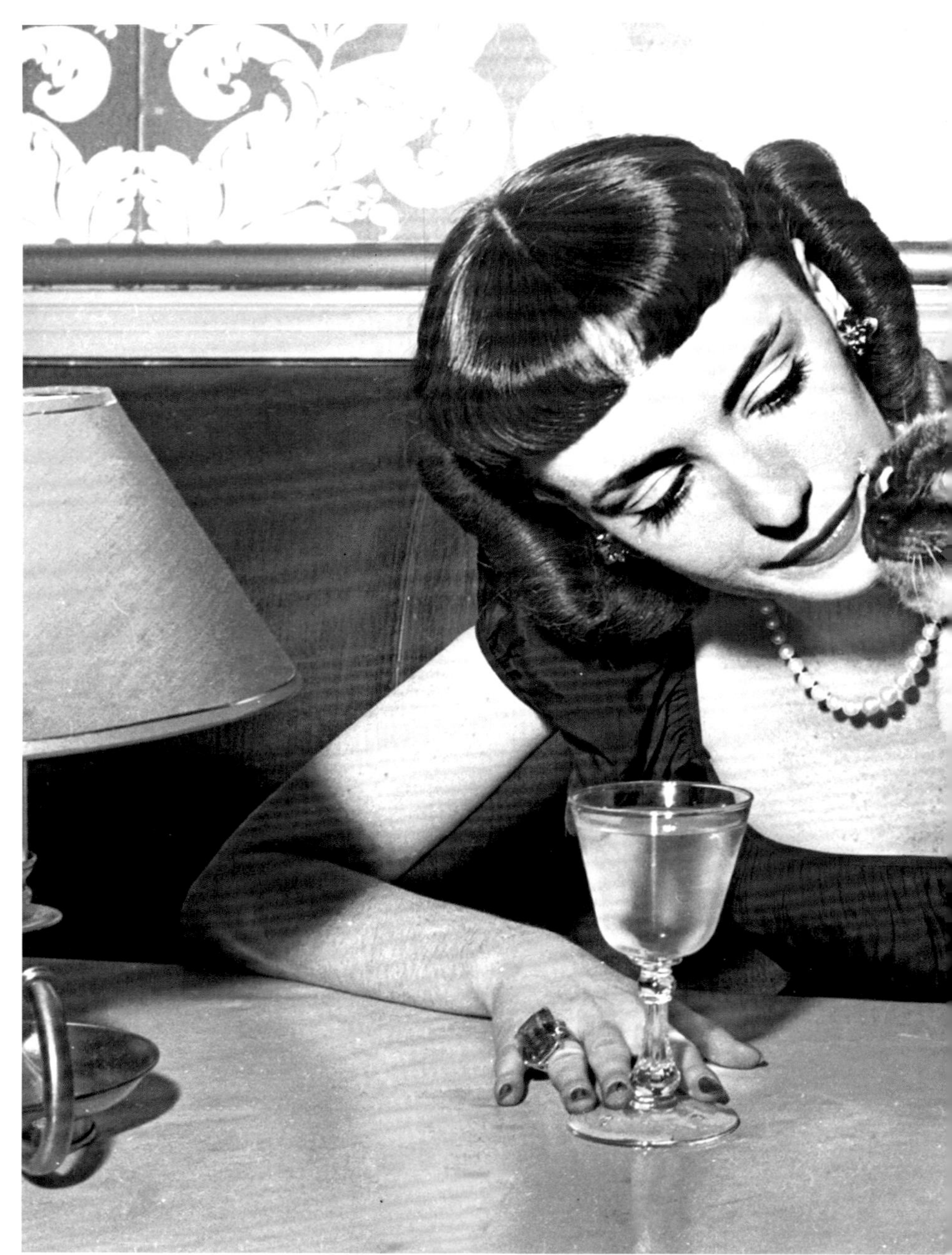

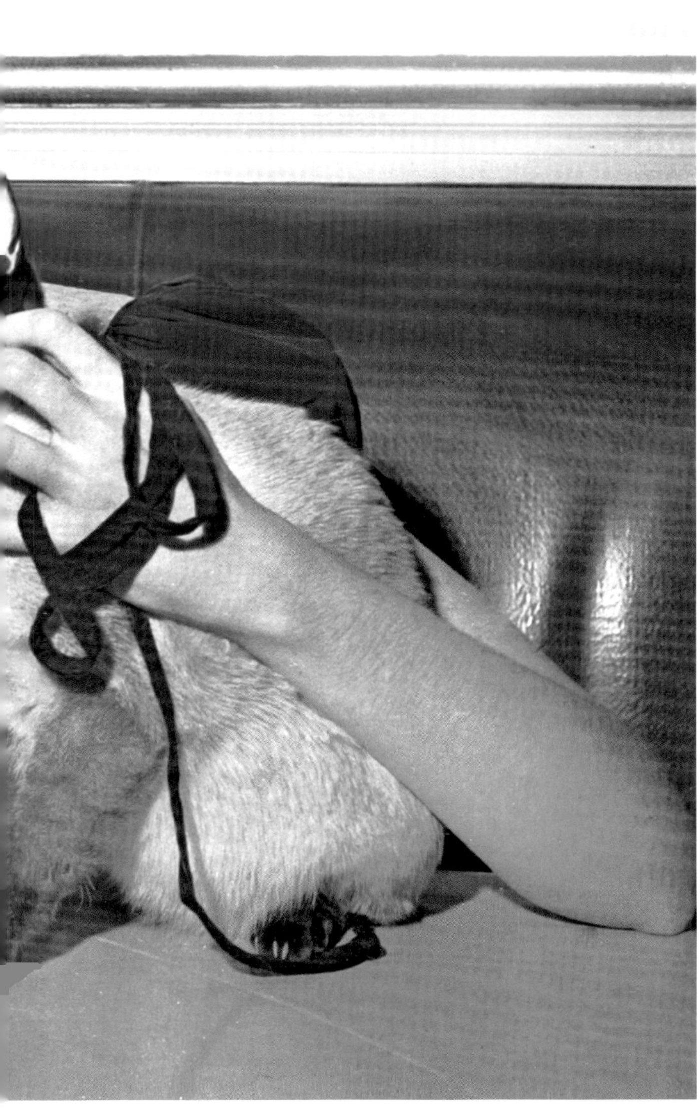

Siamese,
New York City, 1950.

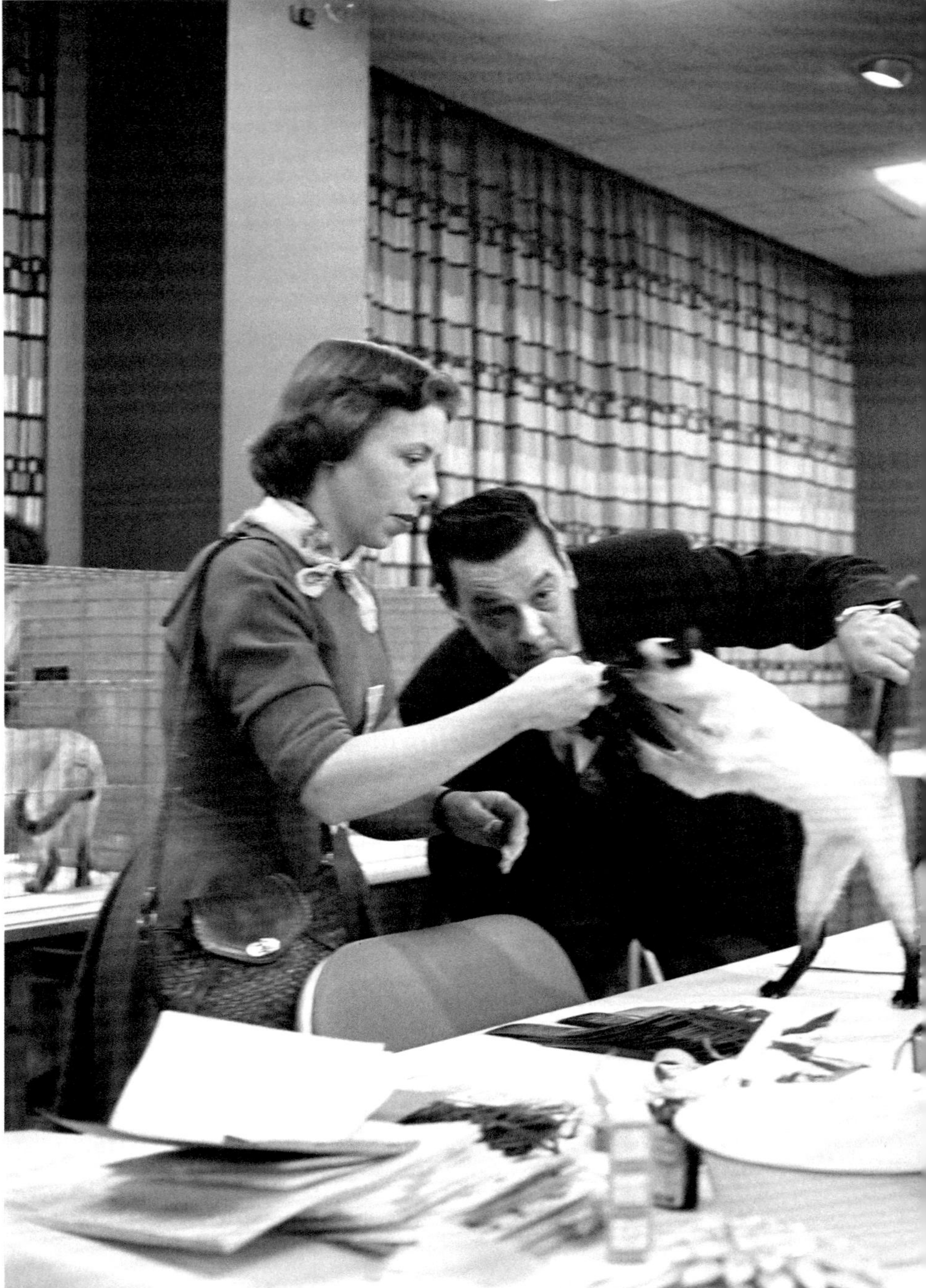

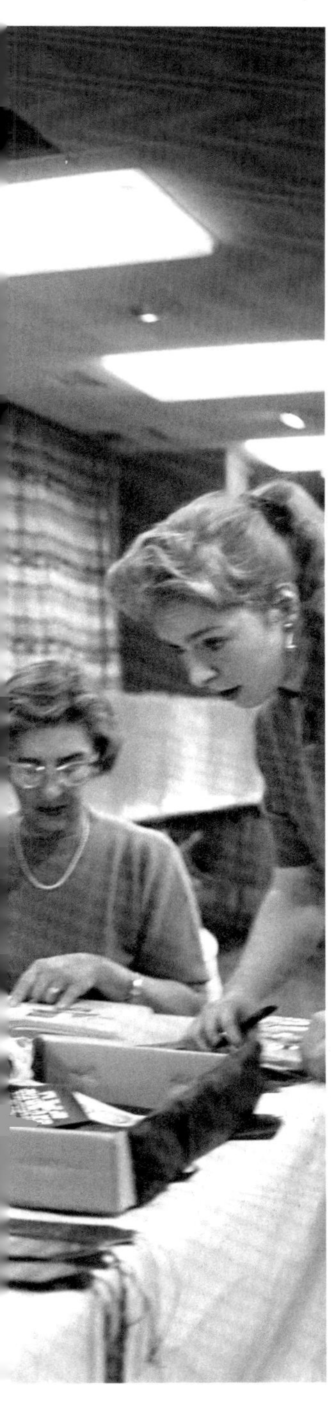

Cat show judges, New York City, 1957.

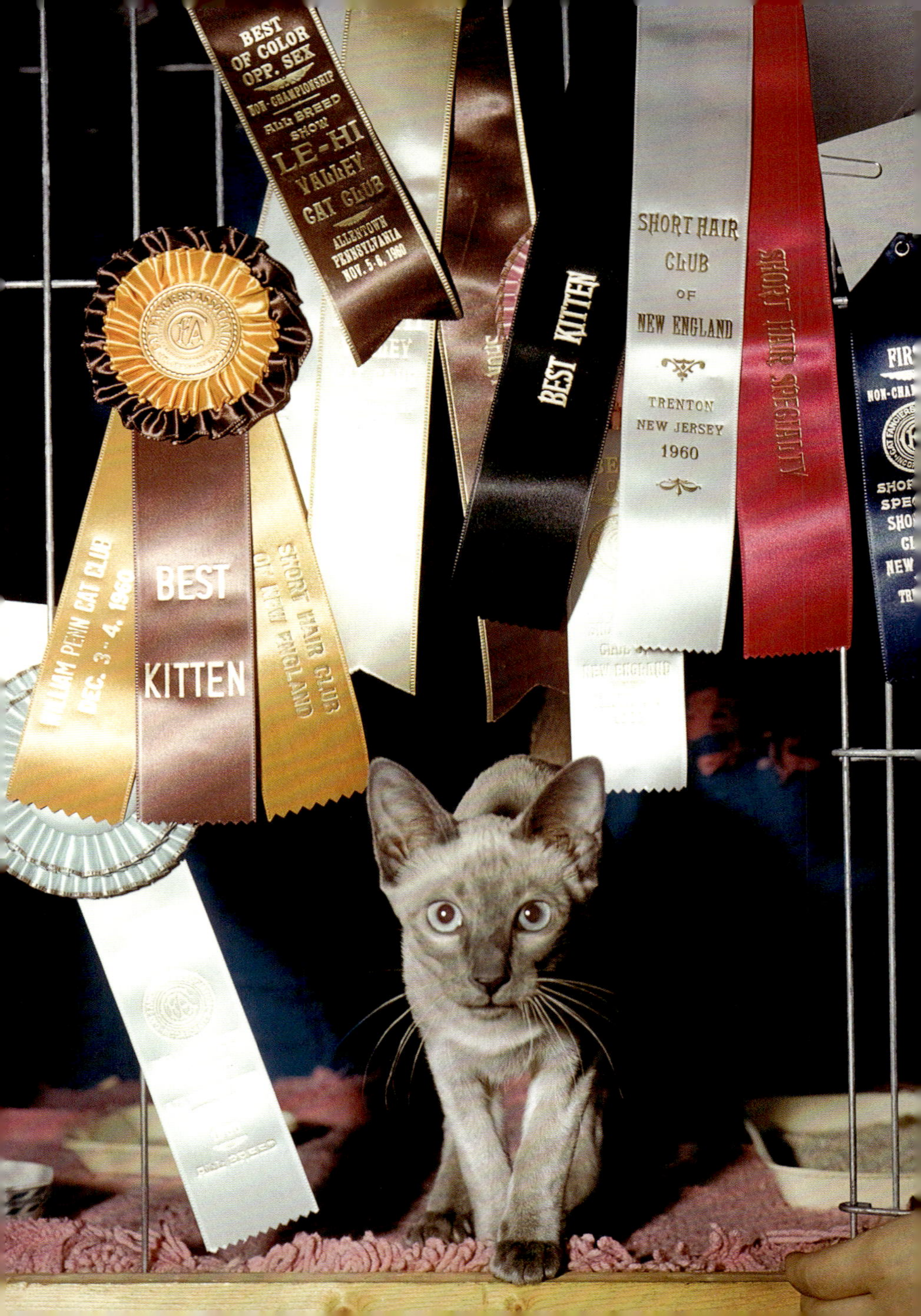

BEST OF COLOR OPP. SEX
NON-CHAMPIONSHIP
ALL-BREED SHOW
LE-HI VALLEY CAT CLUB
ALLENTOWN PENNSYLVANIA
NOV. 5 - 6, 1960
CAT FANCIERS ASSOCIATION
CFA
BEST KITTEN
WILLIAM PENN CAT CLUB
DEC. 3 - 4, 1960
SHORT HAIR CLUB OF NEW ENGLAND
BEST KITTEN
SHORT HAIR CLUB OF NEW ENGLAND
TRENTON NEW JERSEY 1960
SHORT HAIR SPECIALTY
FIRST
NON-CHAMPIONSHIP

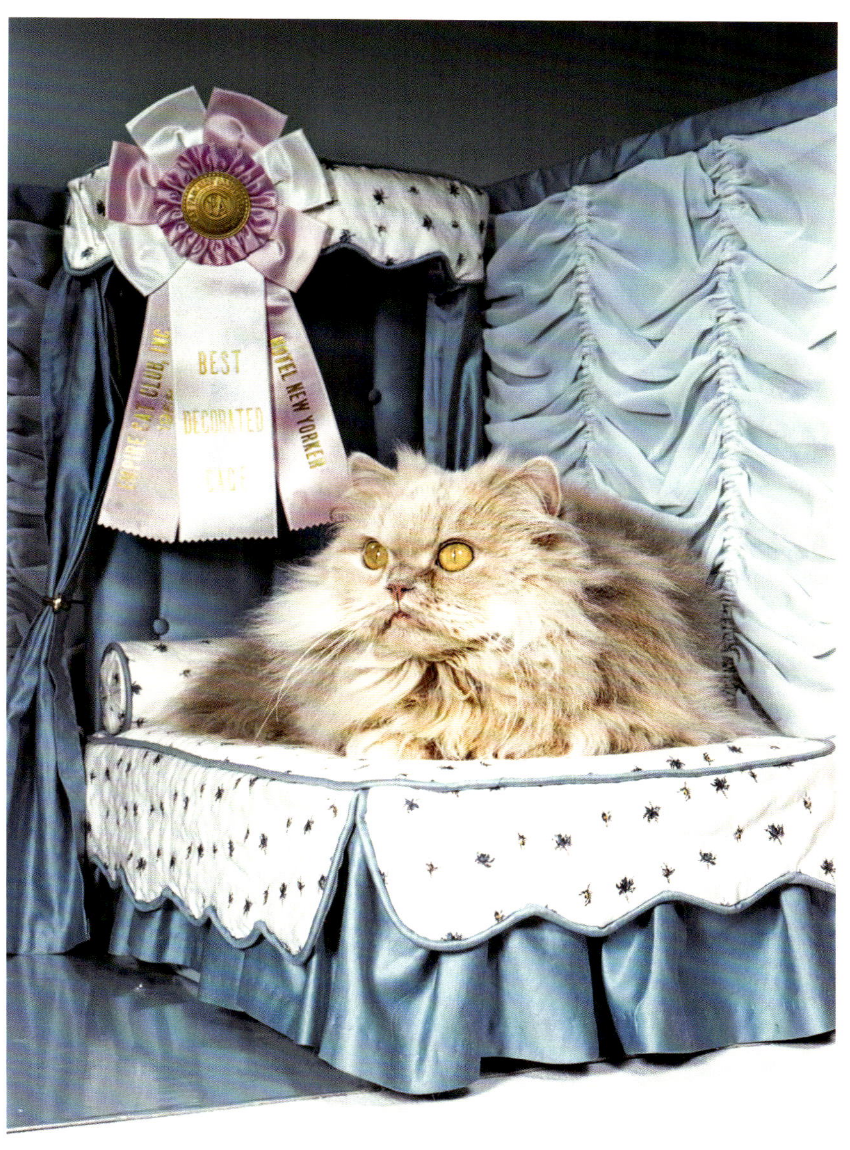

Siamese kitten, New Jersey, 1960.
Golden Persian, New York City, 1960.

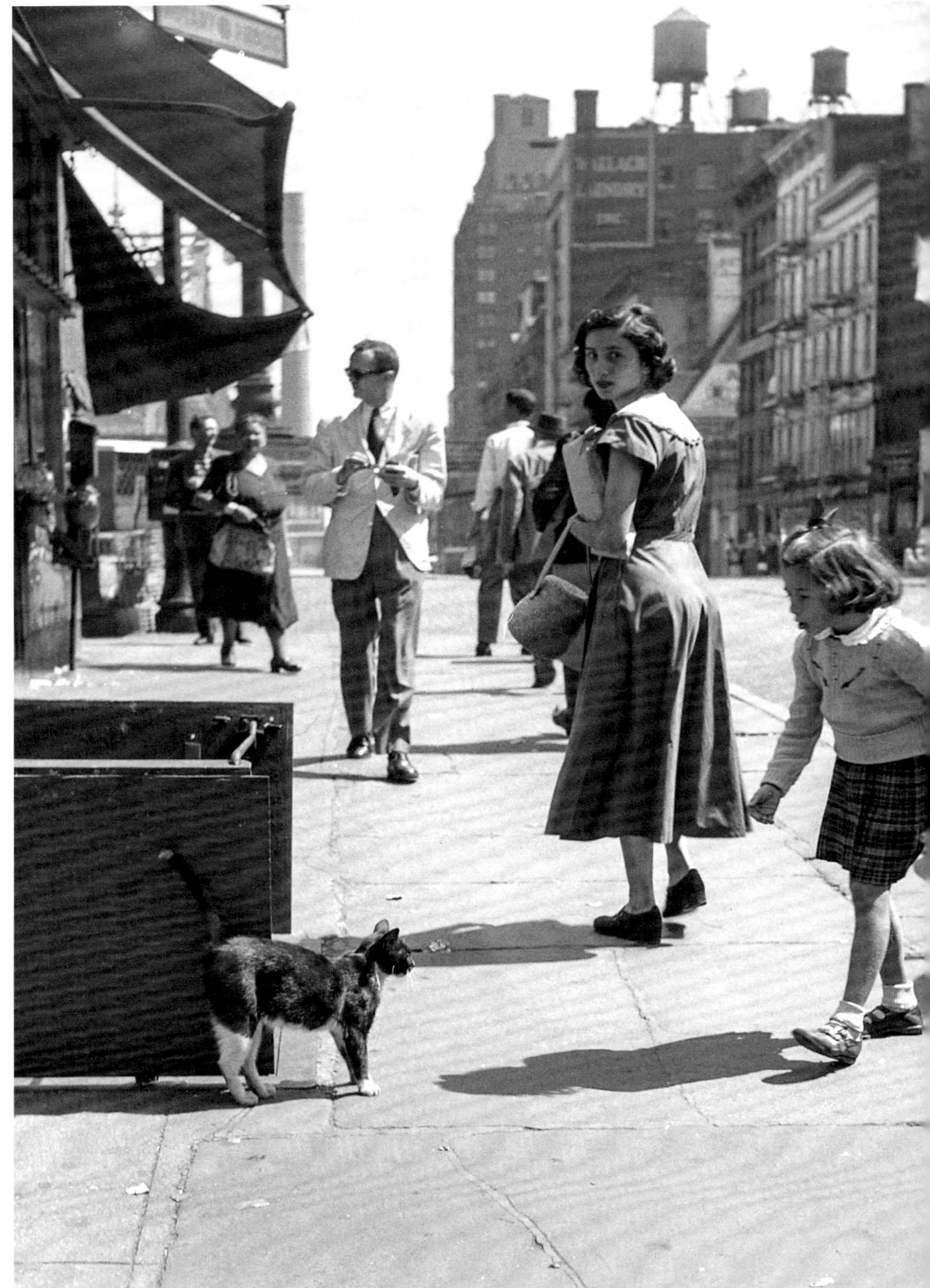

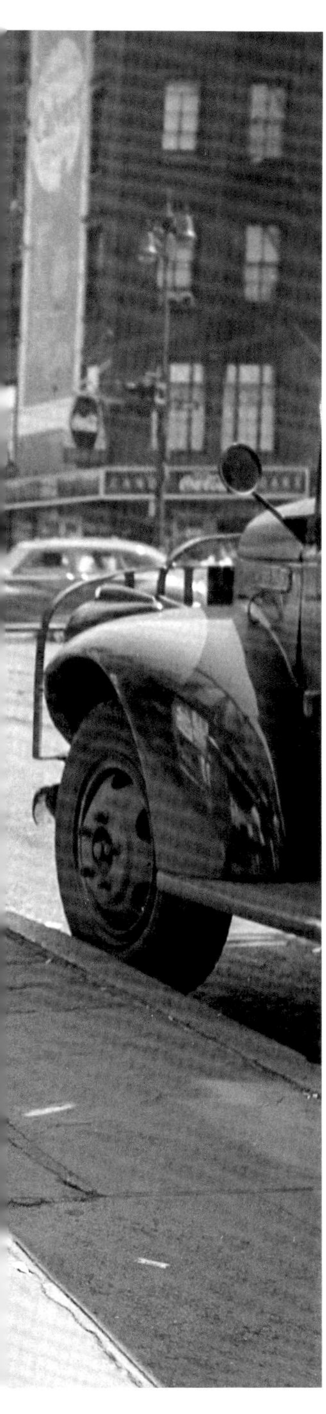

Stray, New York City, 1950.

Iceman and Domestic shorthair,
New York City, 1950.

Following: Domestic shorthairs,
New York City, 1982.

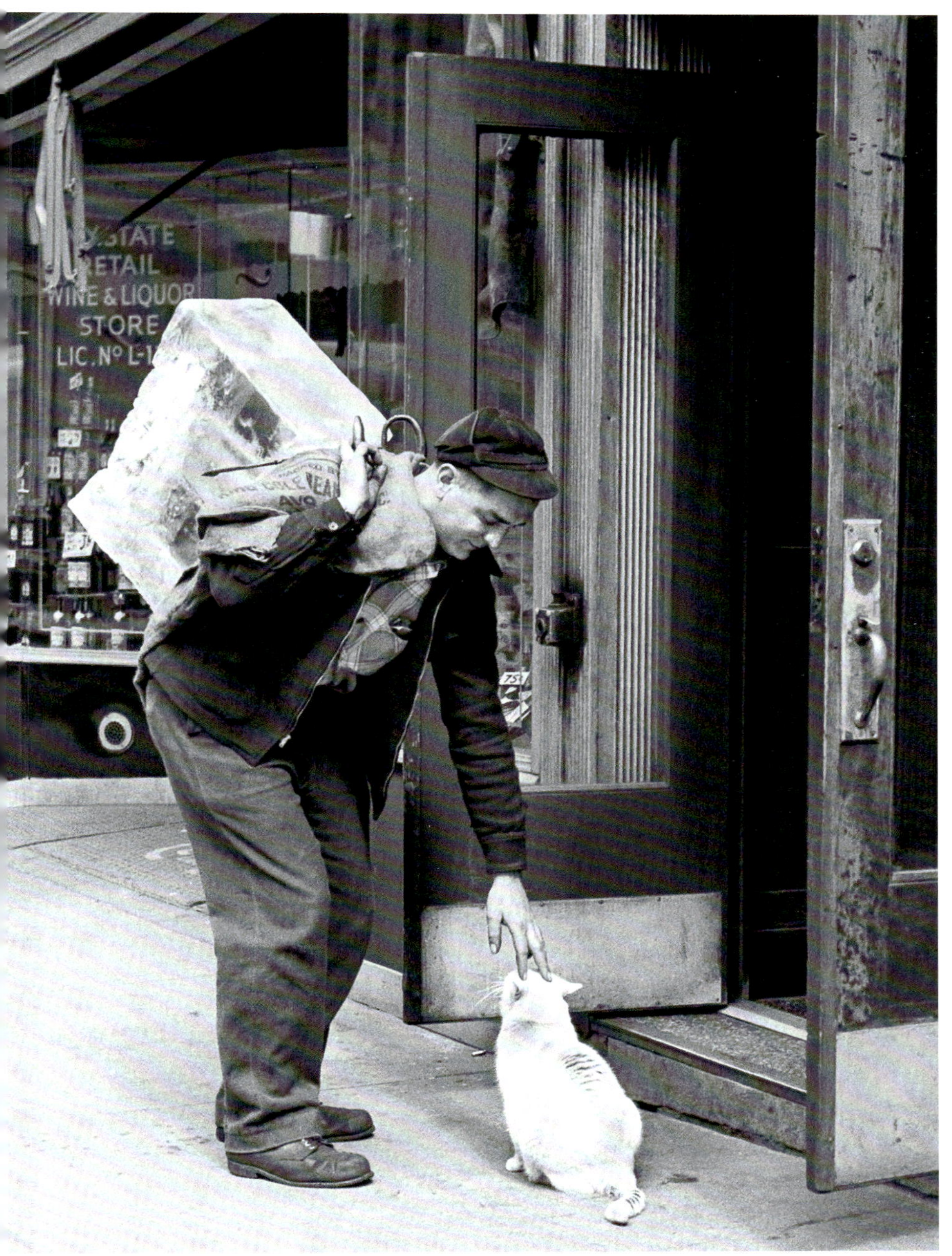
Y STATE
RETAIL
WINE & LIQUOR
STORE
LIC. No L-1

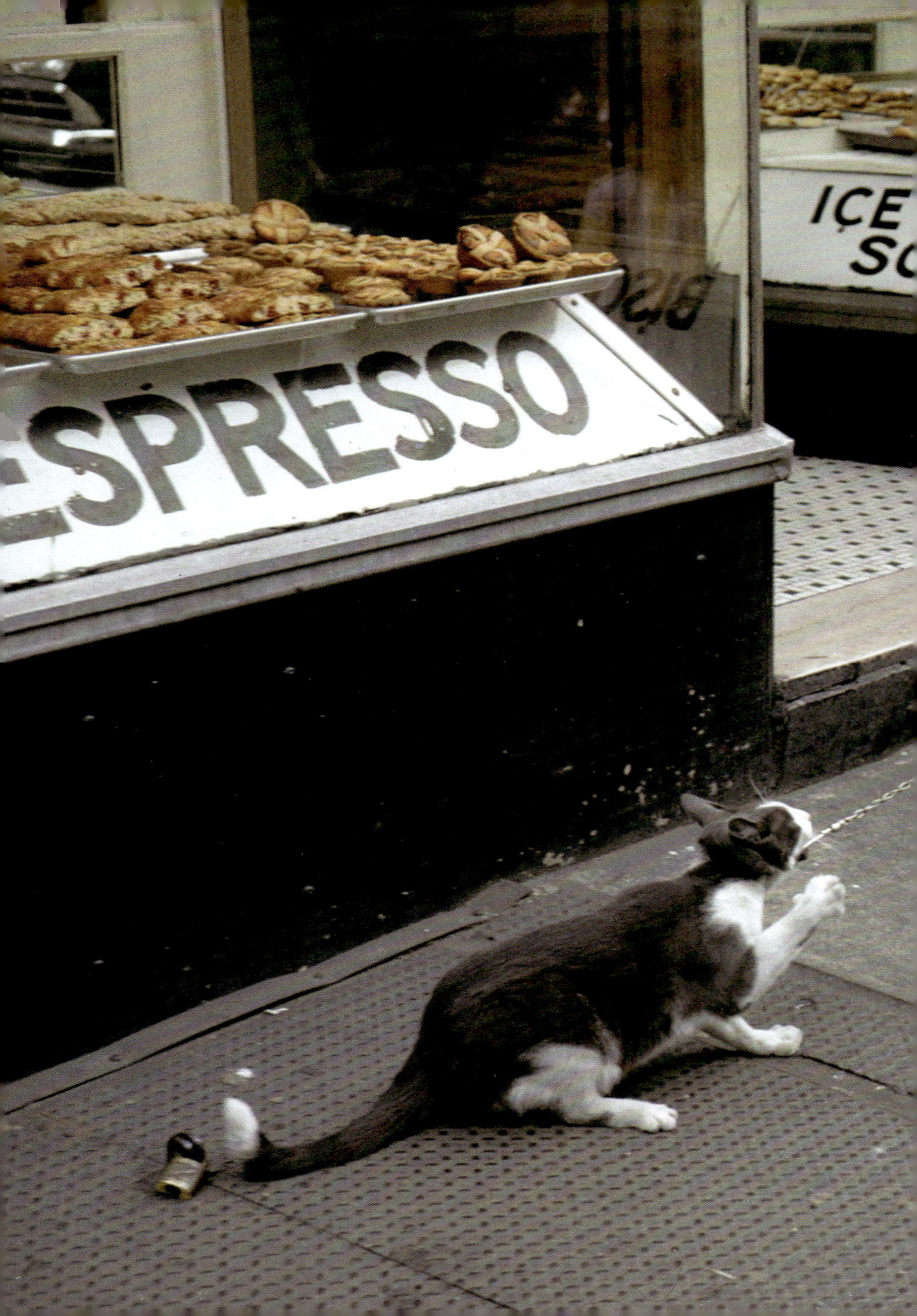

ESPRESSO
IÇE
S

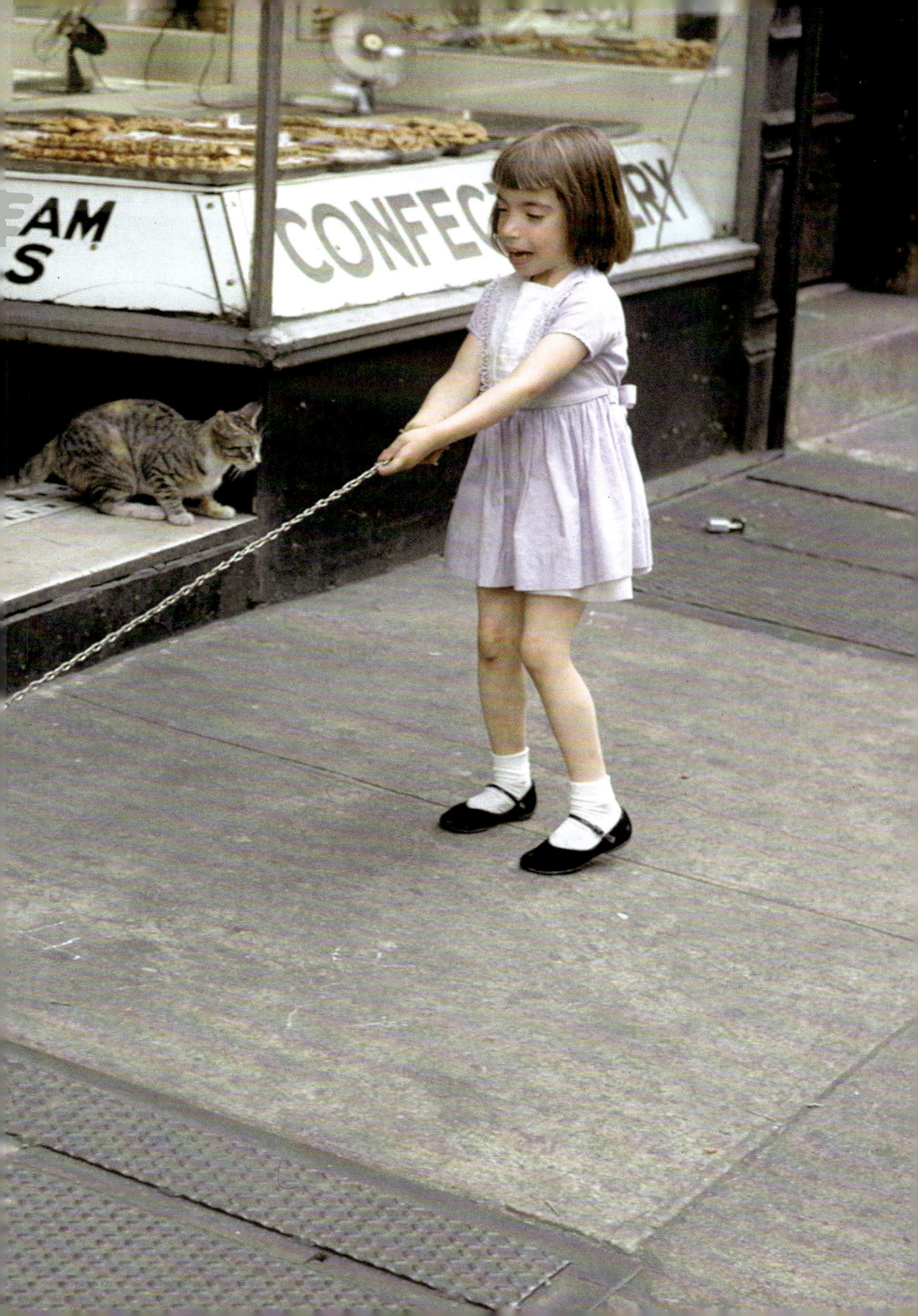
AM
S
CONFEC   RX

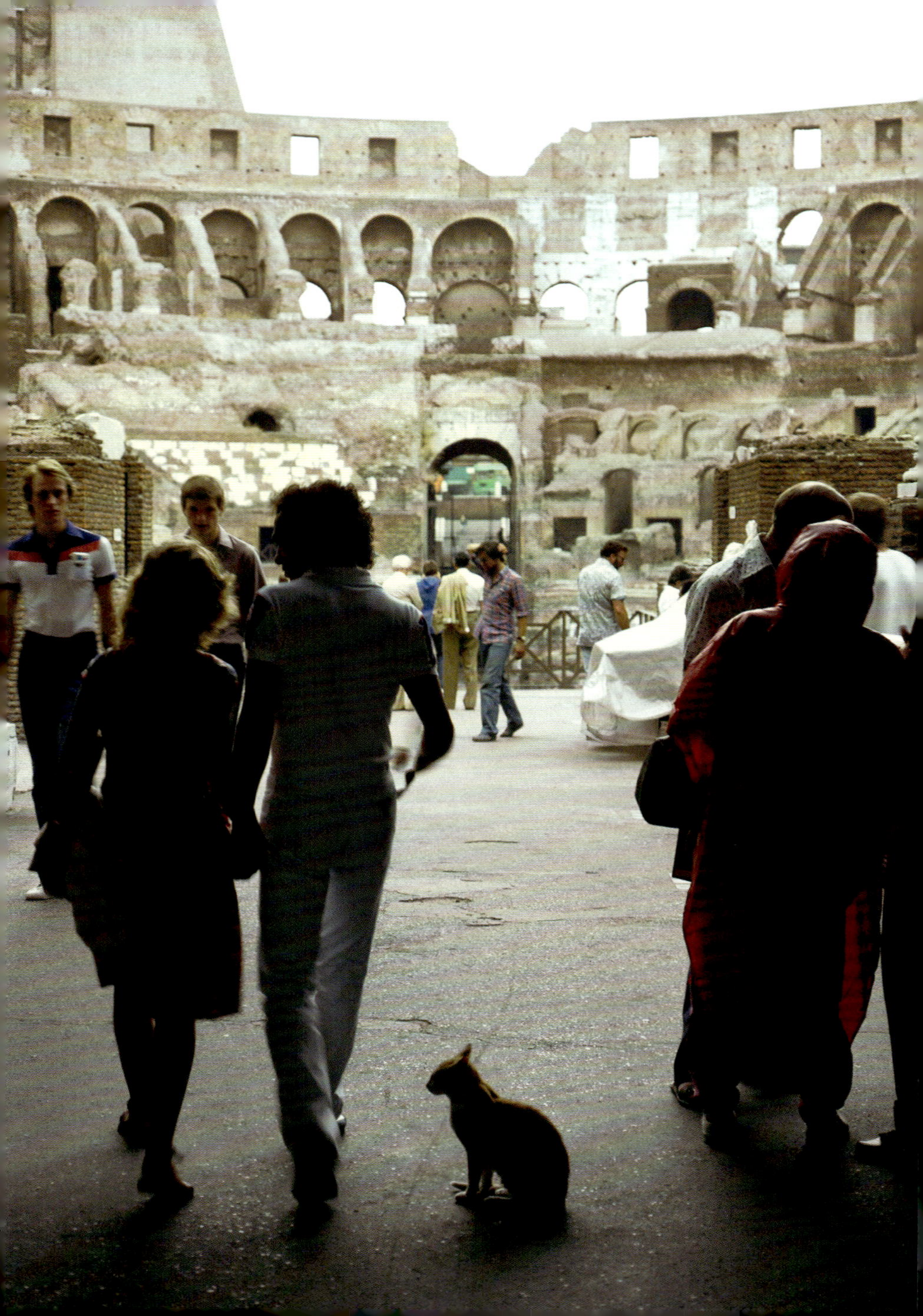

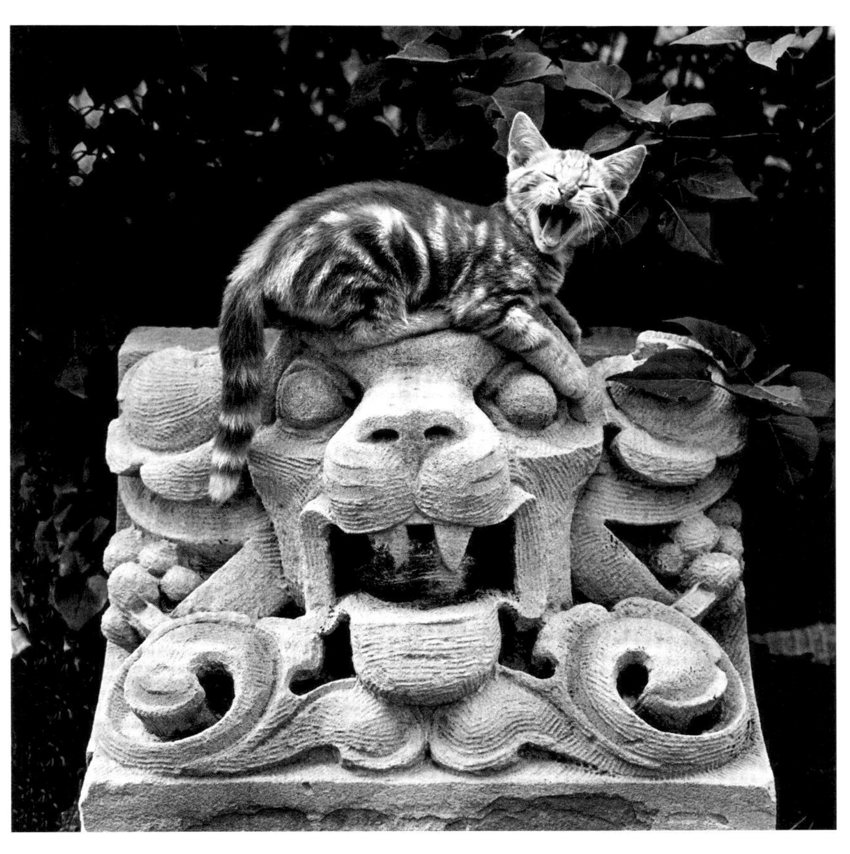

Stray, the Coliseum, Rome, Italy, 1981.
Domestic shorthair, New Jersey, 1977.

Stray, Alberobello, Italy, 1981.

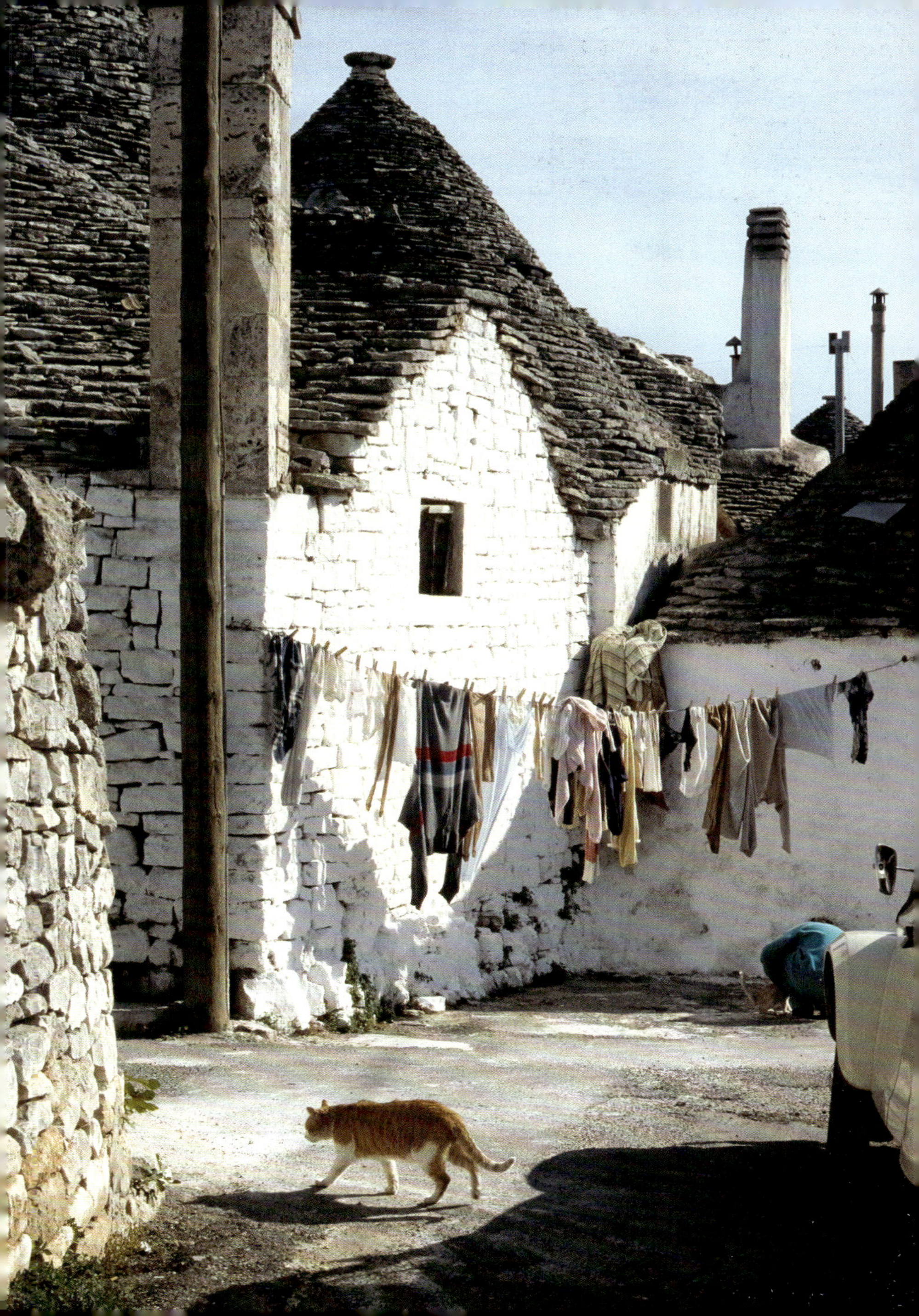

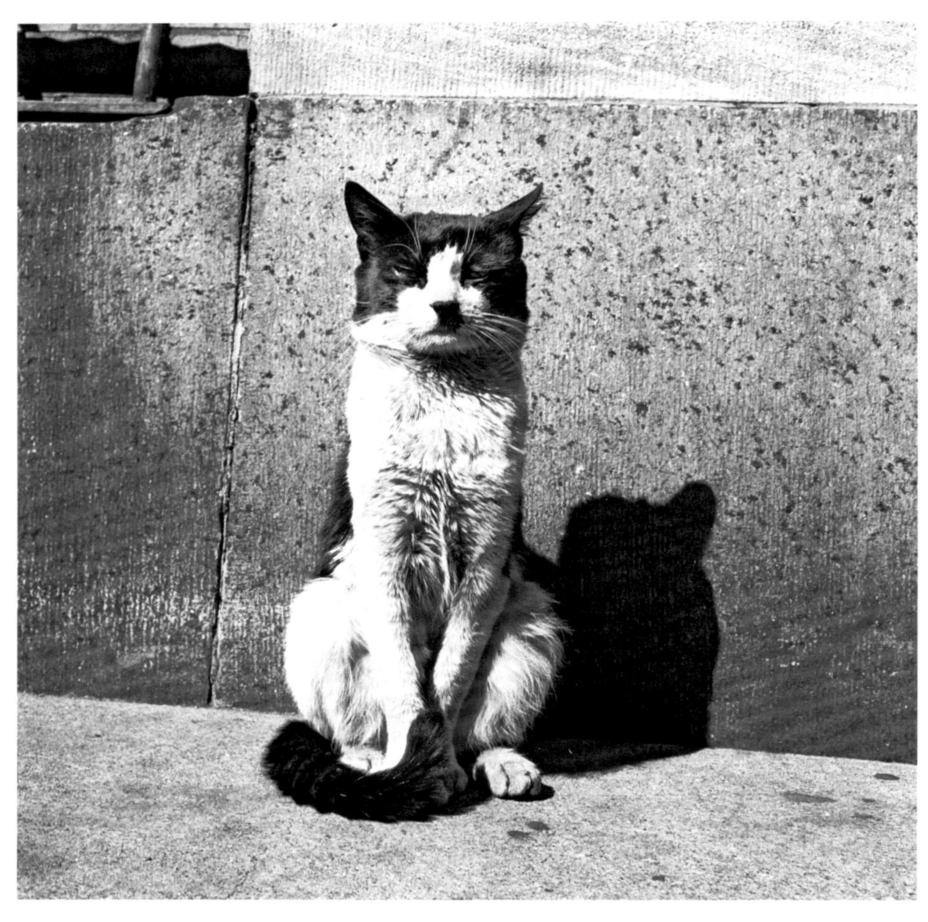

Stray, New York City, 1949.

Domestic shorthair, New Jersey, 1976.

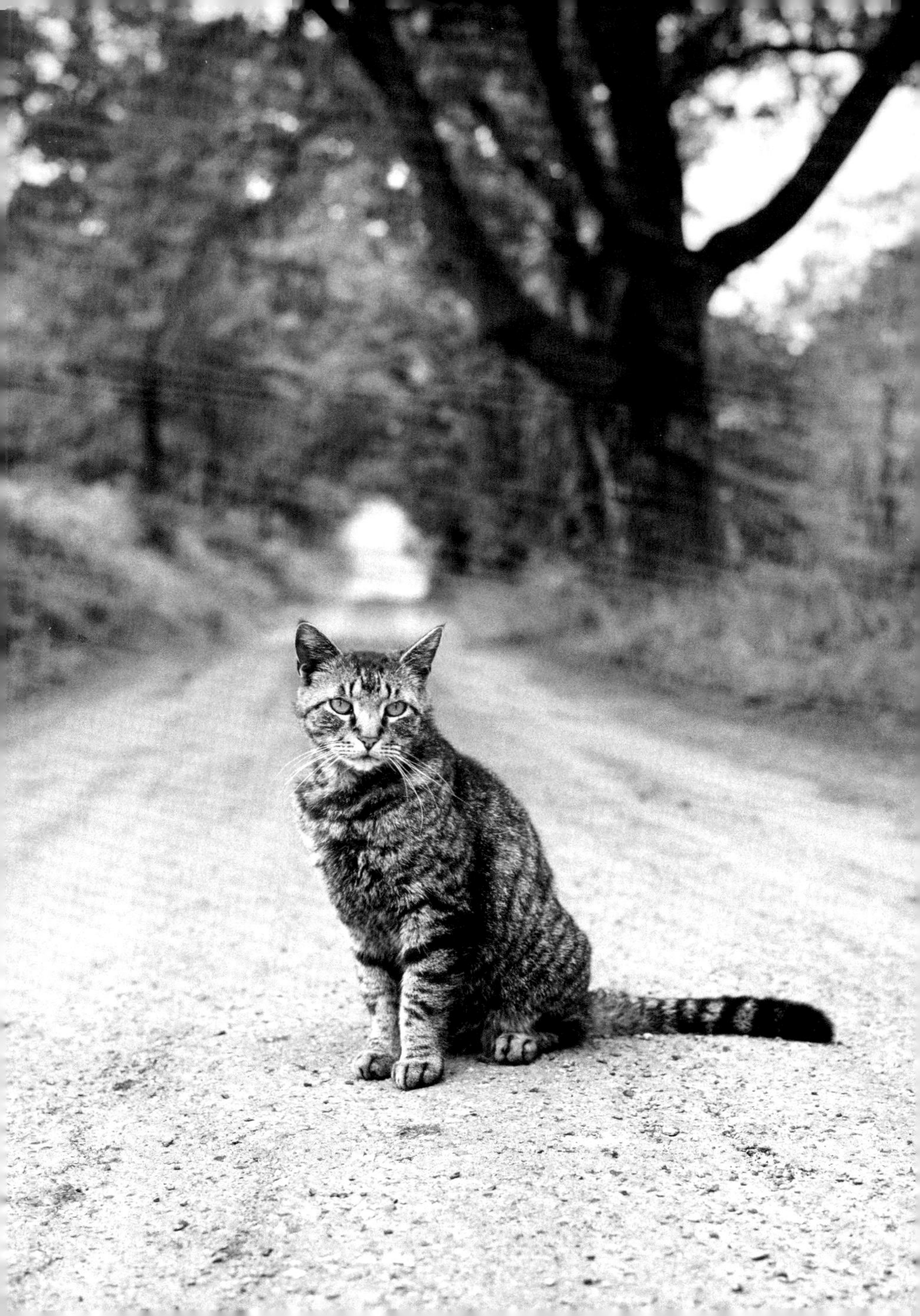

"Most people like to consider cats as loners.
They're actually very gregarious. They
will group together just as a family will."
The Mob, New Jersey, 1961.

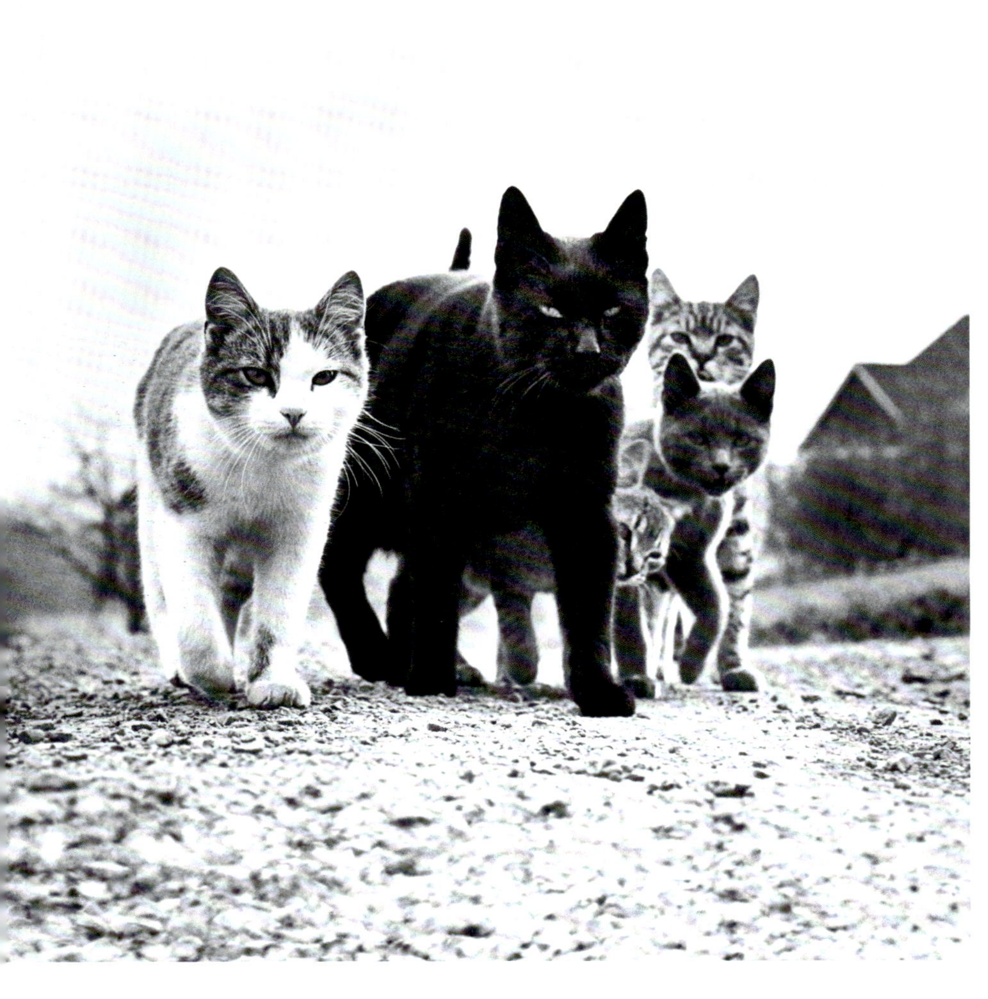

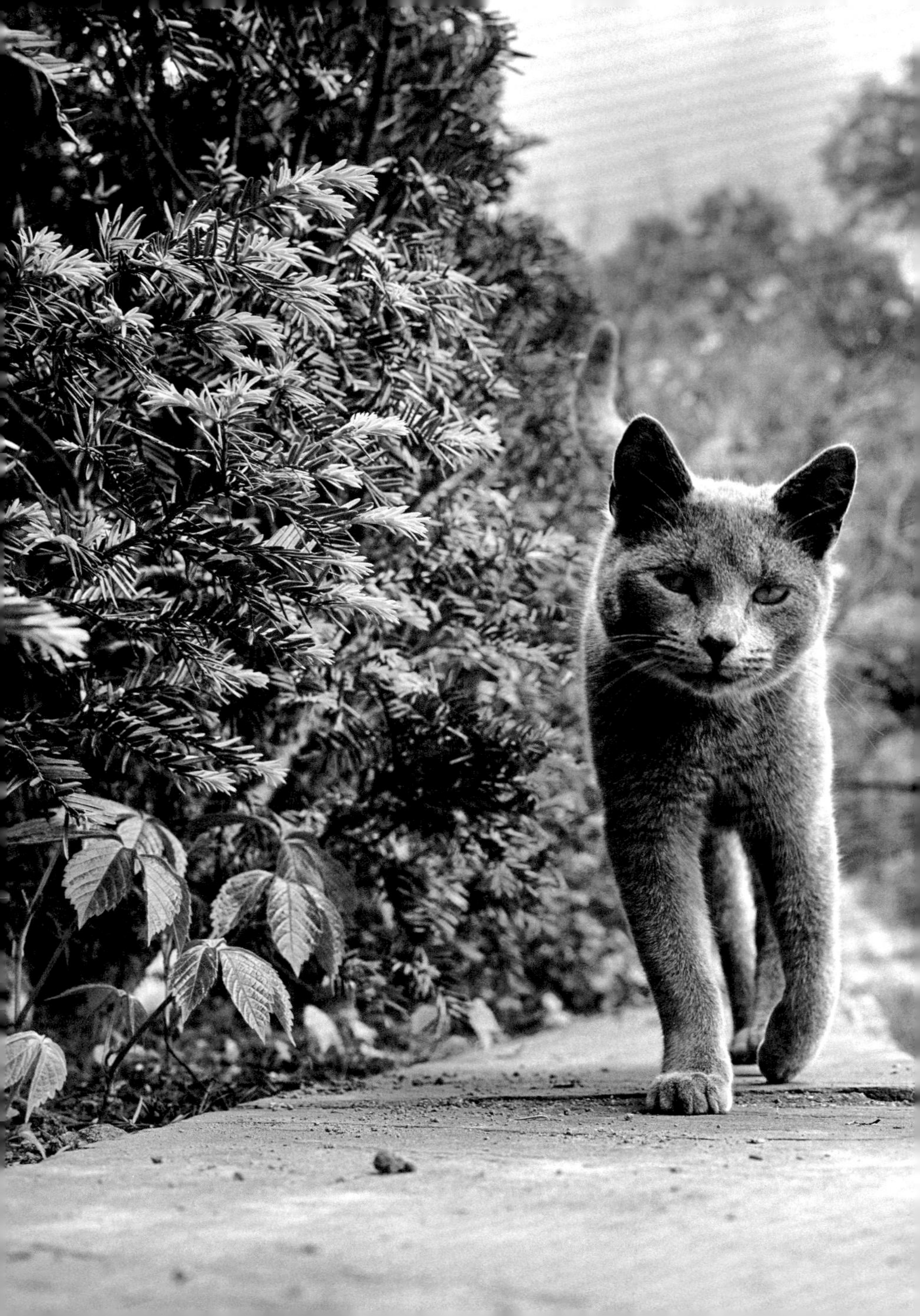

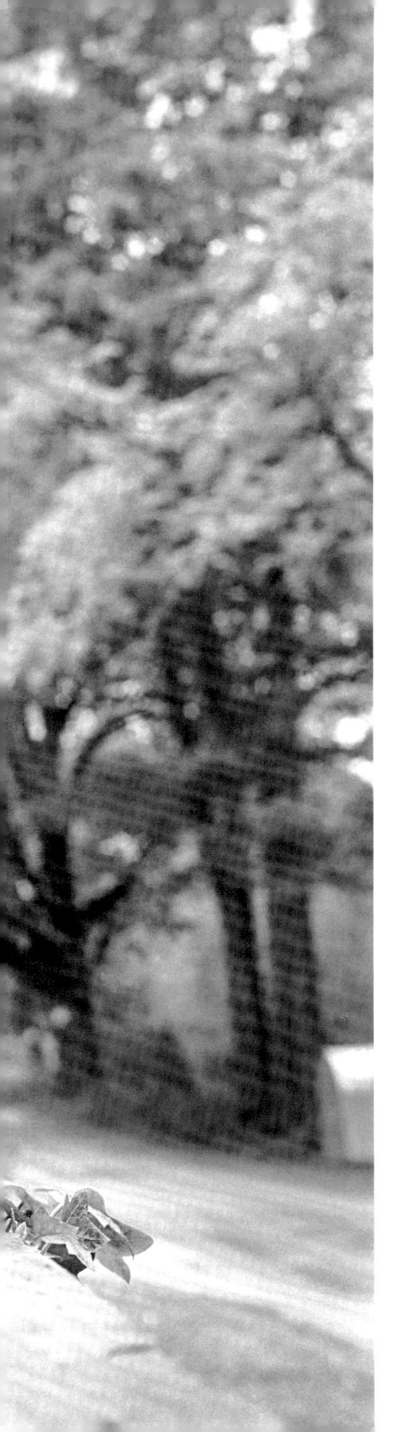

Loco, New Jersey, 1961.

Following: Domestic shorthair,
New Jersey, 1970.

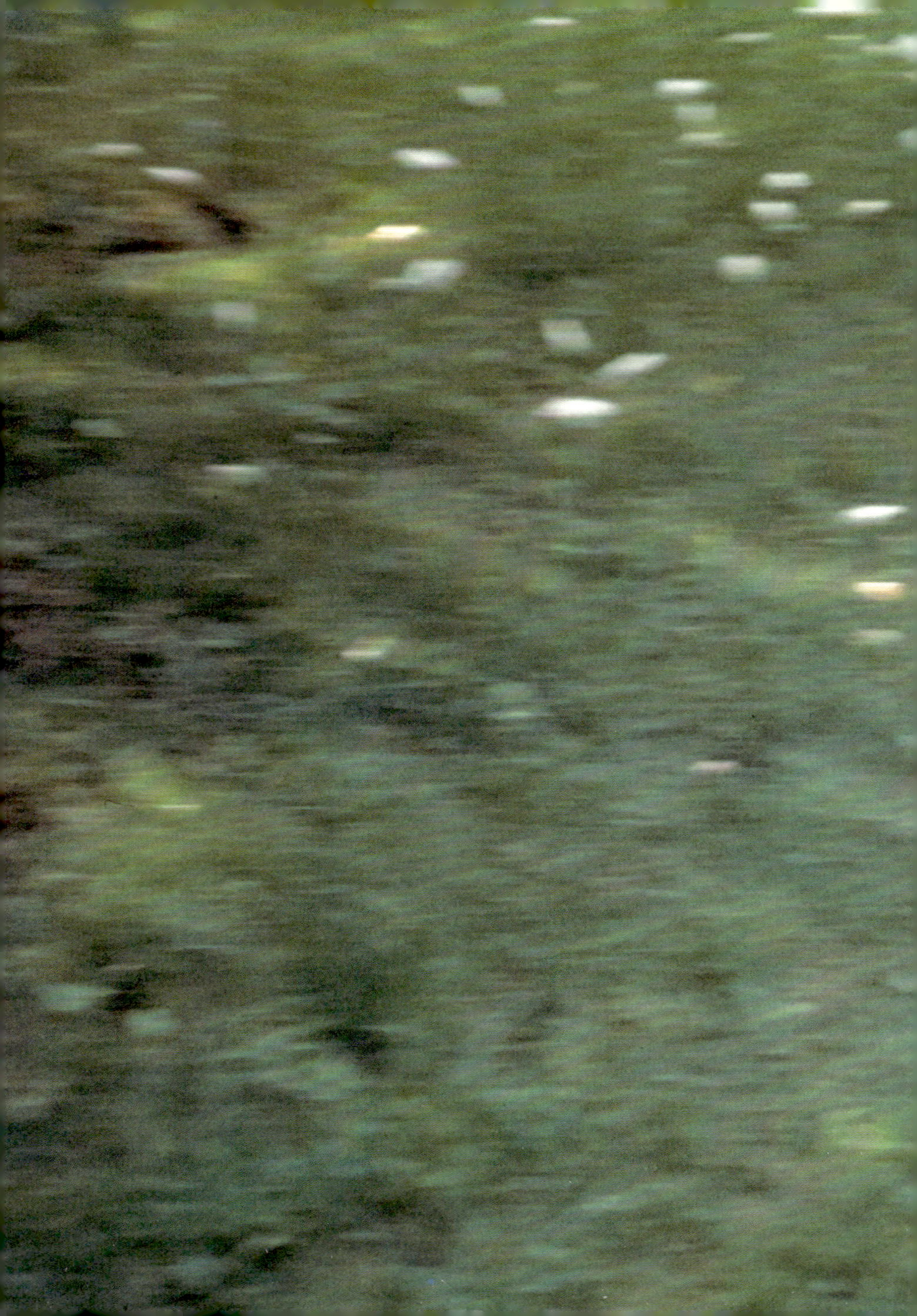

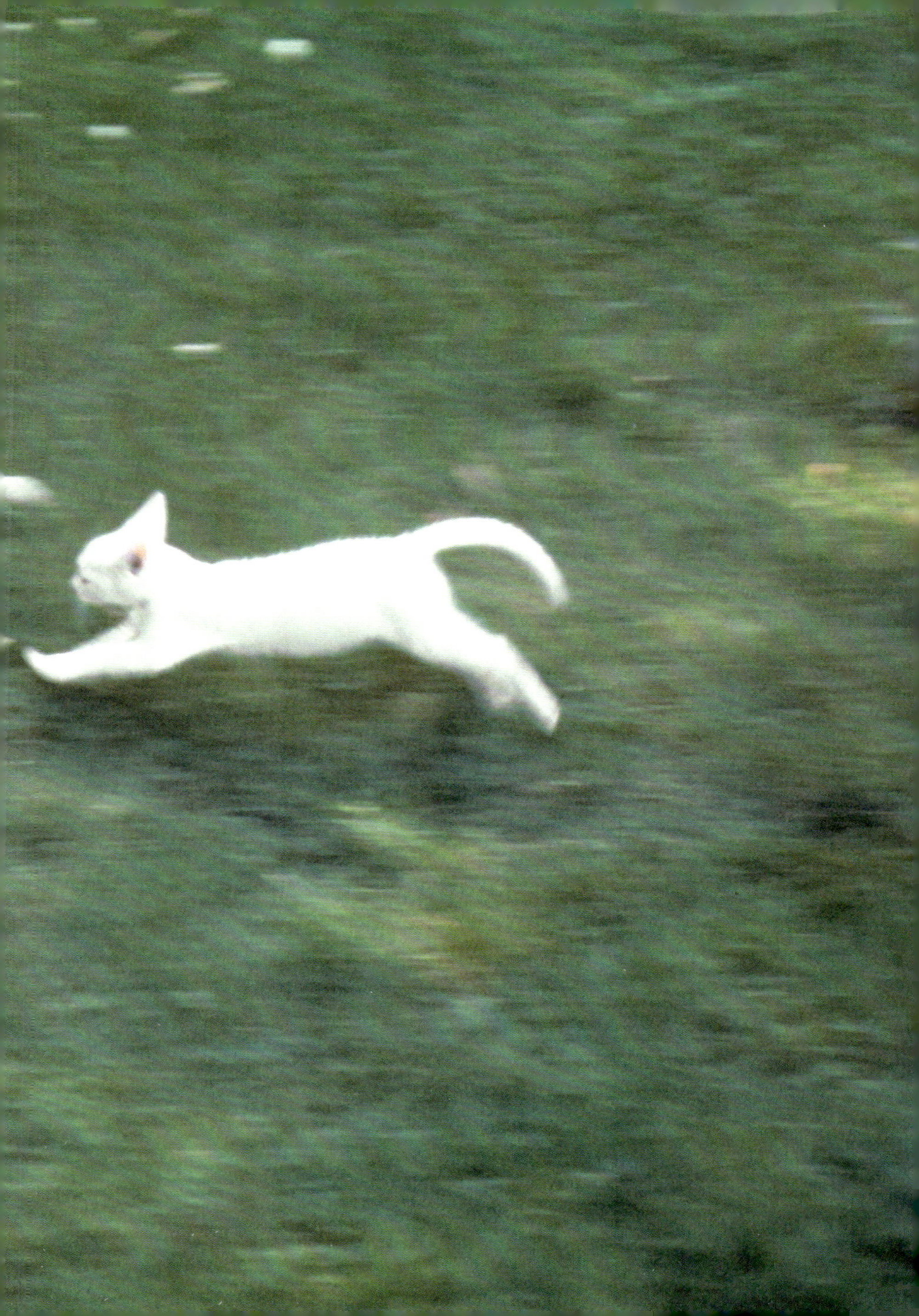

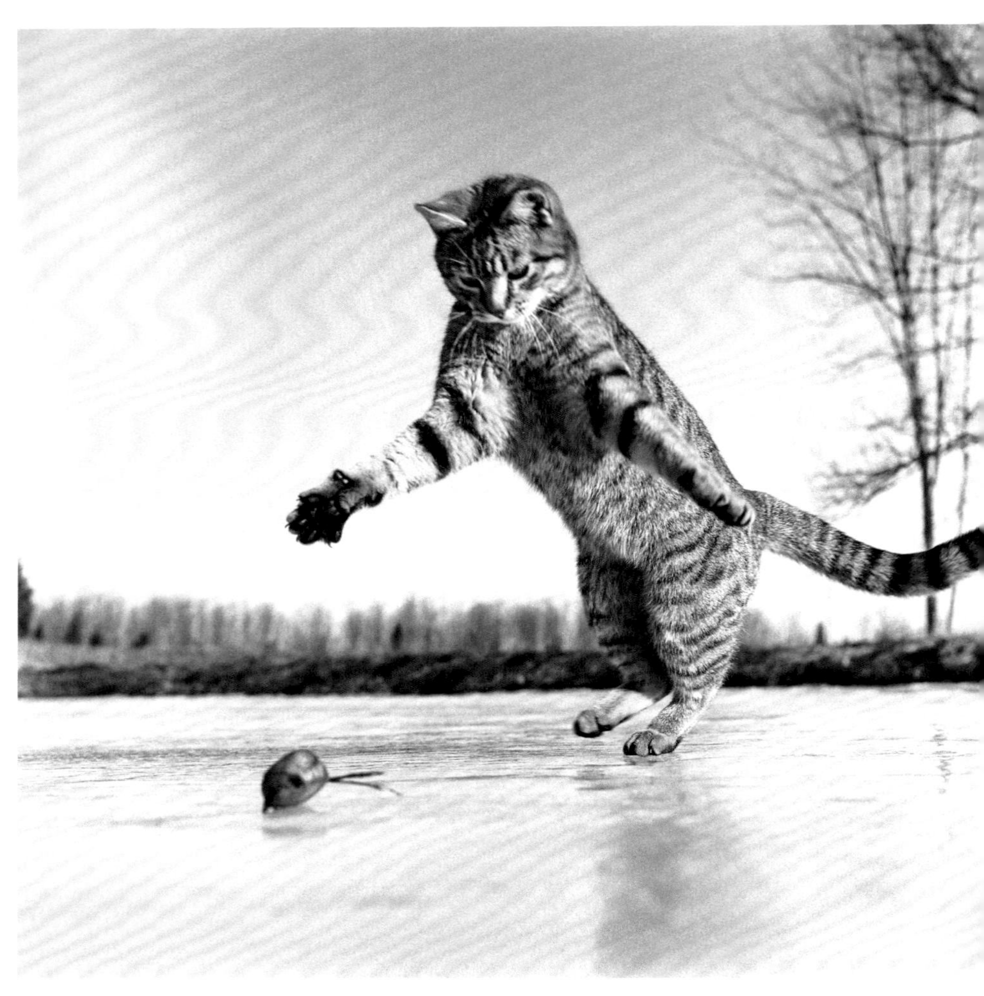

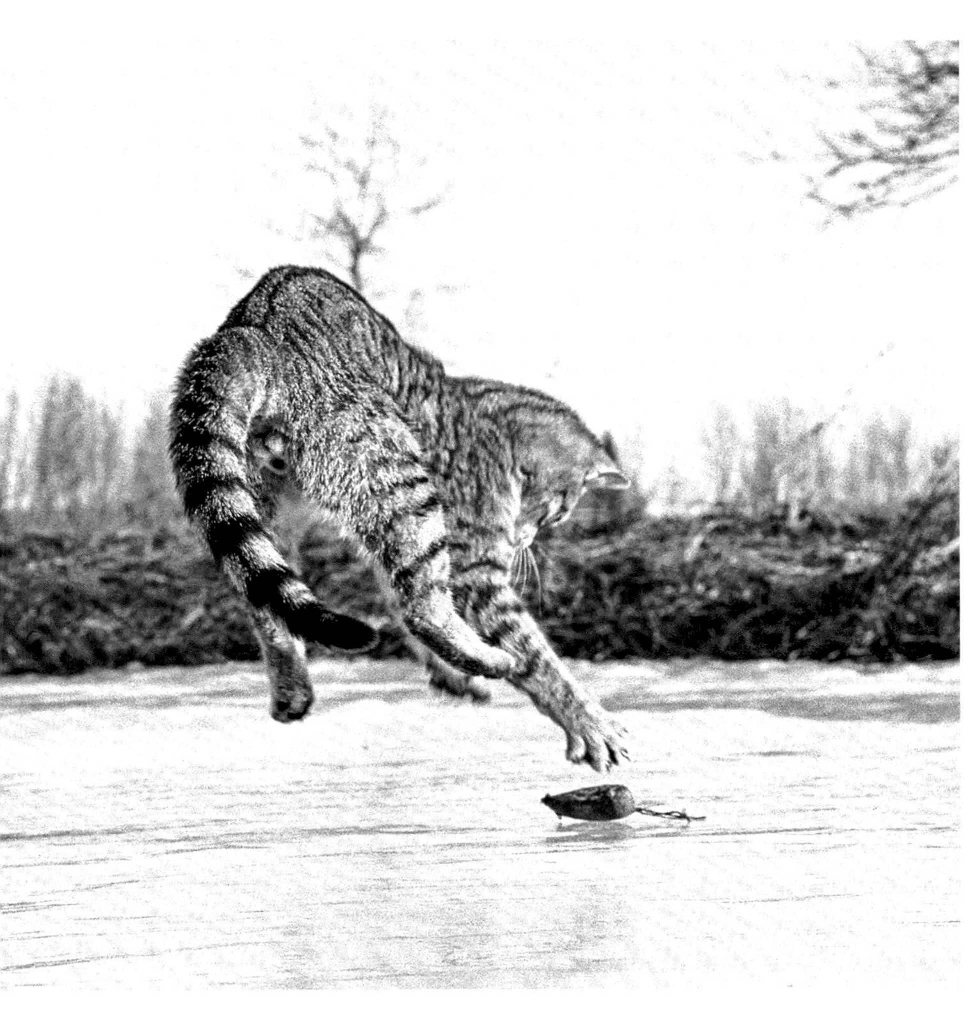

This spread and following:
Domestic shorthair, New Jersey, 1960.

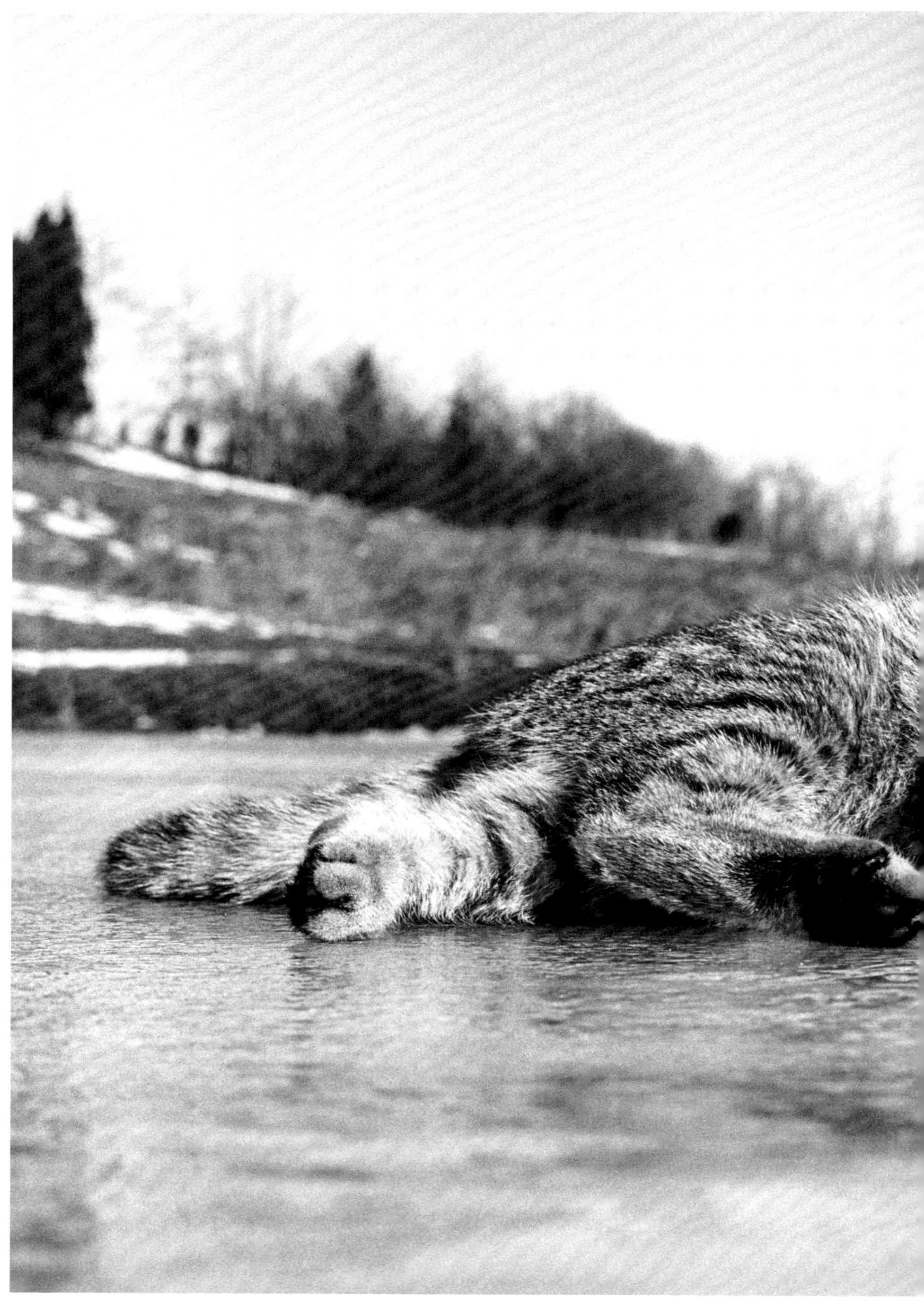

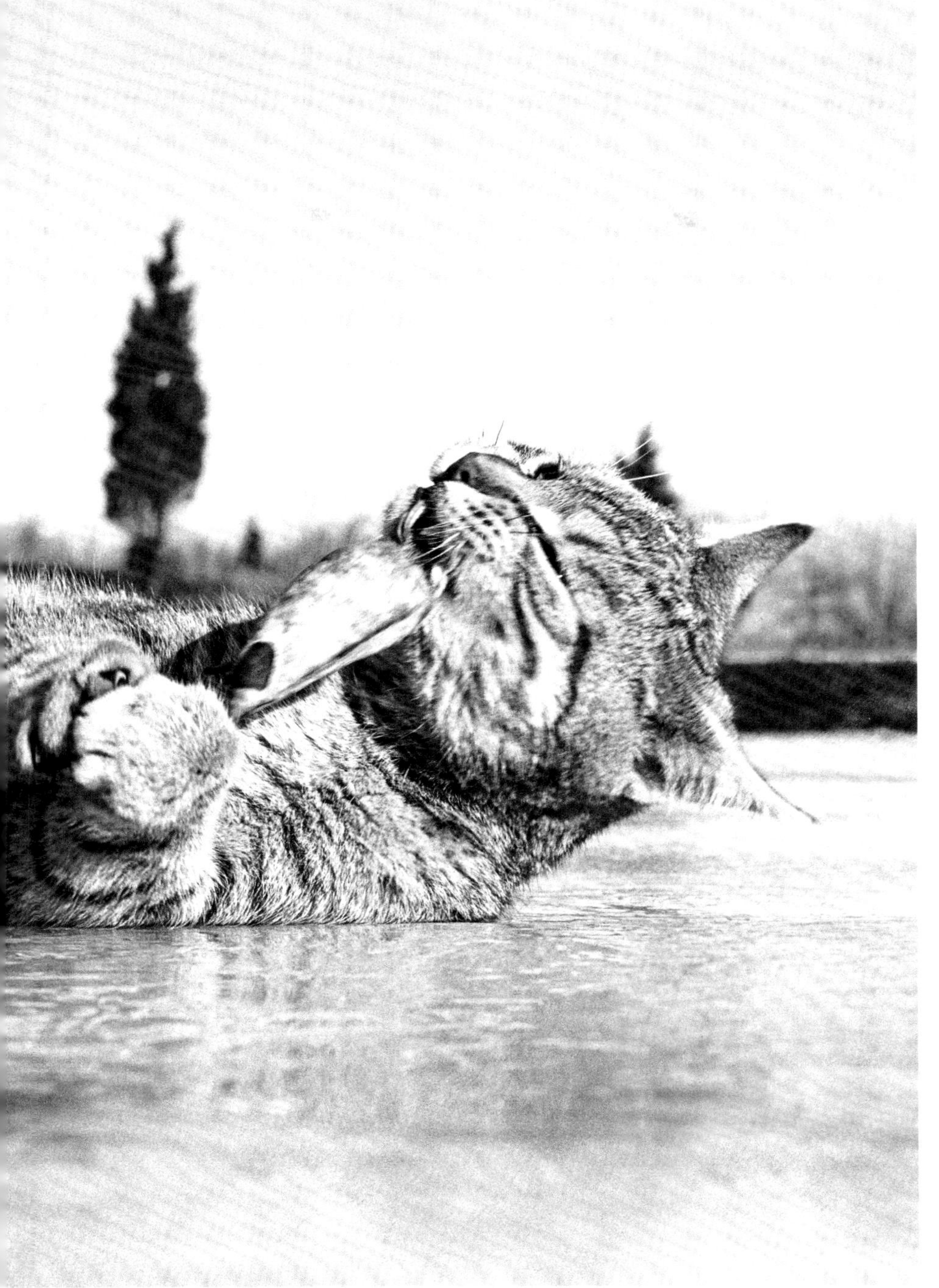

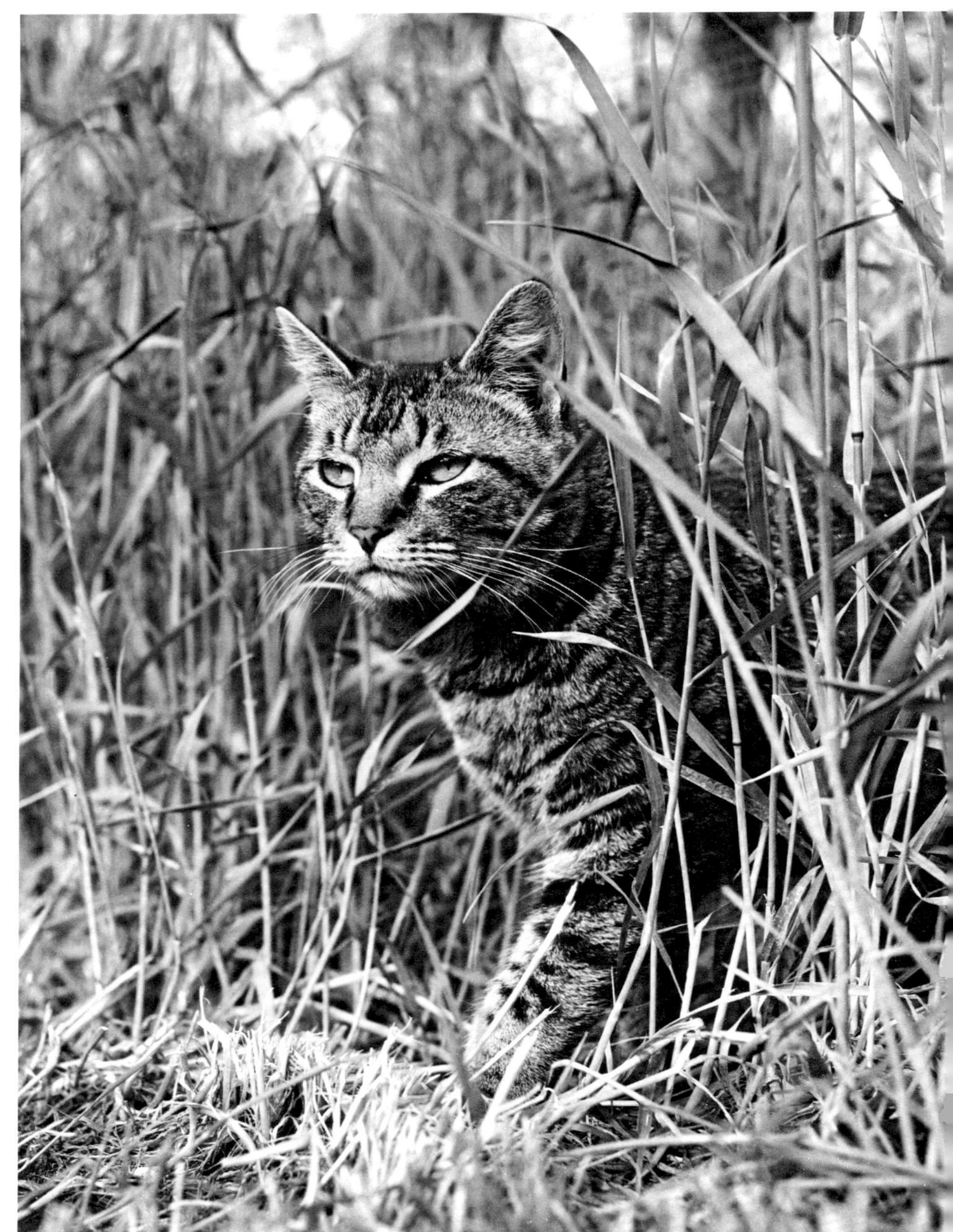

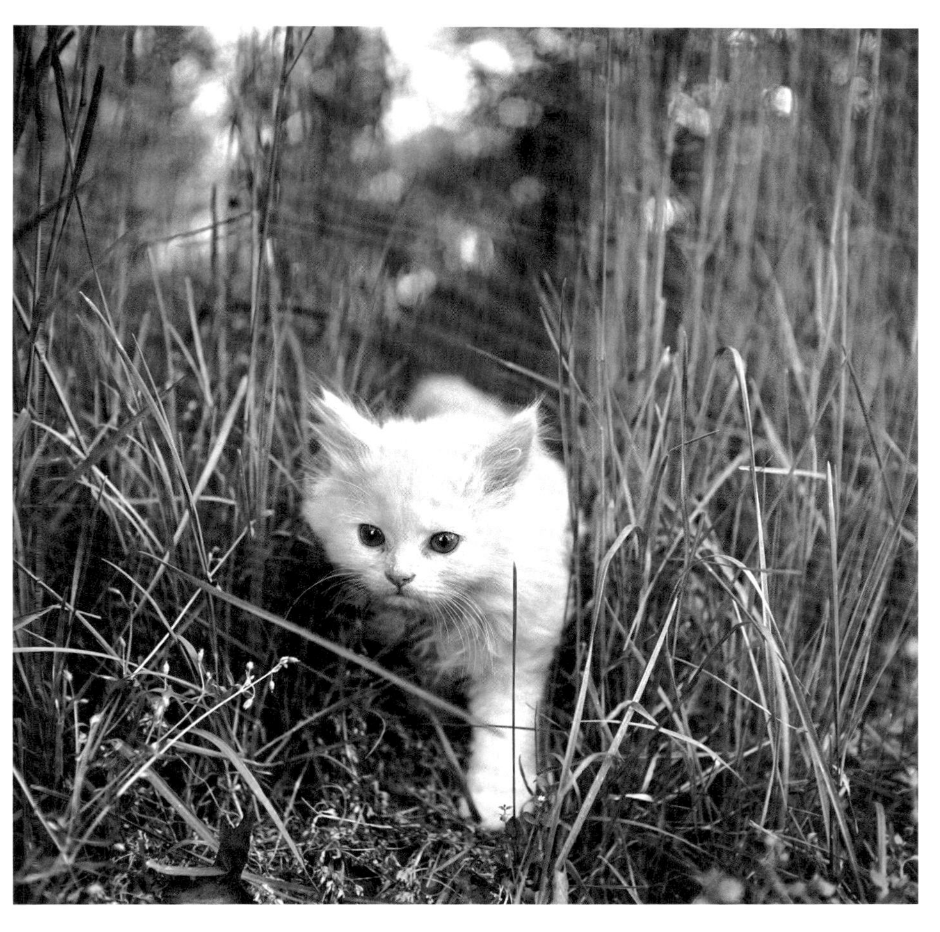

Domestic shorthair, New Jersey, 1963.

Persian, Long Island, 1955.

Following: Loco, New Jersey, 1962.

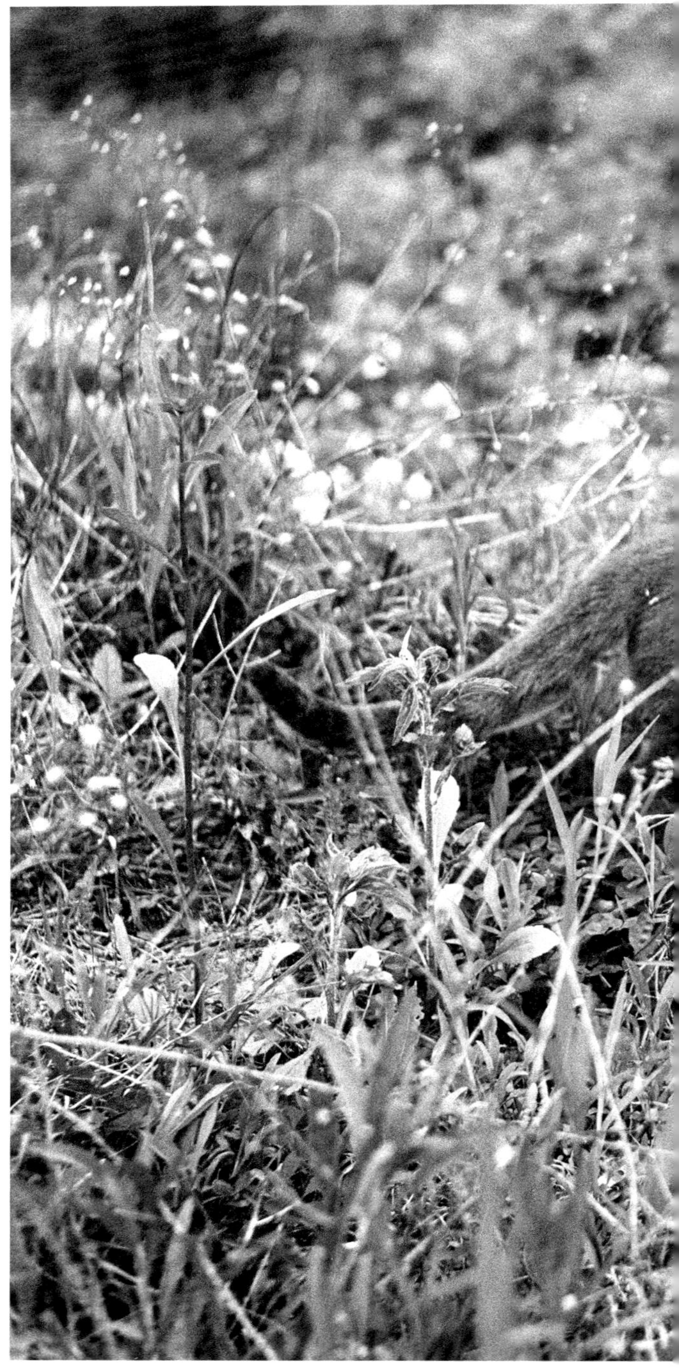

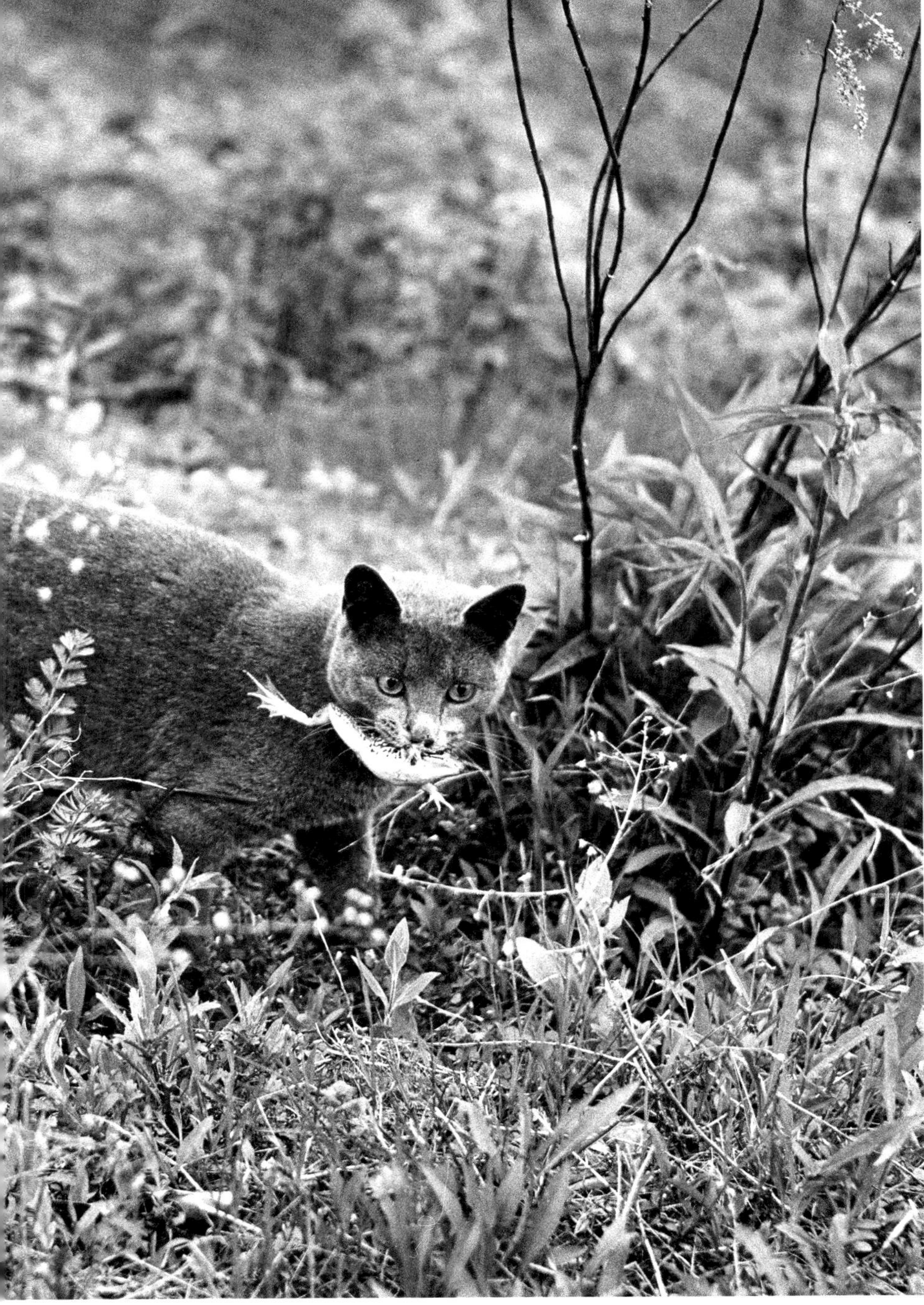

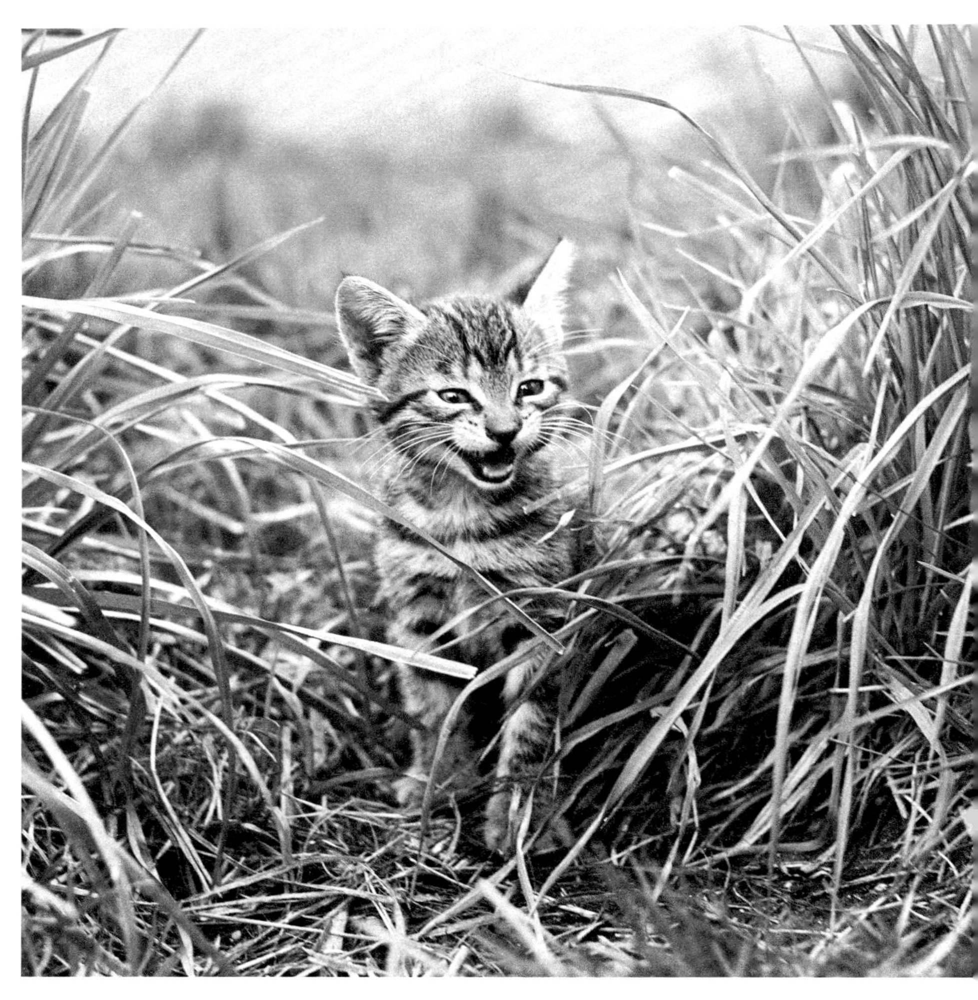

Domestic shorthair, New Jersey, 1965.

Domestic shorthair, Long Island, 1955.

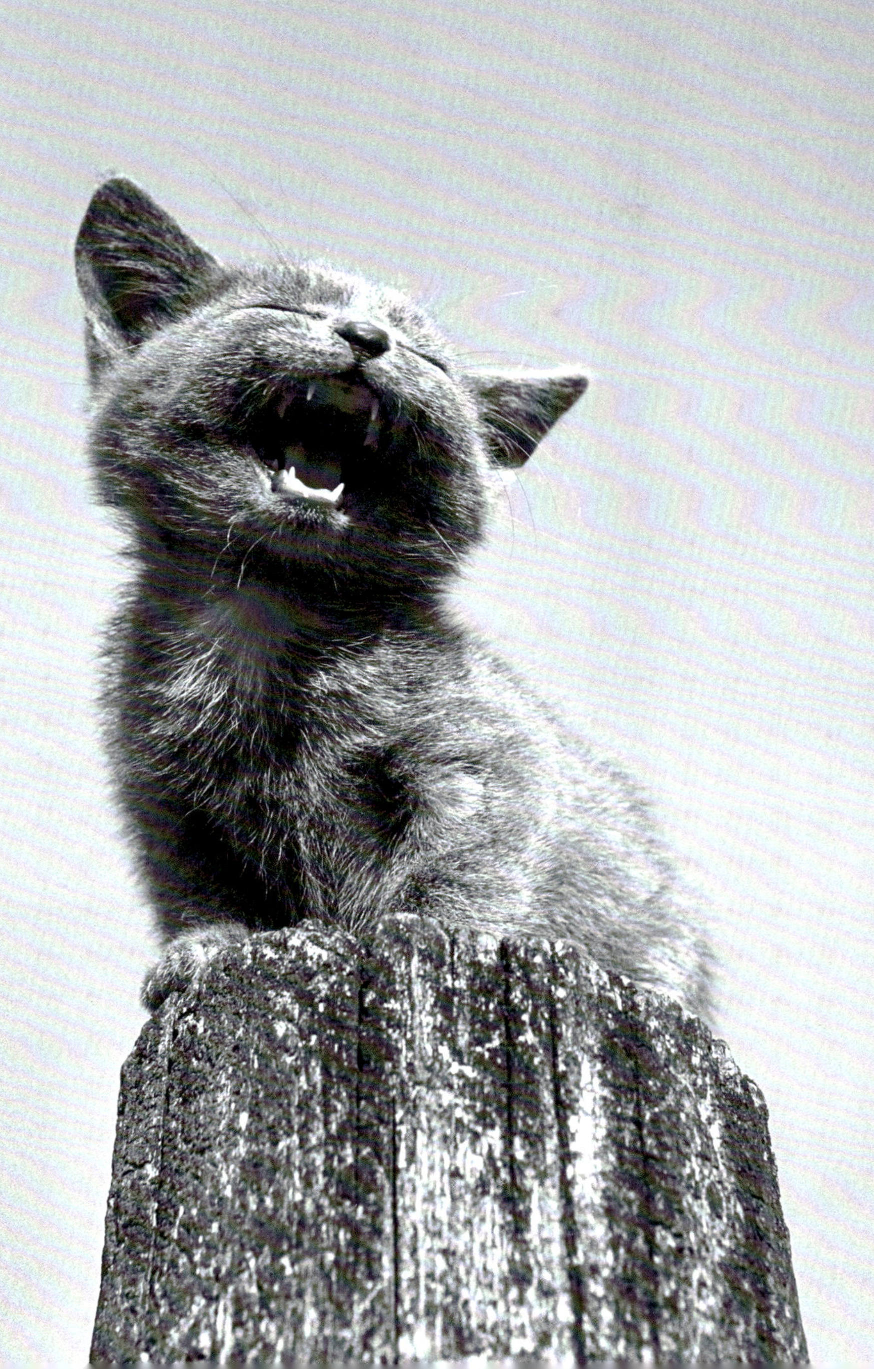

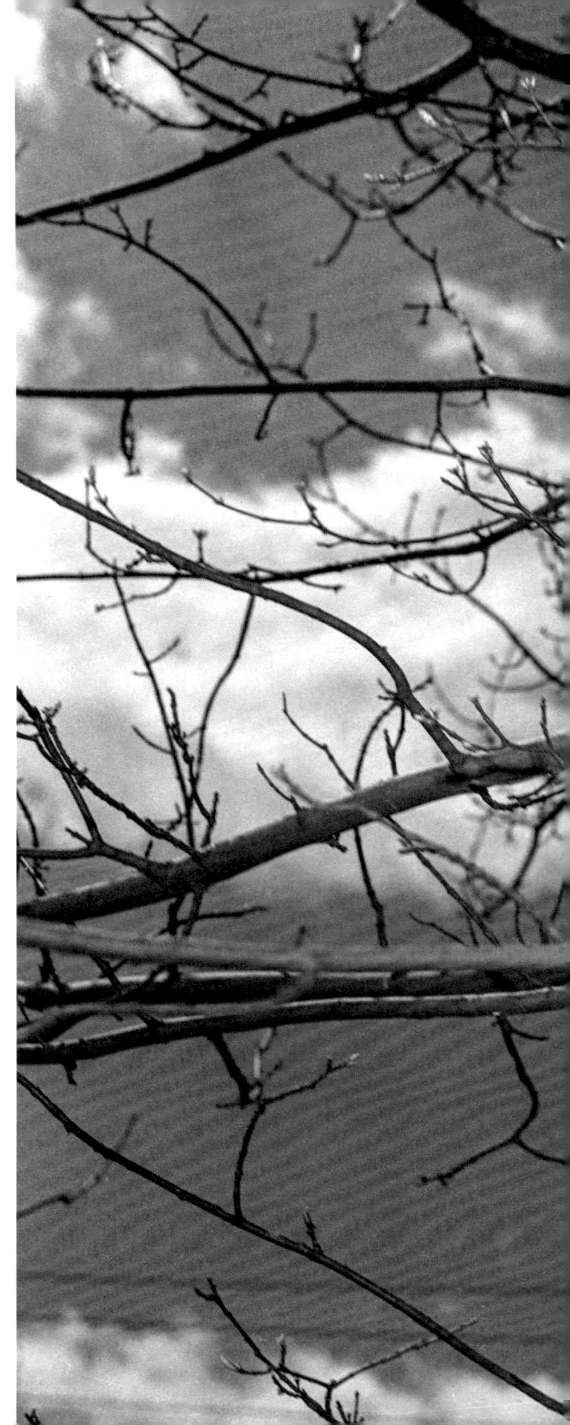

Domestic shorthair,
New Jersey, 1942.

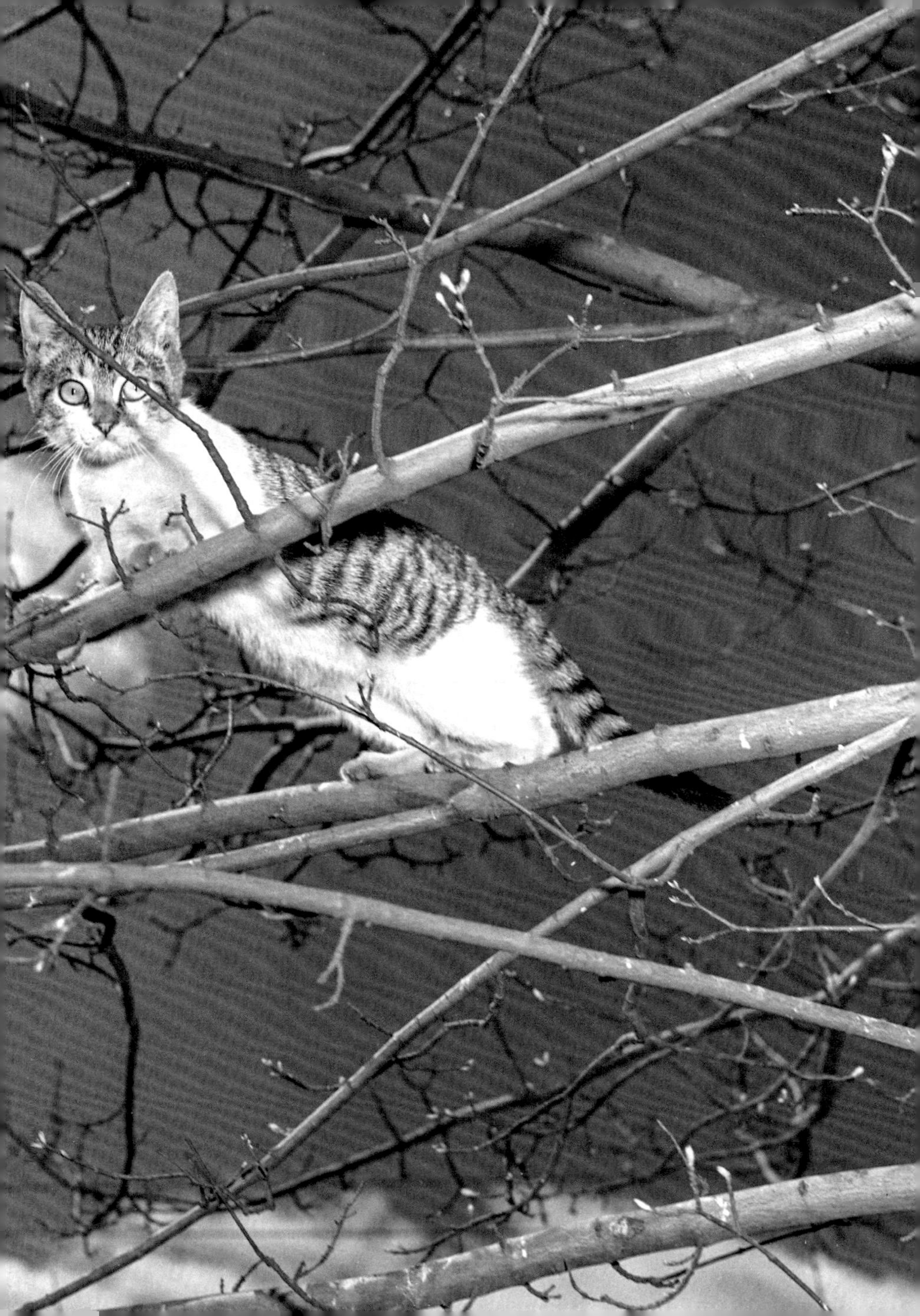

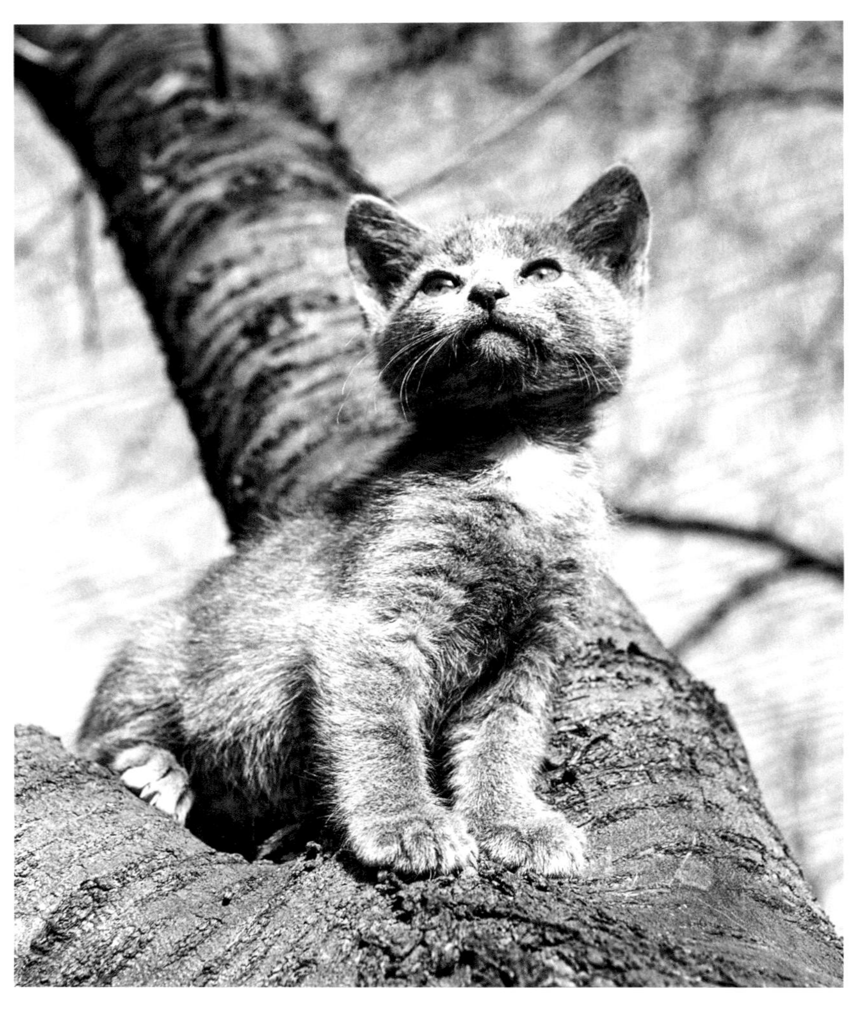

Domestic shorthair, Long Island, 1955.

Stray, New York City, 1950.

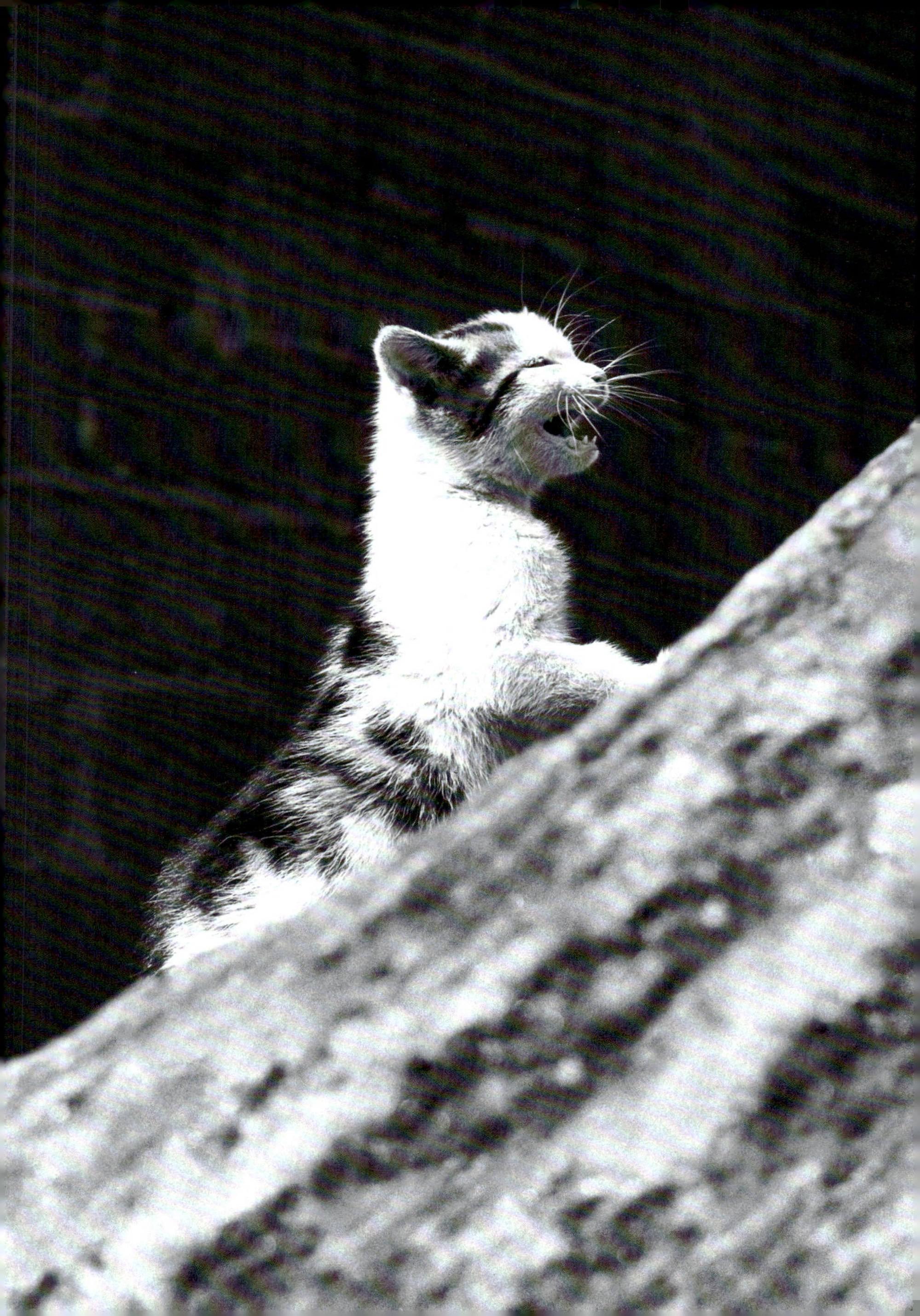

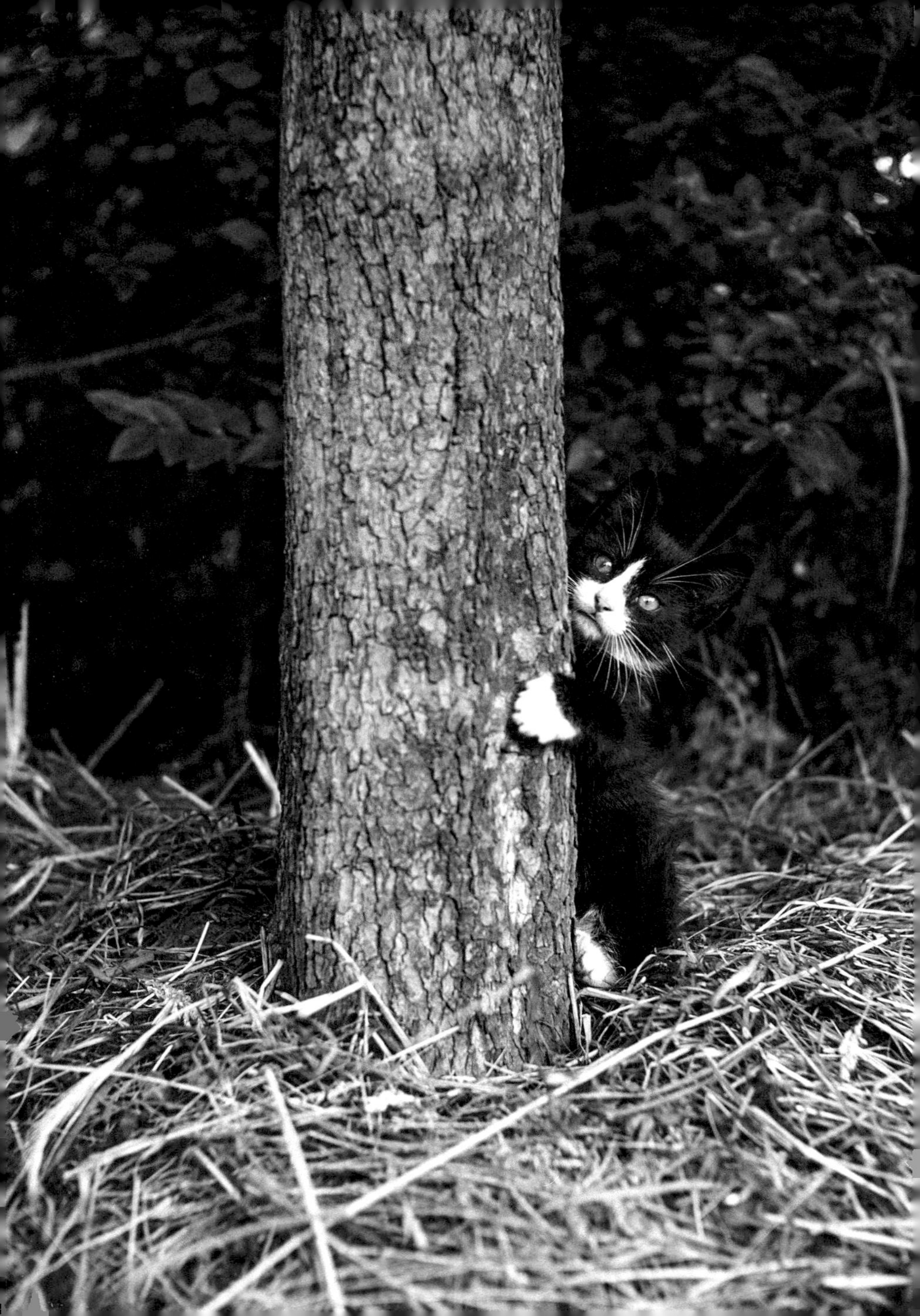

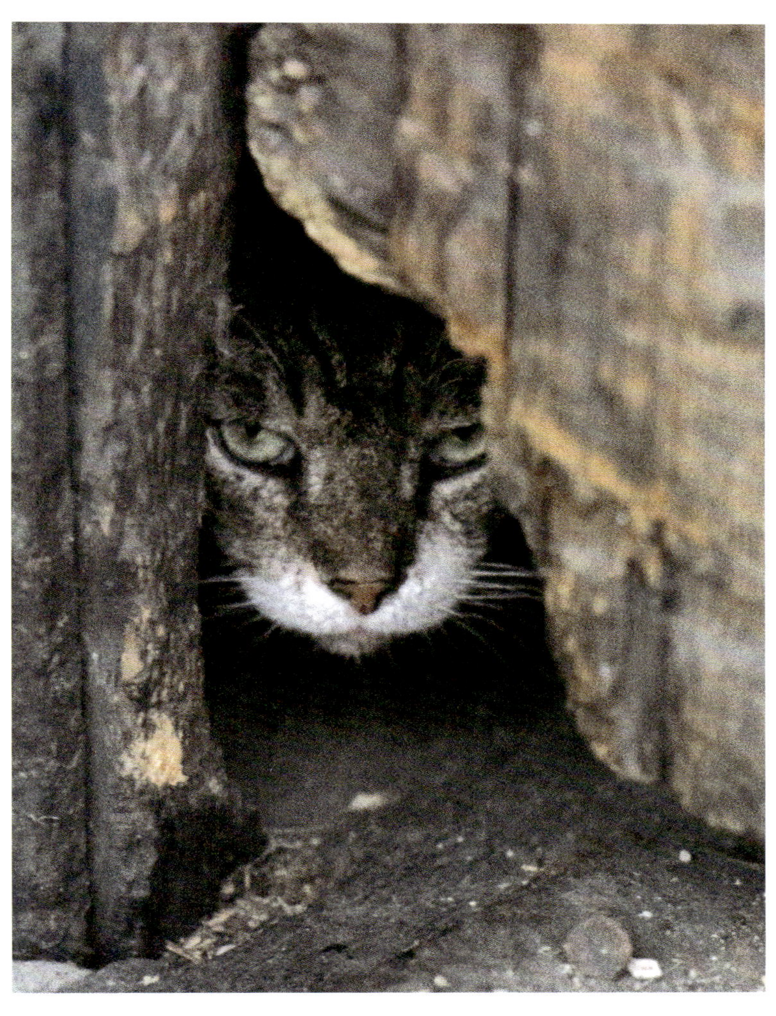

Domestic shorthair, Long Island, 1954.
Stray, New York City, 1962.

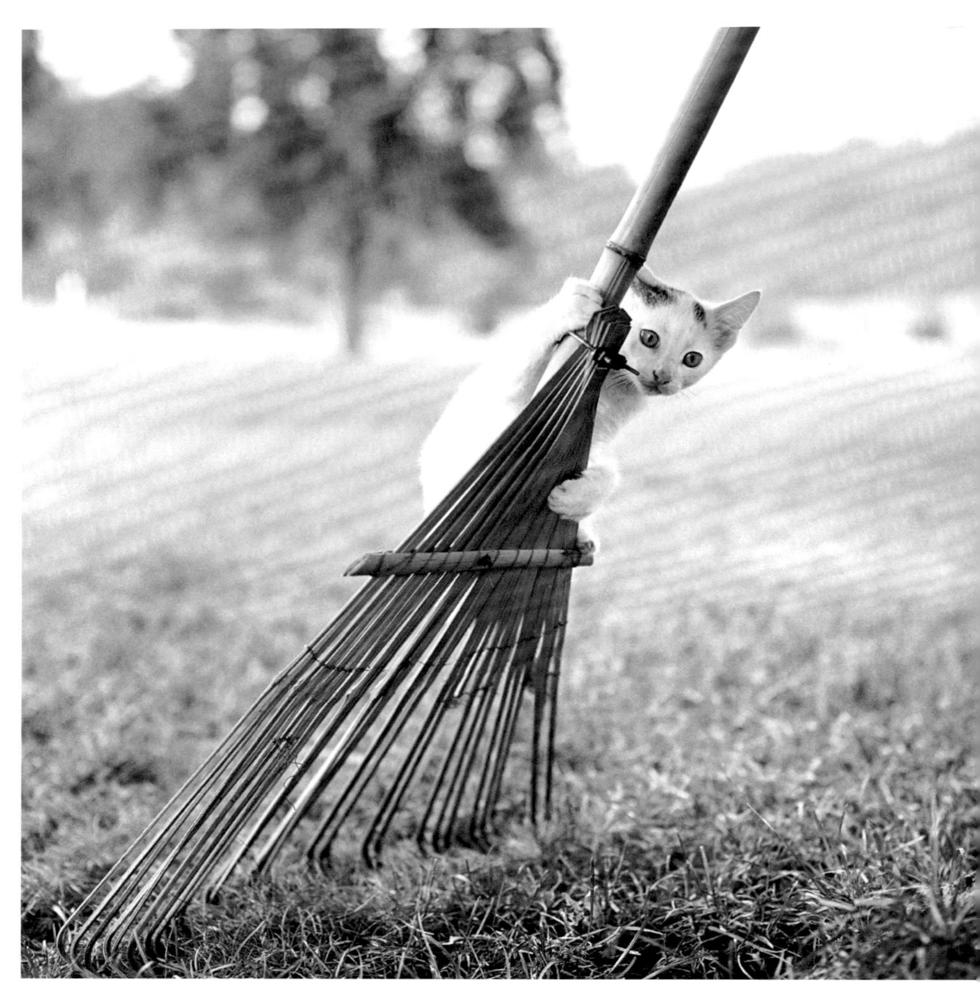

Domestic shorthair, New Jersey, 1961.

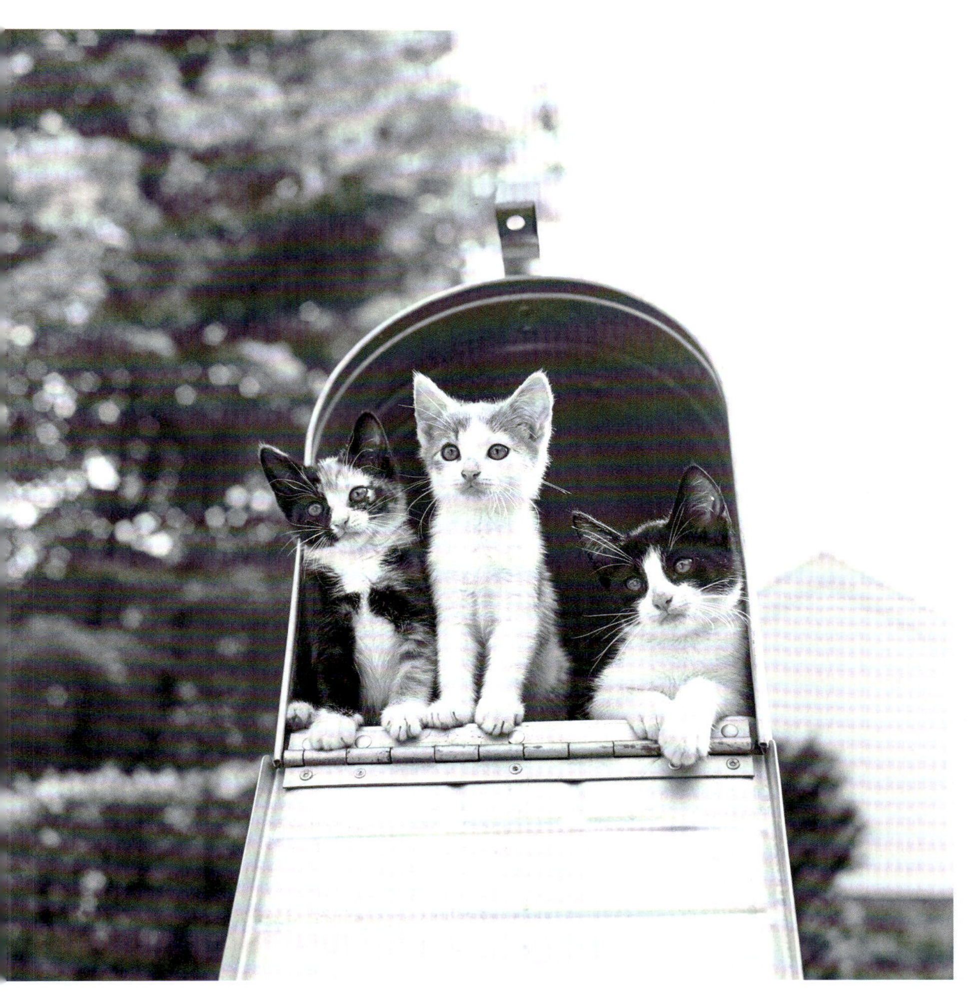

Domestic shorthair, New Jersey, 1962.

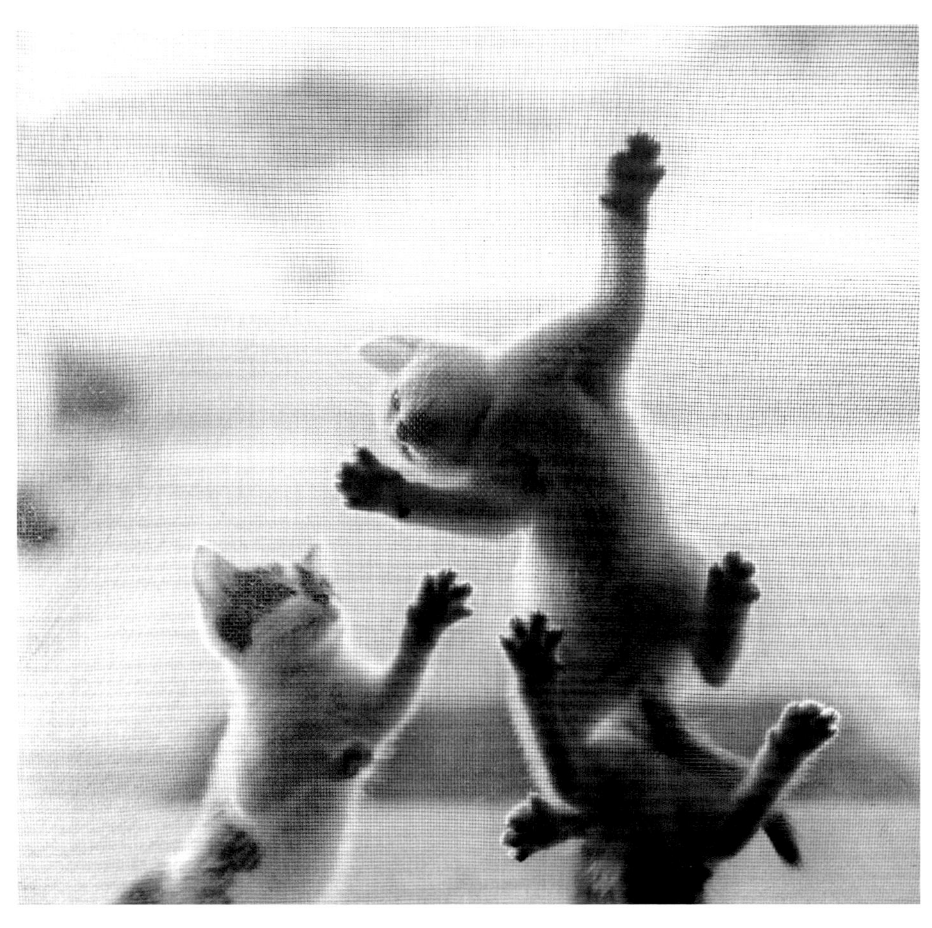

Domestic shorthair, New Jersey, 1962.
Domestic shorthair, Long Island, 1957.

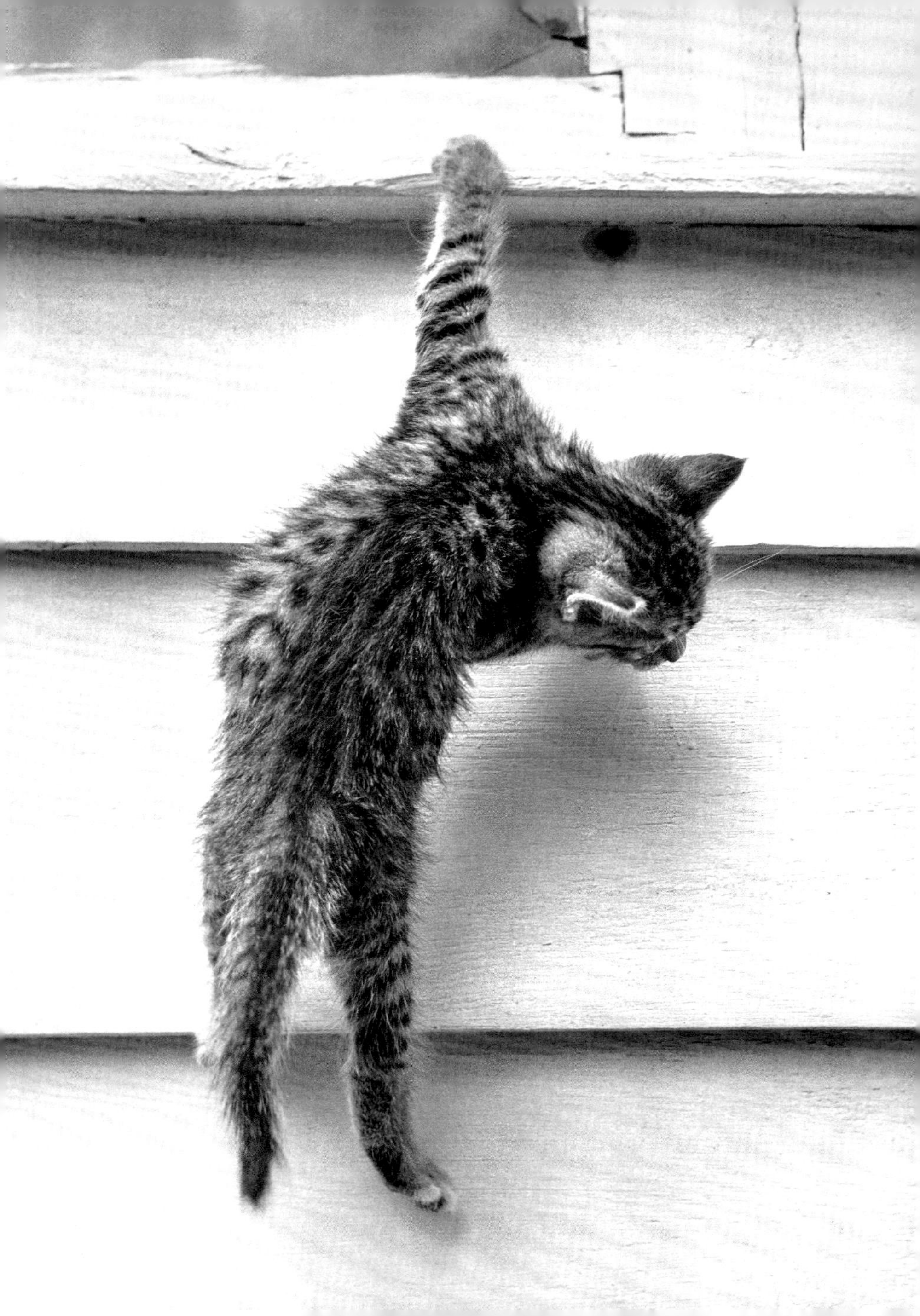

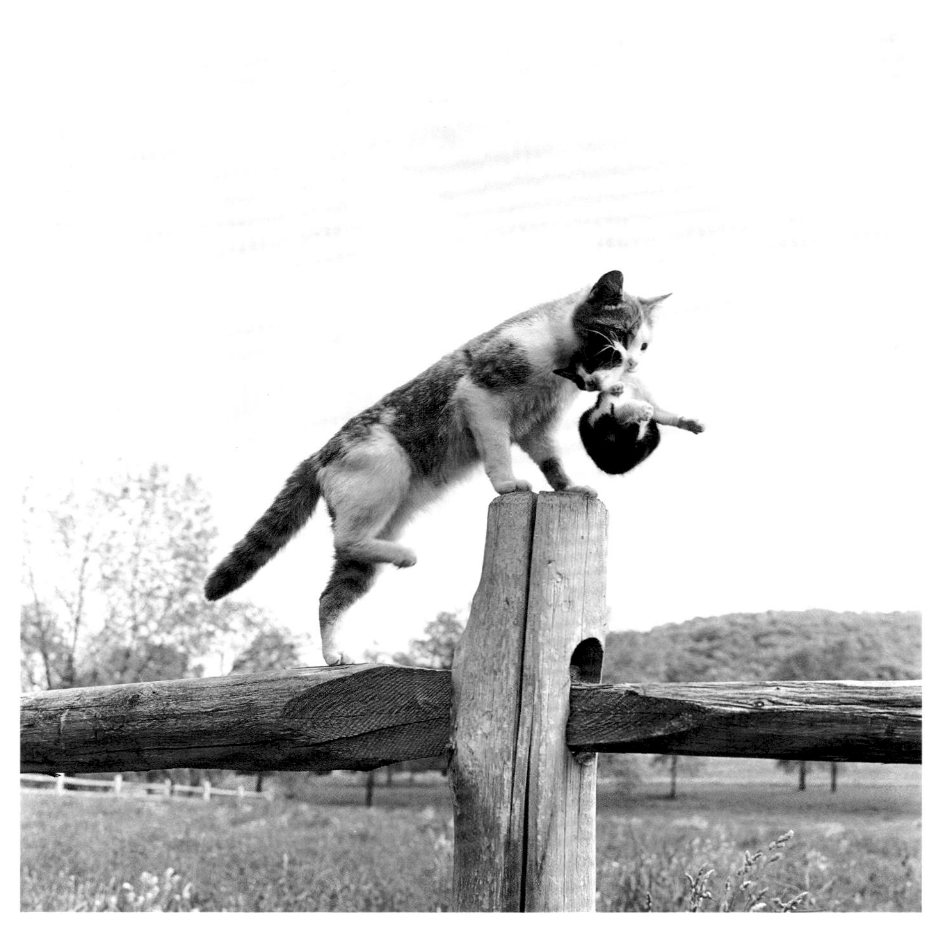

Domestic shorthair and kitten,
New Jersey, 1961.

Minnie and kitten, Domestic shorthairs,
Long Island, 1958.

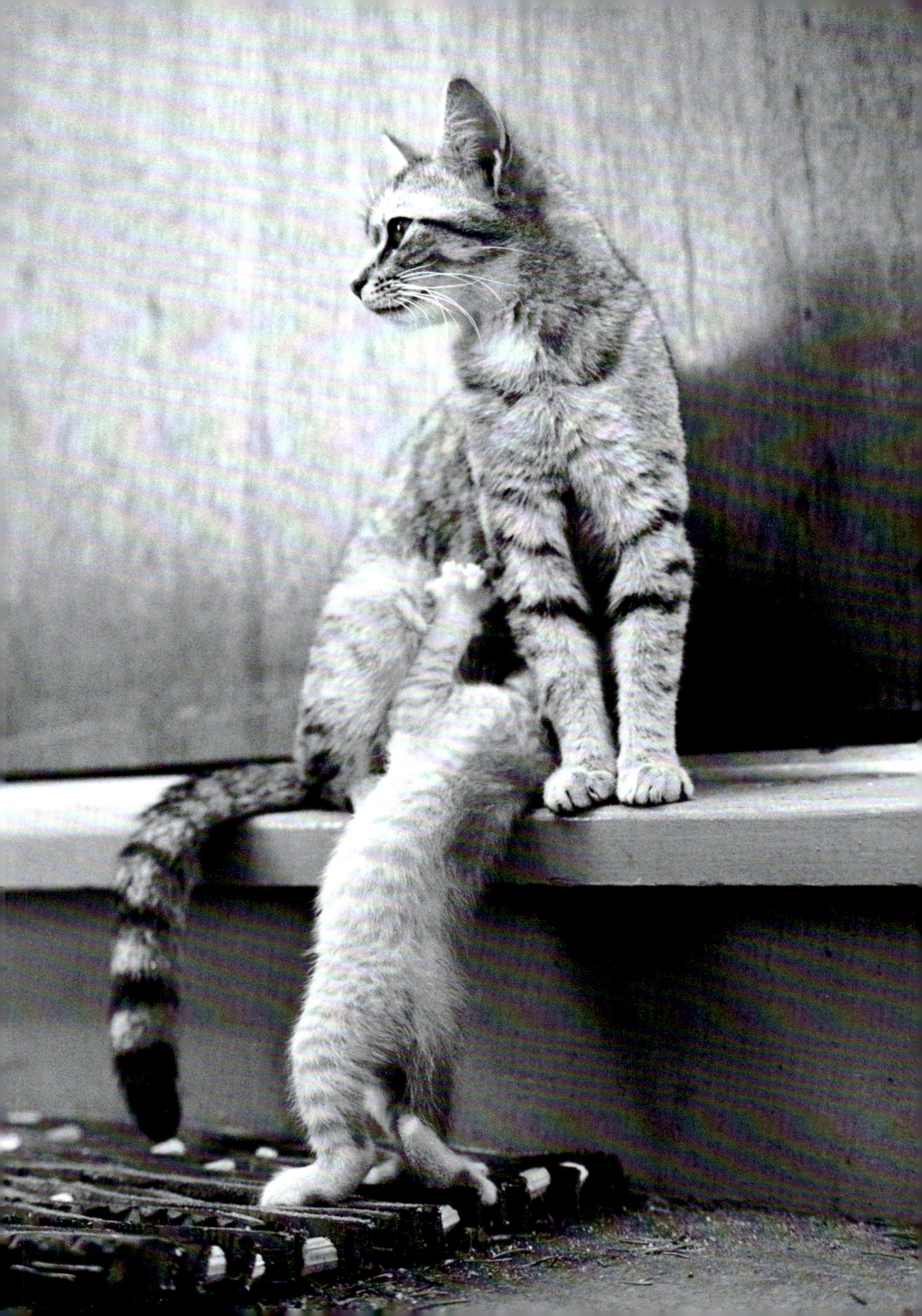

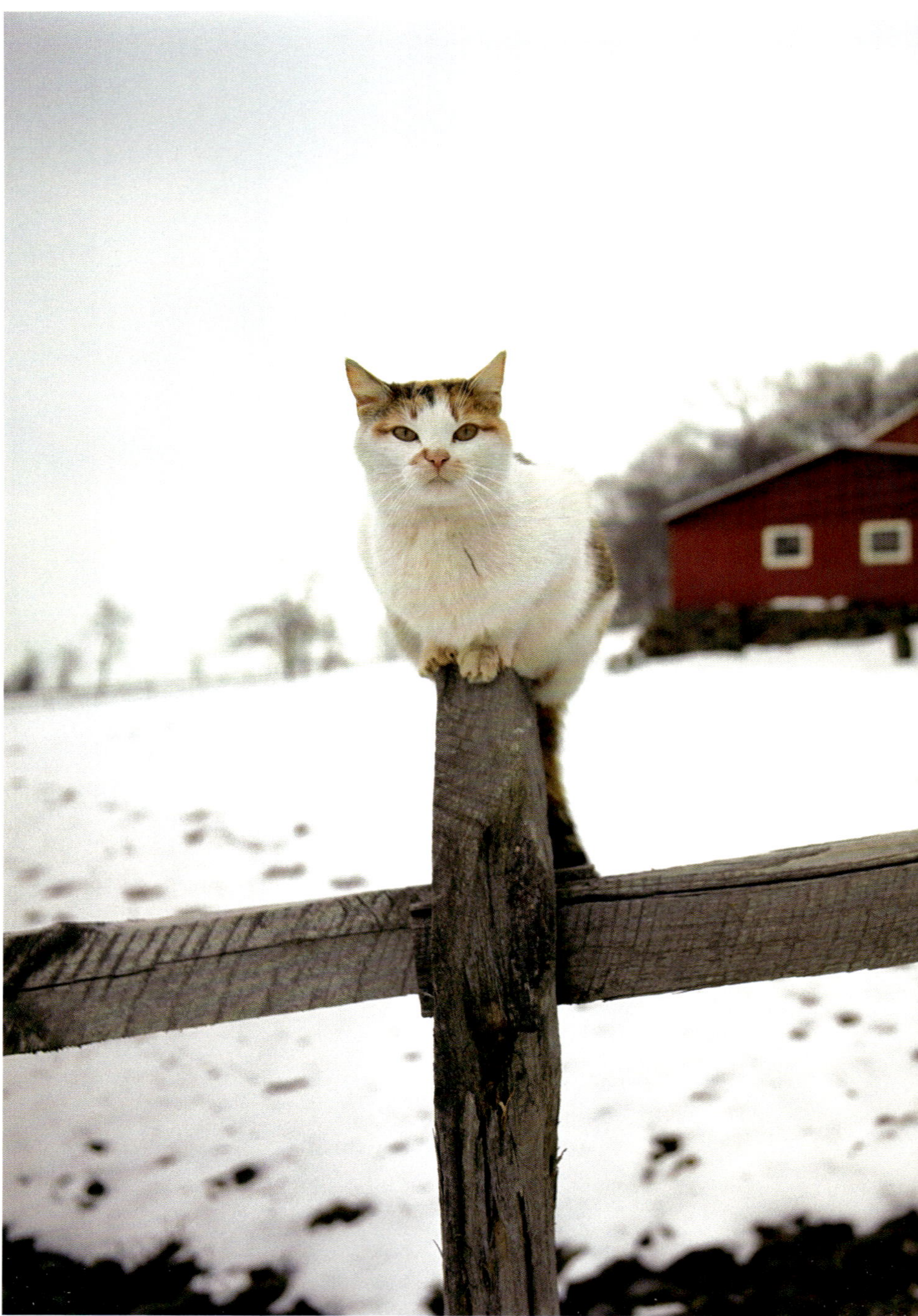

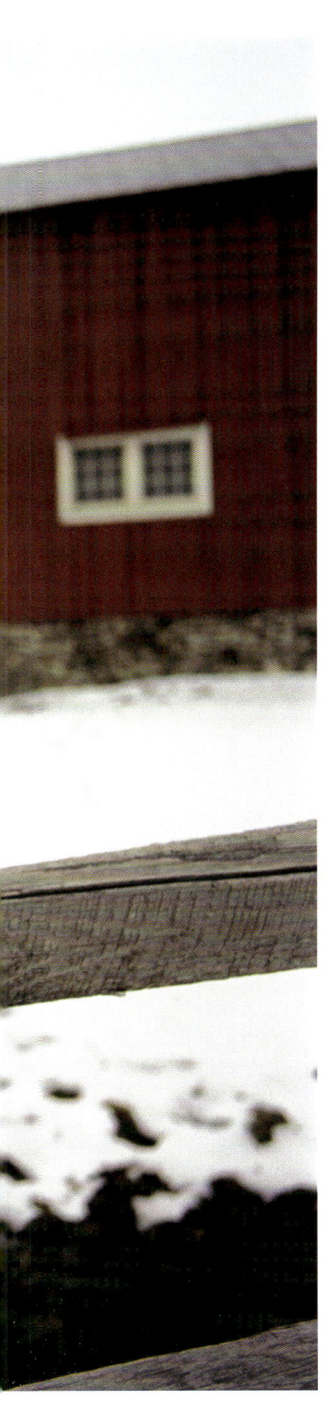

Barn cat, Domestic shorthair,
New Jersey, 1970.

Barn cats, Domestic shorthairs,
New Jersey, 1982.

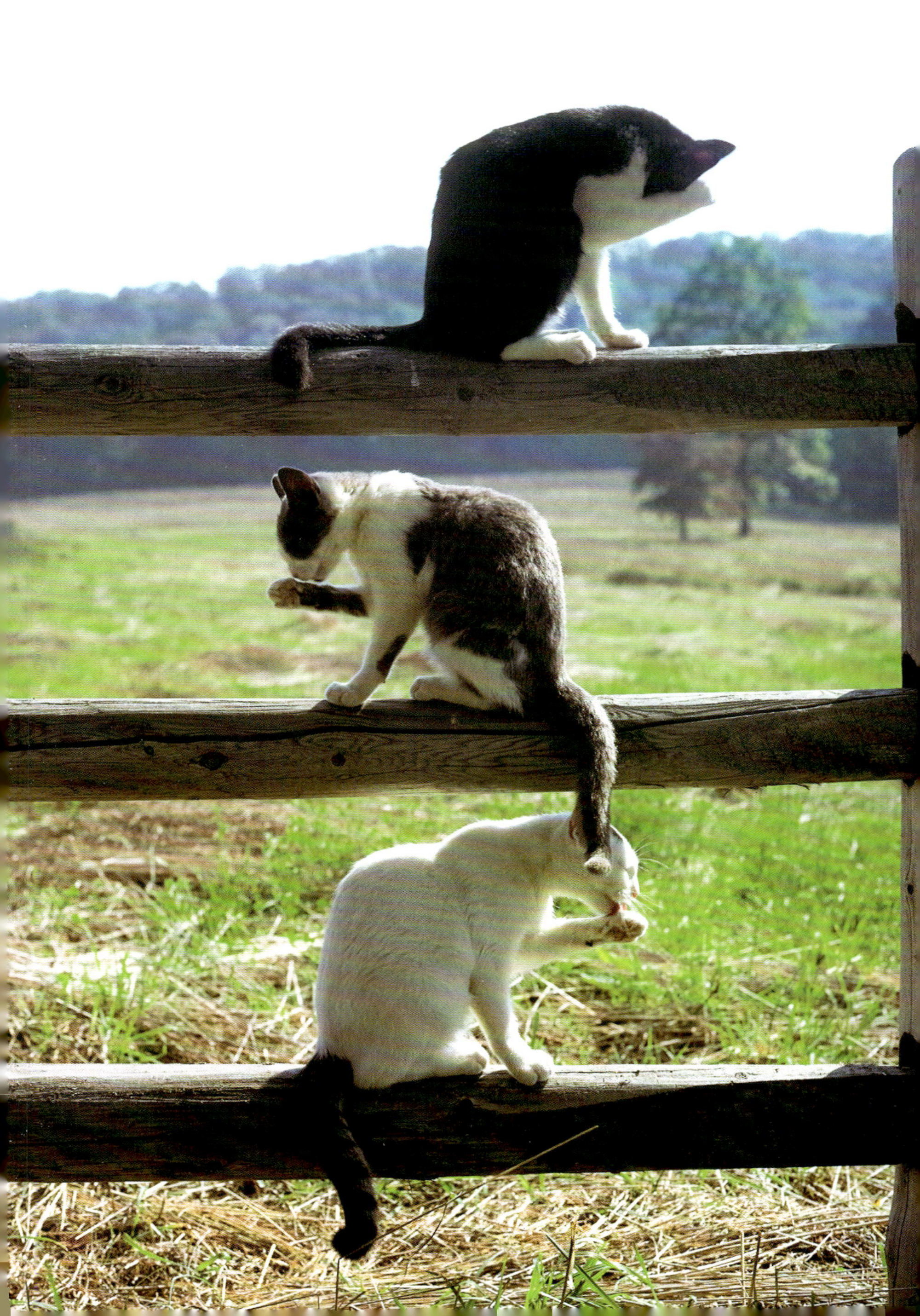

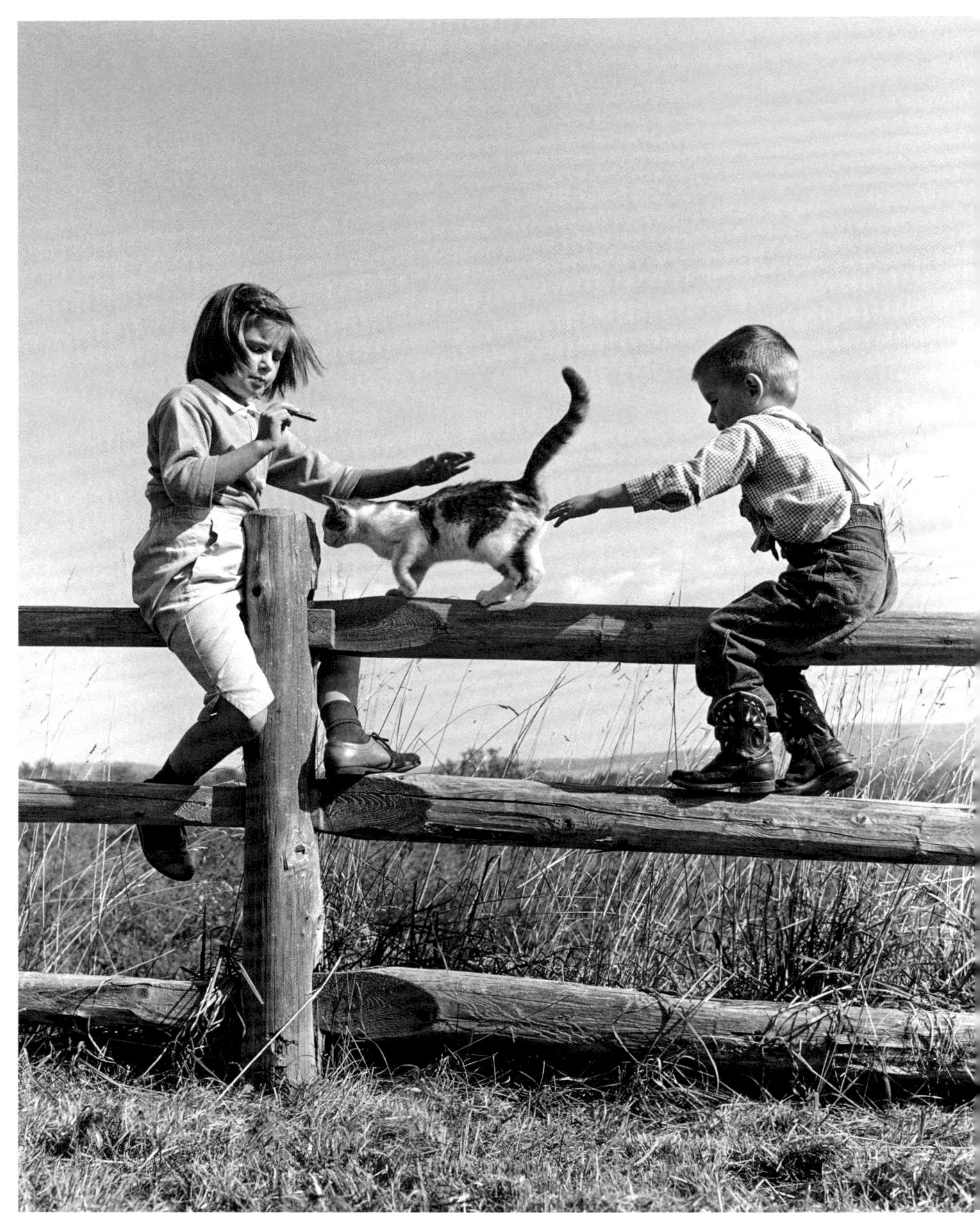

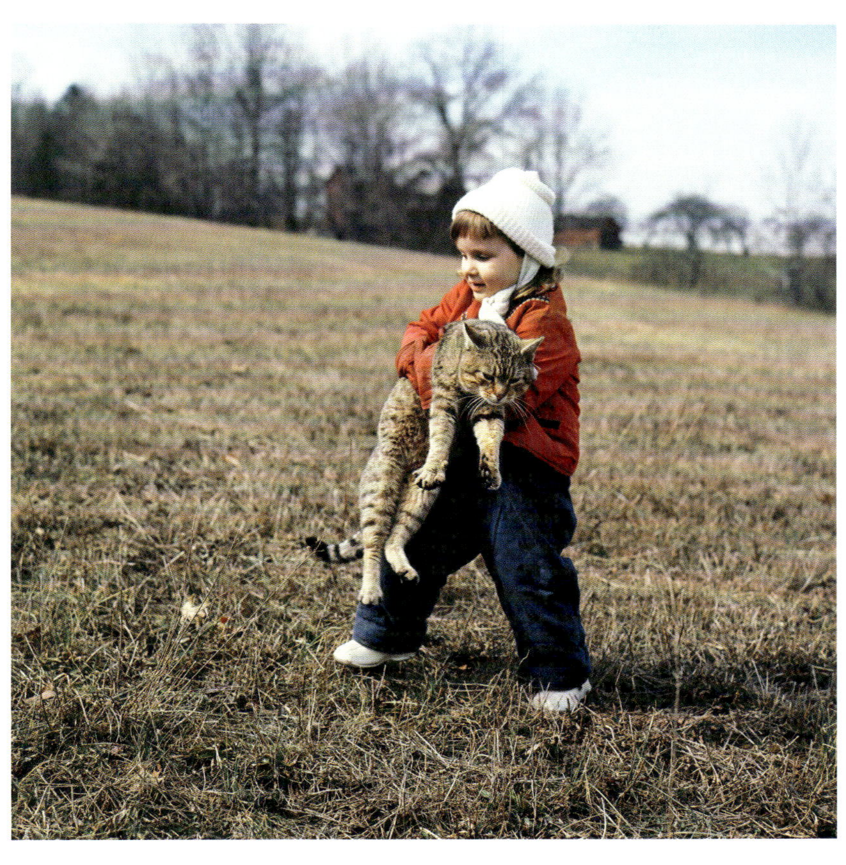

Daughter Maria and son Sam with a family cat,
Domestic shorthair, New Jersey, 1960.

Daughter Chiara and Tiger, New Jersey, 1965.

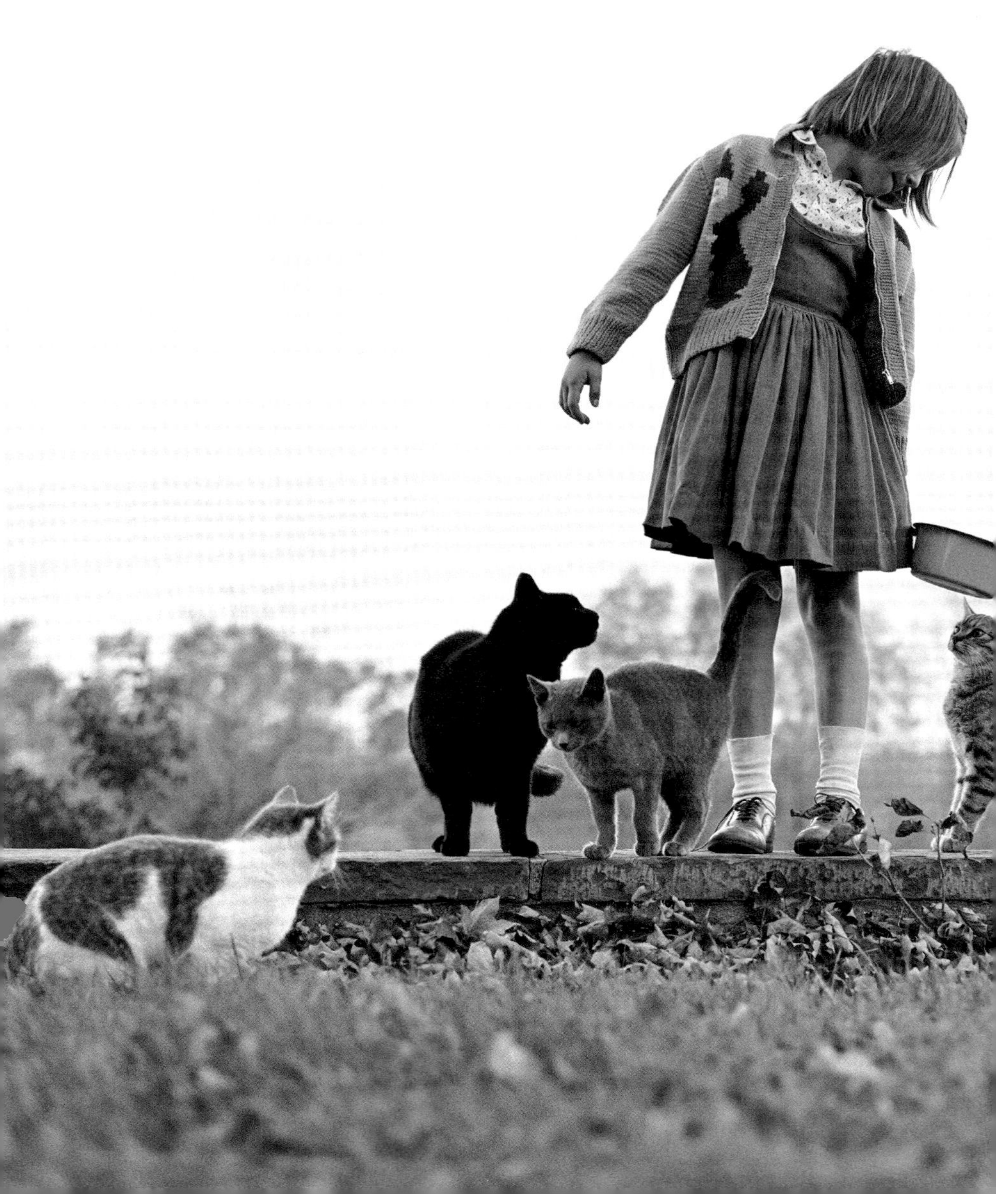

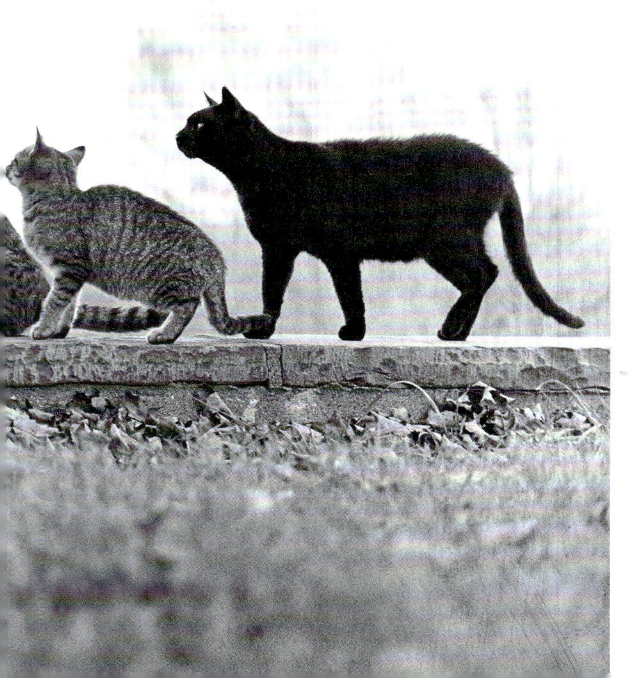

Daughter Maria and family cats, New Jersey, 1962.

Daughter Maria and one of the family cats,
Domestic shorthair, New Jersey, 1962.

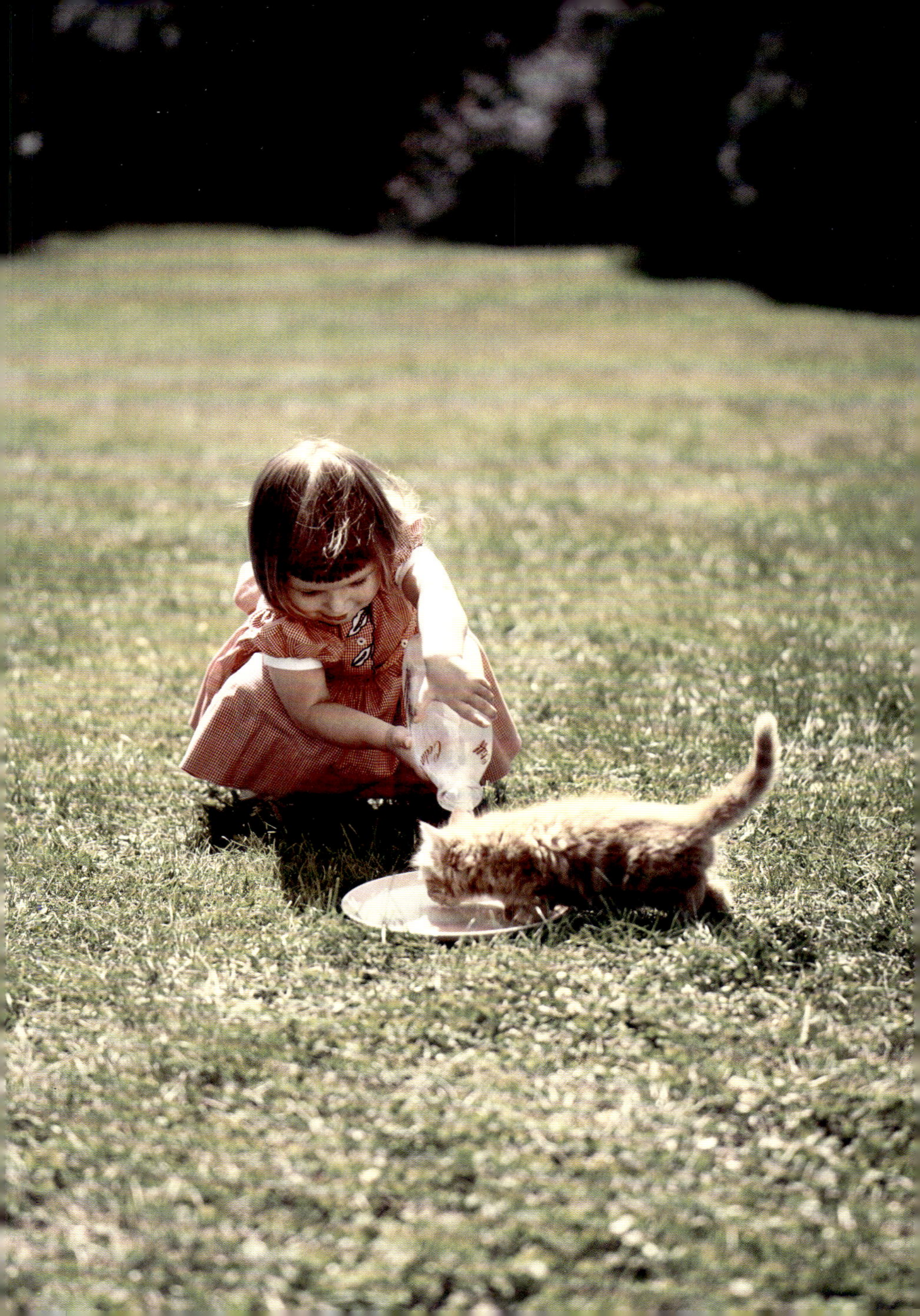

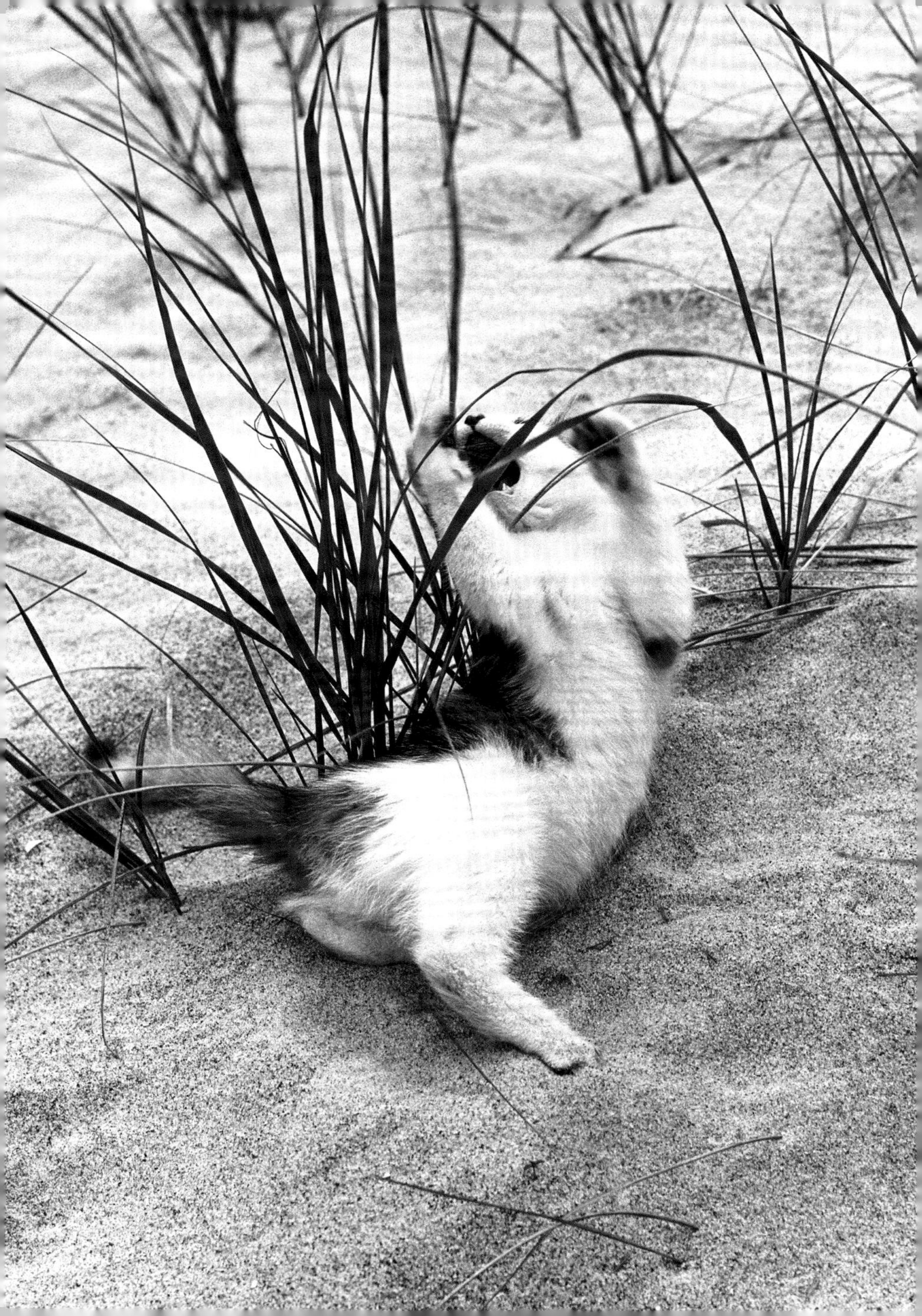

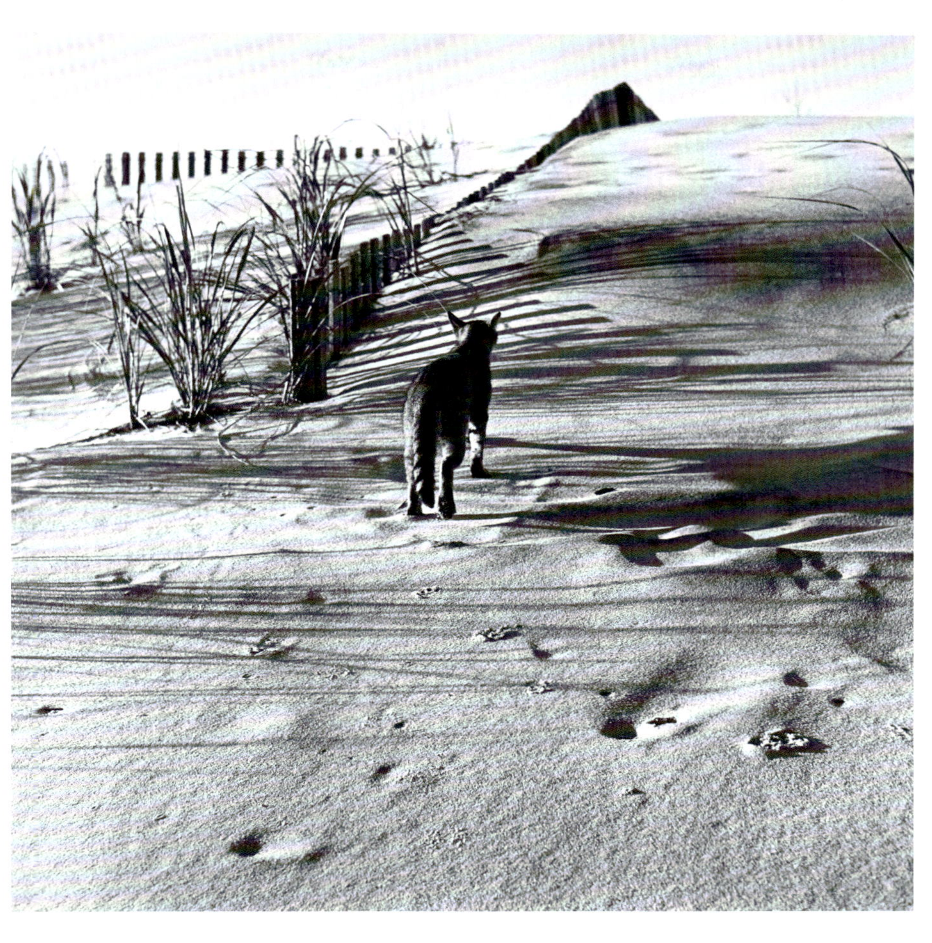

Domestic shorthair kitten, Long Island, 1959.

Above and following:
Minnie, Domestic shorthair, Long Island, 1959.

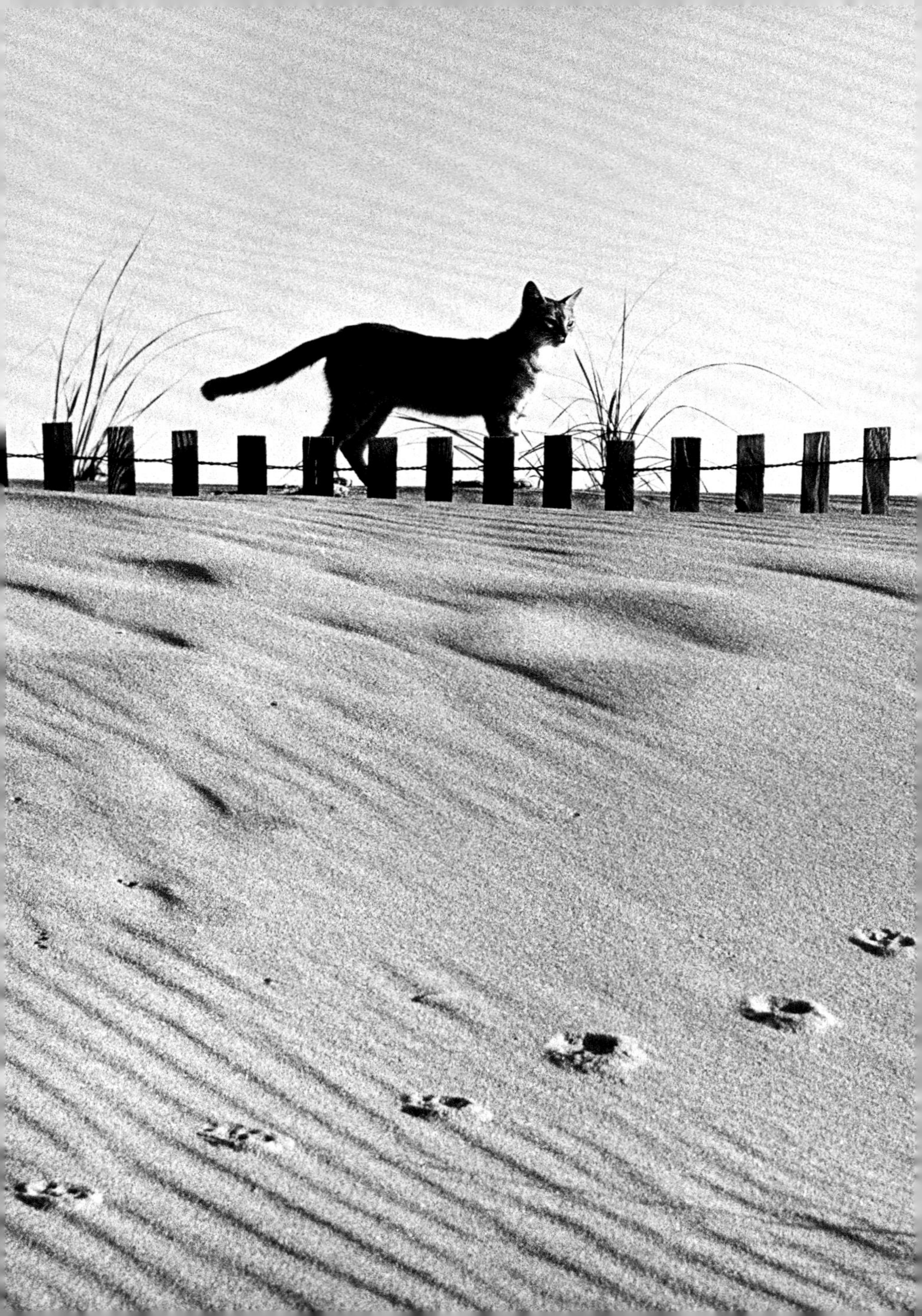

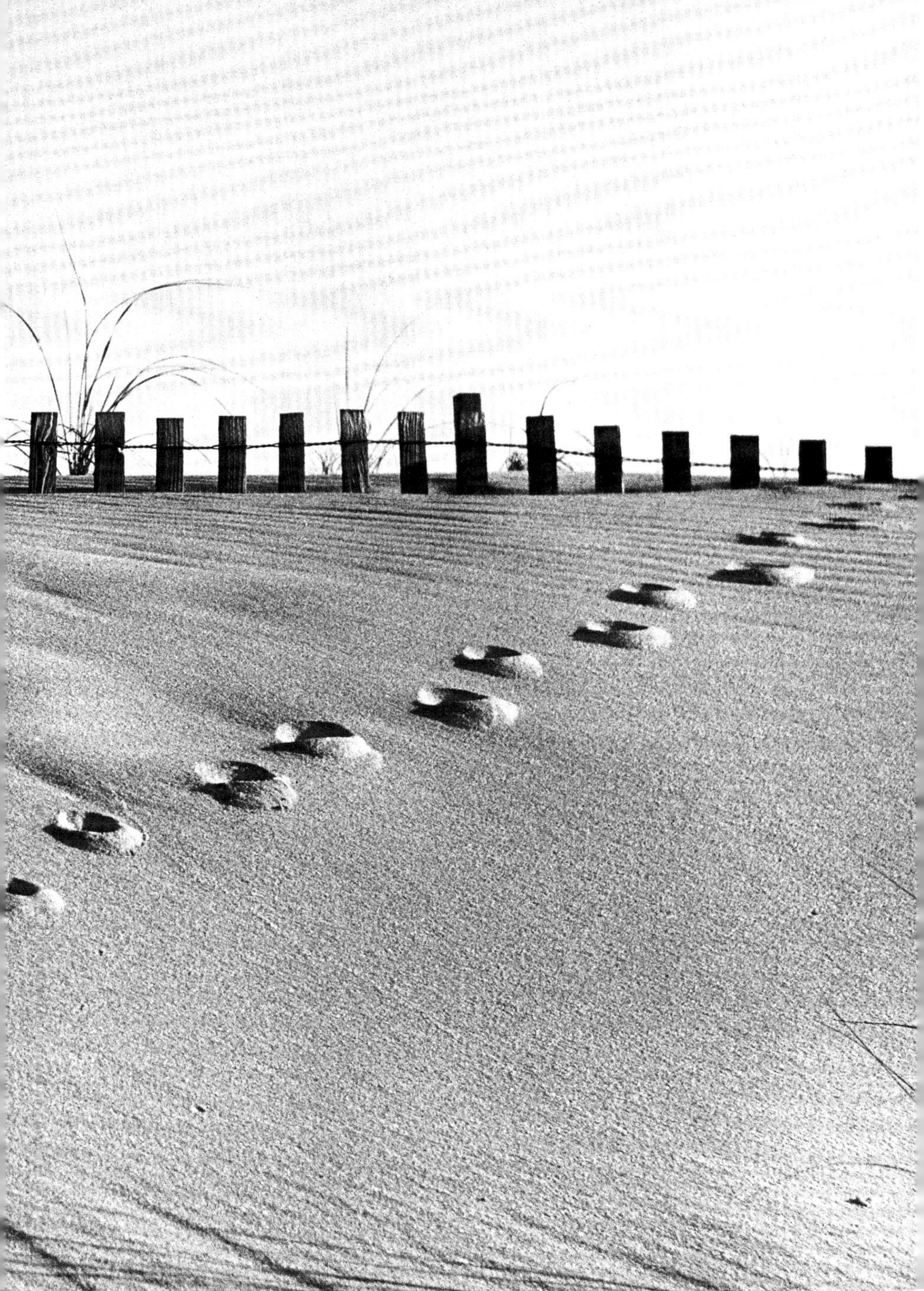

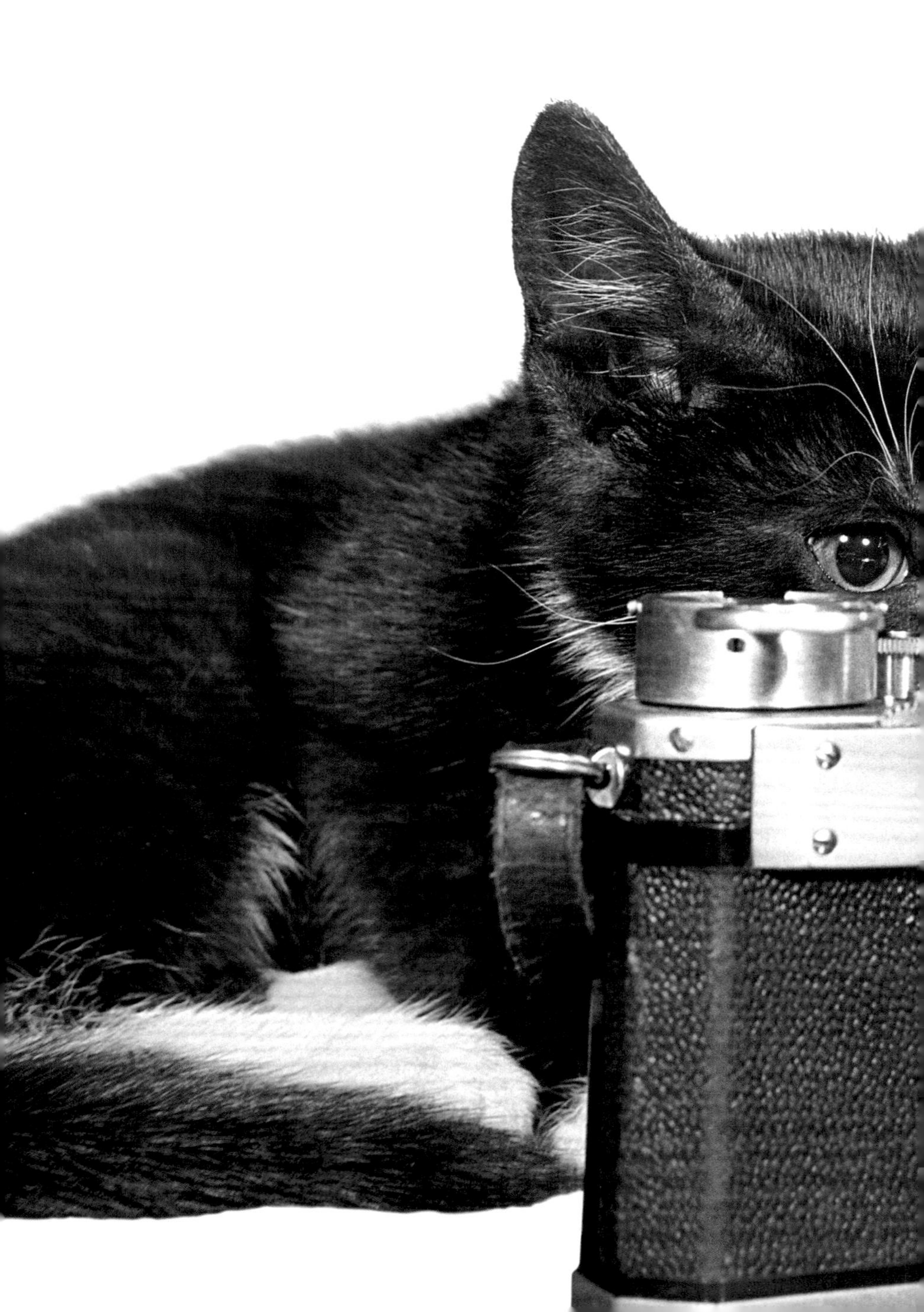

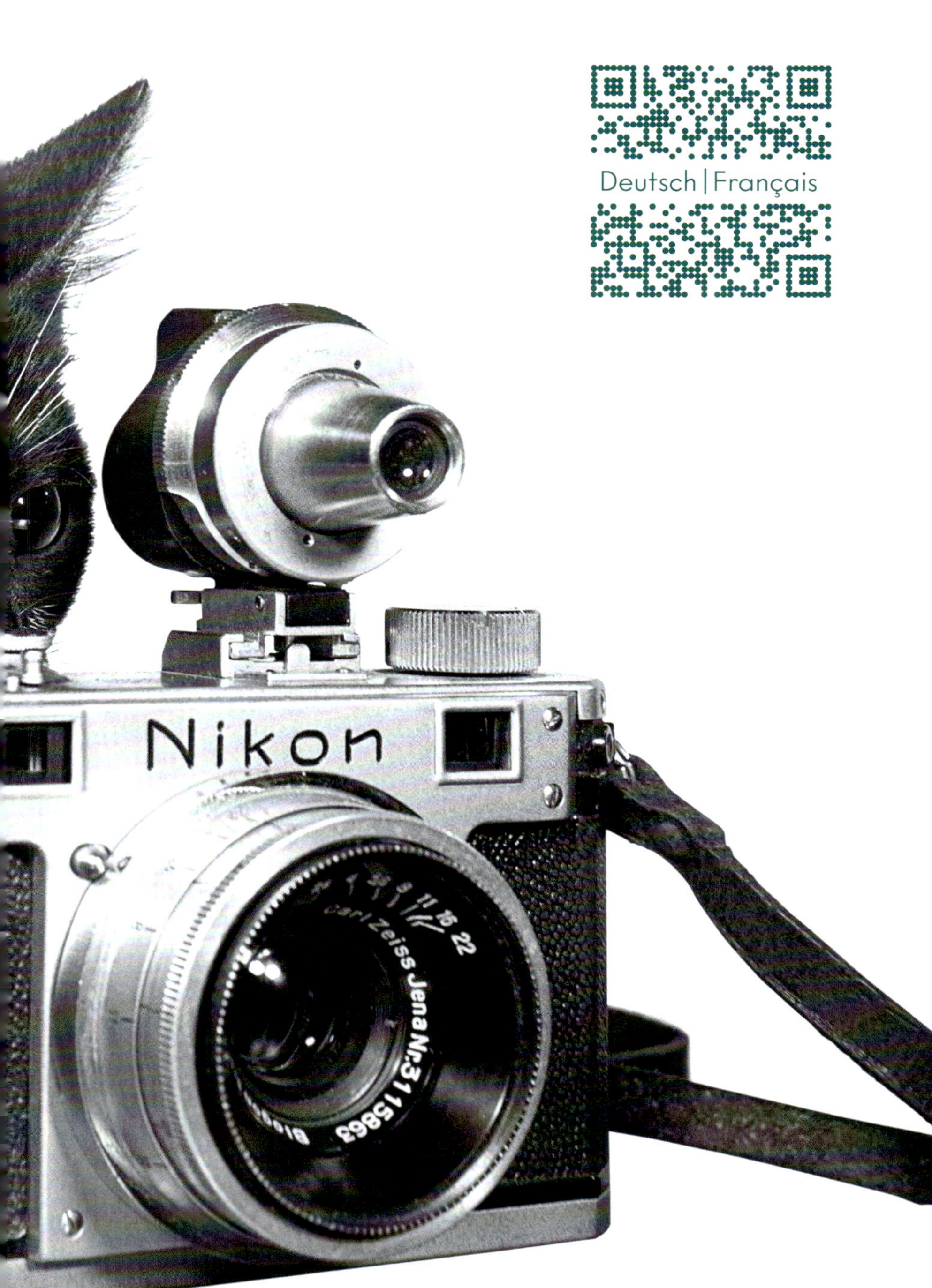
Deutsch | Français
Nikon
Carl Zeiss Jena Nr.31 5863 Biot
11 15 22

**EACH AND EVERY TASCHEN BOOK
PLANTS A SEED!**
TASCHEN is a carbon neutral publisher. Each
year, we offset our annual carbon emissions
with carbon credits at the Instituto Terra, a
reforestation program in Minas Gerais, Brazil,
founded by Lélia and Sebastião Salgado. To
find out more about this ecological partnership,
please check: *taschen.com/zerocarbon*
Inspiration: unlimited.
Carbon footprint: zero.

Want to see more? Visit *taschen.com* to view
our current publications, browse our latest
magazine, and subscribe to our newsletter.

© 2025 TASCHEN GmbH
Hohenzollernring 53, D-50672 Köln
taschen.com

Original edition:
© 2019 TASCHEN GmbH

Edited by: Sarah Wrigley
and Reuel Golden, New York

Printed in Italy
ISBN 978–3–8365–9531–5

Previous: Domestic shorthair, Long Island, 1953.

Right: Chandoha's New Jersey studio, 1968.

Front cover: Persian, New Jersey, 1961.

Back cover: Fabulous Felines pet store, New York City, 1961.

Endpapers: Photo shoot for a Friskies campaign,
Domestic shorthair, New Jersey, 1966.

Page 1: Domestic shorthair, New Jersey, 1979.

Pages 2–3: Domestic shorthairs, Long Island, 1952.

Following: Domestic shorthairs, Long Island, 1953.

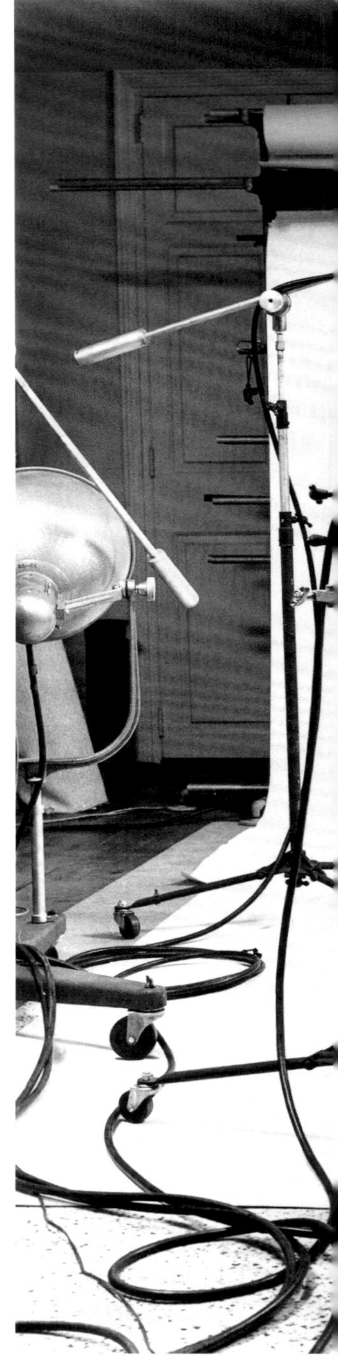

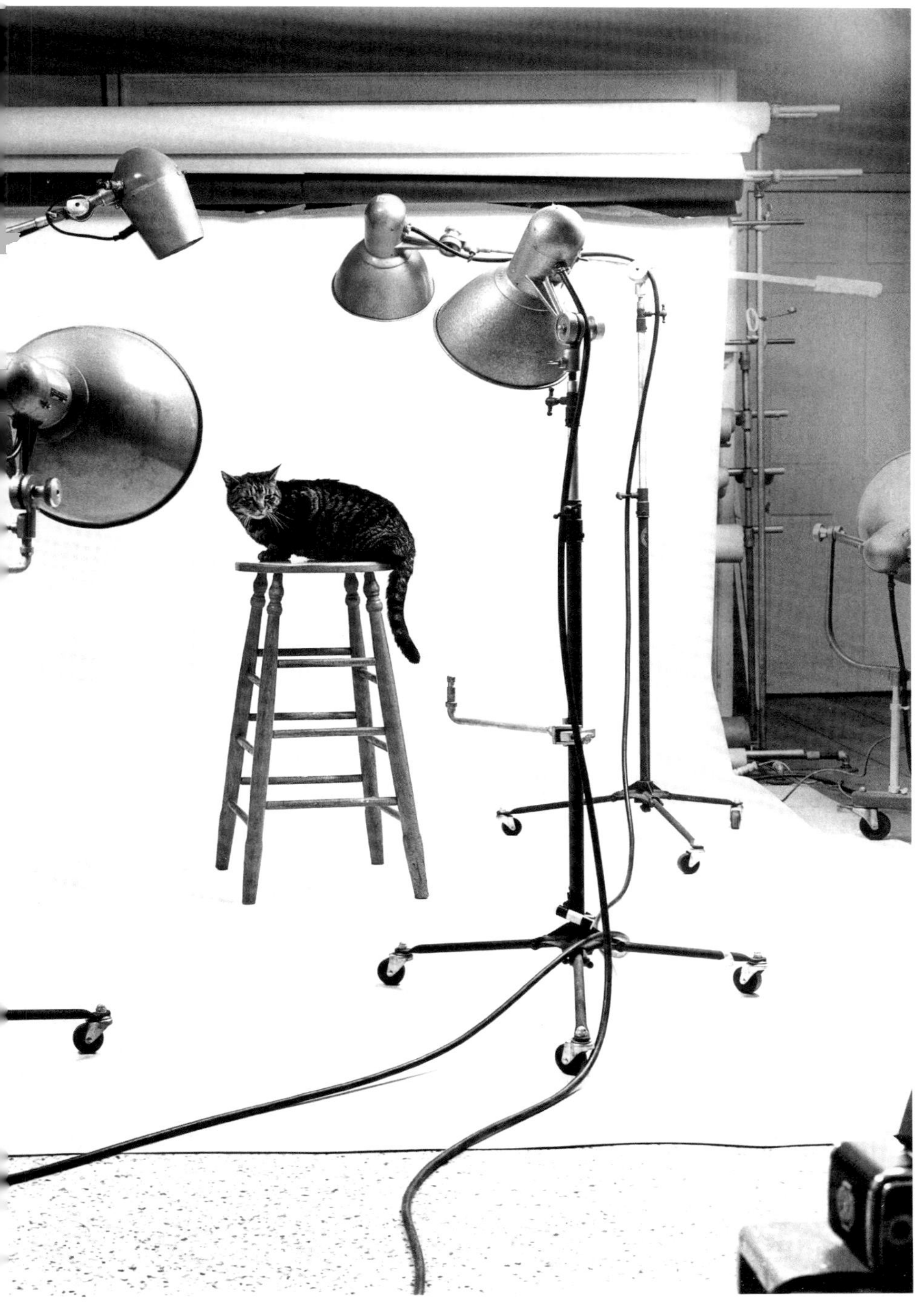

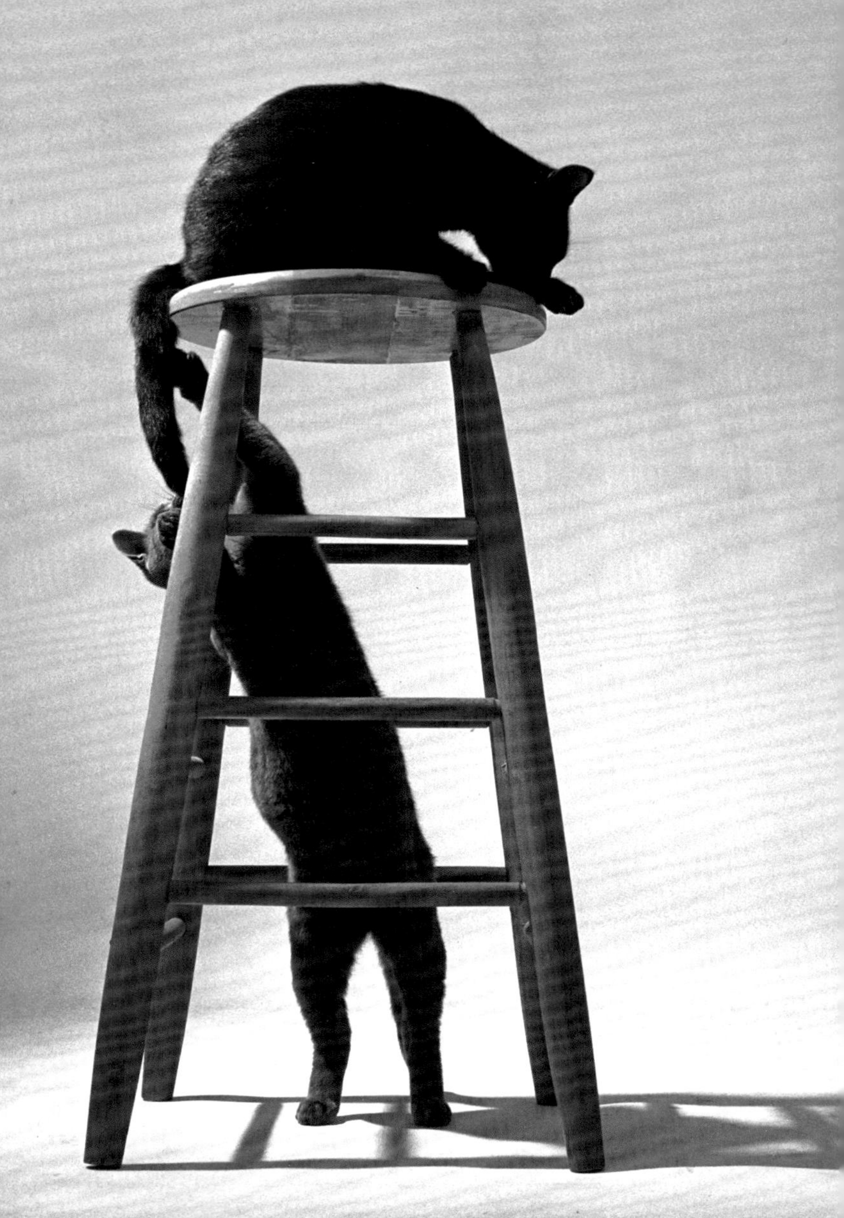

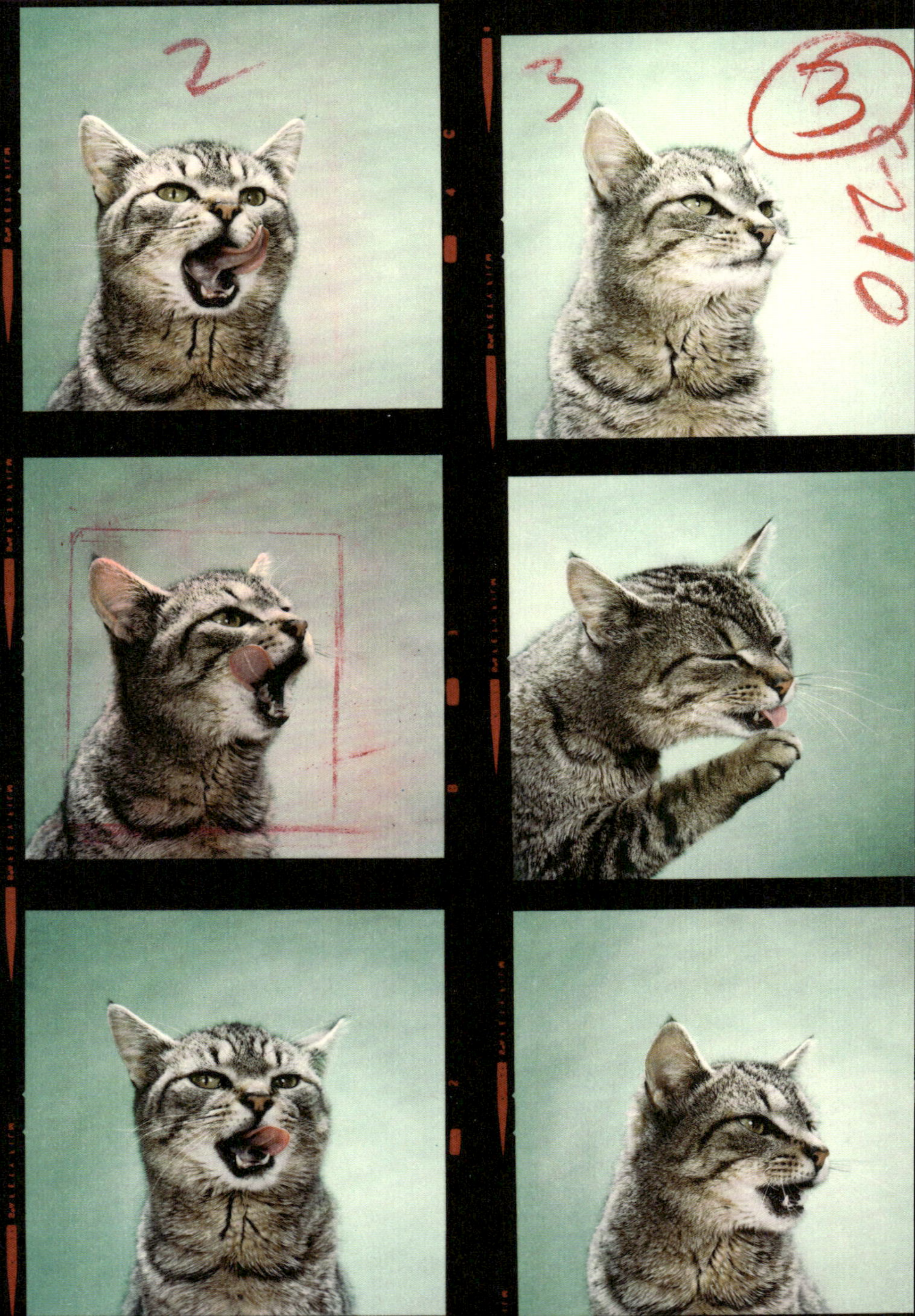
2
3
3